Parenting and Professing: Balancing Family Work with an Academic Career

Parenting and Professing

Balancing Family Work with an Academic Career

Edited by Rachel Hile Bassett

Vanderbilt University Press

NASHVILLE

10 09 08 07 06 05   1 2 3 4 5

This book is printed on acid-free paper.
Manufactured in the United States of America

Library of Congress Cataloging-in-Publication Data

Parenting and professing : balancing family work
with an academic career / edited by Rachel Hile Bassett.— 1st ed.
    p. cm.
Includes bibliographical references and index.
ISBN 0-8265-1477-4 (cloth : alk. paper
ISBN 0-8265-1478-2 (pbk. : alk. paper)
1.   Women college teachers—United States—
     Family relationships—Case studies.
2.   Women college teachers—United States—
     Social conditions—Case studies.
3.   Parenting—Social aspects—United States—Case studies.
4.   Working mothers—United States—Case studies.
     I. Bassett, Rachel Hile, 1971-
LB2332.32.P37 2005
378.1'2'082—dc22

                              2004029426

*This book is dedicated
to Joseph Everet and Helen St. Clare,
and to all the other children
celebrated in these pages.*

Contents

PART II
Possibilities   89

PART III
Change   169

Acknowledgments

The Department of English at the University of Kansas provided financial support for this book through the Zarel and Ruth Spears Scholarship. I am grateful for this tangible support, as well as for the intangible support and interest of professors and colleagues in the department as I worked on this book. I especially wish to acknowledge Margaret Arnold, David Bergeron, Geraldo de Sousa, Richard Hardin, and Tom Lorenz for their advice and support.

I am thankful to have had the opportunity to work with the fine contributors to this volume, in particular those whose contributions do not appear here but who participated fully in the process for two years before the project took its current, shorter form. The ideas, optimism, and encouragement of all these writers have made immeasurable contributions to the volume as a whole.

This book has benefited from the careful attention and intelligent suggestions of many readers: thank you to Amy Cummins, Anita Ilta Garey, Karen Hellekson, Andrea O'Reilly, and Sara Running Danger. Many thanks to Michael Ames at Vanderbilt University Press, whose commitment to this book and to life writing in general has contributed greatly to the body of work on academic lives. Thanks are also due to VUP's Jeremy Rehwaldt-Alexander for his graceful editing and to Dariel Mayer for her care in shepherding the book through production.

Finally, I want to thank the communities and people who have sustained me while working on this book: my and my husband's extended families, the attachment parenting group of Lawrence, Kansas, Kathleen Bryson, Susan Dunn-Hensley, Lara Hernandez;Corkrey, Charlotte Ostermann, and all the others who have patiently listened as I talked at length about the status of women and mothers in academia. Thank you to Jim and Linda Bassett, Ralph and Mary Anne Hile, Darlene Koger, and Stephanie Stuhlsatz for child care. Special thanks go to my most supportive community: Troy J. Bassett, whose countless hours of child care and housework made this book possible and whose input made it better, and Joseph and Helen Bassett, who make changing the world seem a worthwhile—and possible—goal.

Foreword

Andrea O'Reilly

The subject of motherhood and employment, particularly that of professional women, has emerged on the public agenda in the United States over the last several years. With the publication of best-selling books such as Ann Crittenden's *The Price of Motherhood* (2001) and Sylvia Ann Hewlett's *Creating a Life: Professional Women and the Quest for Children* (2002), the subject of motherhood and employment is now being discussed by individuals as diverse as talk-show hosts, policy makers, scholars, and newspaper columnists. Headlines ask: "Can Women Really Have It All?: A Career and Family," and terms such as "the biological clock," "the mommy tax," "the price of motherhood," "time crunch," and the "on-track/off-track career" may be heard in everyday conversations. These concerns and concepts are not new; the "second-shift," "the double day," and "the pink ghetto" have been studied for more than 20 years by scholars and policy makers. What is new, however, and what has captured the interest of the media and general public is that the women now under discussion, particularly in the two books noted above, are women who should, by virtue of their privileged status as the first generation of college-educated baby boomer women, be able to "have it all."

Recent studies demonstrate, however, as Crittenden (2001) and Hewlett (2002) note, that professional women have been unsuccessful in their attempts to wed motherhood with a career. A study cited by Crittenden shows that fewer than 20% of college-educated baby boomer women have managed to achieve both motherhood and a career by their late 30s or 40s; another study shows "that baby boomer women without children have been twice as successful in achieving a career as the women with children" (cited in Crittenden, p. 32). Hewlett's study found that "across a range of professions, high achieving women continue to have an exceedingly hard time combining career and family: thirty-three percent of high-achieving woman and forty-nine percent of ultra-achieving women are childless at age 40; (this compares to twenty-five percent of high-achieving men and nineteen percent of ultra-achieving men)" (p. 86). Hewlett concludes that "the more successful the woman, the less likely it is she will find a husband or bear a child. For men the reverse is true. The more successful the man, the more likely he is to be married with children" (p. 42). Investigating professions as diverse as medicine, law, business, and government service, Crittenden found that although women were entering these professions in record numbers, few women were represented at the senior levels of the profession, and most of these women were childless.

A significant, and to many a surprising, finding of Hewlett's research was the fact that among professionals, female academics have the *highest* rate of childlessness: 43 percent (p. 97). Surprising, because, as Rachel Hile Bassett notes in the introduction, professors enjoy benefits unimagined by the average worker: flexible work schedules, the ability to do work from home, and summers off. Such working conditions would suggest that being a professor is the ideal career for mothers. However, as the research shows, nothing could be further from the truth. One study that looked at the effect of early babies on women's academic careers, cited by Hile Bassett in the introduction, reveals that "women with early babies are less likely to achieve tenure than women with late babies or no children." Another study, the 1988 Canadian Association of University Teachers bulletin, reported that "of all the professions, that of university teaching is the one in which women have the least number of children" (cited in Innis Dagg & Thompson, 1988, p. 84). The American Association of University Professors confirmed in their "Statement of Principles on Family Responsibility and Academic Work" (2001) that "although increasing numbers of women have entered academia, their academic status has been slow to improve: women remain disproportionately represented within instructor, lecturer, and unranked positions; more than 57 percent of those holding such positions are women. . . . In contrast, among full professors only 26 percent are women." Likewise, "among full-time faculty women, only 48 percent are tenured whereas 68 percent of full-time men are tenured." Although more women are earning their doctorates, as Alice Fothergill and Kathryn Felty (2003) note, "the structure of tenure-track jobs has not changed in any real way to accommodate them" (p. 17). Perhaps, they continue, this is why "the number of women in tenure track jobs has *declined:* from 46 percent in 1977 to 32 percent in 1995" (p. 17). This research on motherhood in academia shows, as noted by Angela Simeone (1987), that "marriage and family, while having a positive effect on the [academic] careers of men, has a negative effect on the progress of women's careers. Married women, particularly with children, are more likely to have dropped out of graduate school, have interrupted or abandoned their careers, be unemployed or employed in a job unrelated to their training, or to hold lower academic rank" (p. 12). This research on motherhood and academia seeks to understand why the academic profession is particularly unreceptive to mothers and what can be done to correct this situation.

Parenting and Professing: Balancing Family Work with an Academic Career is a timely and invaluable contribution to this emergent research field. Although one issue of *The Journal of the Association for Research on Mothering* (Vol. 5, No. 2, 2003) examined mothering in the academy, its focus was on research studies on motherhood and the academy. In contrast, what is important about *Parenting and Professing* and what makes it essential to this field of study is that it provides first-person accounts of the *experience* of being a mother (and in two instances a father) in the academy. Divided into three sections—"Challenges," "Possibilities," and "Change"—and made up of 24 essays, the collection revisits the central research questions—why is the profession of the academy particularly unreceptive to mothers, and what can be done to correct this situation—and seeks to answer them by way of personal reflections on lived experiences of parenting and professing. Current research documents well the difficulty of being a parent in academe; this collection, composed as it is of first-person accounts, examines how parents respond to and function in this reality. Across a wide range of universities and disciplines, and from many and diverse perspectives—for example, age, race, class, marital status—the contributors give voice to the discrimination documented in the existing research. In so doing, the collection broadens and deepens our understanding of how and why motherhood is incompatible with academia and, as a result, enables us to better understand what "solutions" are needed.

The importance of stories becomes particularly evident in light of the collection's central finding; namely, that "the obstacles to successfully combining parenting and work result almost entirely from attitudes entrenched in the academic culture, not from the exigencies of the work itself." As discussed in the introduction and demonstrated in the chapters, family-friendly policies have not been widely adopted and utilization rates are low, often because parents "fear professional repercussions for using them." The prevailing ethos of academic culture is that the career is to be prioritized above all else. To do otherwise is to risk being perceived as not committed to your profession, or worse, to risk not being taken seriously as a "real" scholar. Mothers on the tenure track thus must practice what is termed "discrimination avoidance"; that is, "behaviors intended to minimize any apparent or actual intrusions of family life on academic commitments." Such behaviors, as Hile Bassett explains, "can include opting out of partnering and children altogether, delaying childbearing or limiting the number of children, and attempting to hide one's caregiver status by not taking advantage of family-friendly policies." Women, unable or unwilling to stay in the mother closet, often find themselves marginalized in part-time and non-tenure-track positions. Indeed, as these stories show, women who "choose" marginalized academic work often do so because of family commitments.

The final section of the book, "Change," shows that what is needed is changes in perception—changes, as Hile Bassett explains in the introduction, "in how we conceptualize work and in how employers structure work, such that women and men with significant caregiving responsibilities can be recognized as valuable and effective workers." The achievement of this collection is that it does just that. The stories show that being a parent does not make a professor any less committed to his or her profession. In fact, as the section "Possibilities" confirms, becoming a parent often makes you a better scholar and teacher. And although the stories reveal that speaking truthfully about the real difficulties of parenting within academia may not be the safest course, it is, as Hile Bassett notes, "a necessary one." "Honest stories from people living with these challenges," Hile Bassett writes, "can let others dealing with the same problems know that they are not alone." Additionally, as Hile Bassett continues, "such stories play an important role in changing others' perceptions of parenting in academia." *Parenting and Professing* delineates both the challenges and possibilities of being a parent-professor and details the changes needed to achieve work-family balance in this profession. In so doing, the collection develops and delivers, to paraphrase Hile Bassett, "a sociology of academia and of the family" that enables us—nay empowers us—to imagine and implement changes to both institutions.

REFERENCES

American Association of University Professors. (2001). *Statement of principles on family responsibilities and academic work.* Retrieved May 20, 2004, from www. aaup.org/statements/REPORTS/re01fam.htm

Crittenden, A. (2001). *The price of motherhood: Why motherhood is the most important—and least valued—job in America.* New York: Henry Holt.

Fothergill, A., & Felty, K. (2003). "I've worked very hard and slept very little": Mothers on the tenure track in academia. *Journal of the Association for Research on Mothering, 5*(2), 7–19.

Hewlett, S. A. (2002). *Creating a life: Professional women and the quest for children.* New York: Miramax.

Innis Dagg, A., & Thompson, P. J. (1988). *MisEducation: Women and Canadian universities.* Toronto: OISE Press.

Simeone, S. (1987). *Academic women: Working towards equality.* South Hadley, MA: Bergin & Garvey.

Introduction

Rachel Hile Bassett

For those outside academia who feel pulled between work and family responsibilities, the academic's somewhat flexible schedule looks appealing. Indeed, the popular culture's image of the professorial workload suggests an ideal fit with childbearing and rearing—flexible schedule, ability to do some work from home, and summers off. But those who have more experience with the demands of an academic career can immediately see the downside: the work that never ends, the rigidly prescribed hierarchical career structure, the emphasis on competition and individual achievement.

Looking at parenting issues in the academic workplace is important not only for parents in academia but also for feminists and social scientists interested in work-family issues, because in the academic workplace, obstacles to successfully combining parenting and work result almost entirely from attitudes entrenched in the academic culture, not from the exigencies of the work itself. Academic labor is more flexible in terms of time and location than almost any other type of work—theoretically, at least, this flexibility could extend to family-friendly policies such as part-time tenure-track positions, shared faculty positions, and the option for new parents to stop the tenure clock for a year without penalty. However, such policies have not been widely adopted (Hutton Raabe, 1997), and utilization rates are low, in some cases because parents fear professional repercussions for using them (Drago & Colbeck, 2003). Despite these challenges, recent research and personal accounts suggest the ways that caregiving experience can enrich and inform one's academic work, and academic activists are succeeding in getting administrations to enact policies to warm the "chilly climate" (Sandler & Hall, 1986) of academia for women in general, and for mothers in particular. Change is slow and by no means inevitable, but change is occurring for parents in academia.

Challenges

Research in the 1970s and 1980s found that women received tenure less frequently than men (Menges & Exum, 1983); not surprisingly, this disparity in tenure achievement coincided with the childbearing years (Farber, 1977). More recent research suggests that little has changed in the decades since: Despite increasing representation of women among doctoral degree recipients, the percentage of women among tenured faculty has remained essentially the same for the past three decades (Mason & Goulden, 2002). The most recent data available, found in the American Association of University Professors' (AAUP) "Annual Report on the Economic Status of the Profession, 2003–04," quantify the situation. For all categories of schools combined, the percentage of male assistant professors (14.7%) was similar to that of female assistant professors (12.6%), suggesting institutional efforts to attain gender parity. The disparity at the associate level (16.3% male associate professors versus 10.2% female associate professors) indicates that women face barriers not so much in getting a job as in achieving tenure (AAUP, 2004).

"Early Babies" and "Late Babies": Fitting Childbearing into the Academic Career Model

Childbearing has an undeniable role in the gender disparity in tenure-achievement rates. Mason and Goulden (2002) studied the effects of "early babies" (those who join the household either while the parent is in graduate school or within the first five years after completing the PhD) versus "late babies" (those who join the family more than five years after completion of the PhD) on rates of tenure achievement for male and female faculty. Though having an early baby does not negatively affect men's chances of earning tenure, the timing of babies makes a big difference for women: Women with early babies are less likely to achieve tenure than women with late babies or no children.

Because of data such as these, many junior female professors receive advice to wait until after achieving tenure to have children (Wilson, 1999a). For example, Emily Toth (aka Ms. Mentor), with her very pragmatic stated goal of helping more women to achieve tenure, acknowledges the danger to women of being perceived as too much mother, not enough professional. She advises mothers to remain "in the closet" until tenure, commenting that "when you do not have tenure, you must 'fit in,' and children simply don't" (Toth, 1997, p. 120). Earlier cohorts of female academics tended to avoid or defer family commitments as a way of avoiding professional bias. In the 1950s, a study of 43 female full professors who had received PhD degrees from Radcliffe found that only 4 of the 43 were married, and none had children (Radcliffe College Committee on Graduate Education for Women, 1956). Female professors continue to have lower rates of childbearing than the already low rates of other professional women (Hewlett, 2002).

But the advice to delay childbearing ignores very real risks, and evidence suggests that many in the younger cohort of academic women are less willing to defer or avoid childbearing (Sorcinelli, 1992). Amy Varner (2000) details the potential problems for female professors who wait to conceive: Maternal age over 35 carries increased health risks for the mother, increased risk of miscarriage and birth defects, and increased likelihood of requiring expensive and emotionally draining infertility treatments to become pregnant.

Faculty women who decide not to risk deferring pregnancy and become parents before achieving tenure face a work culture that is remarkably intolerant of employment interruptions. In *The Young Woman's Guide to an Academic Career,* published in 1974, Marjorie Farnsworth advises her readers:

> After having obtained a position, you may decide to have a family. You may also entertain the idea of leaving the university for one or several years or until your children are of school age, and then going back to your former position. If so, you are indulging in wishful thinking. You can never go back. Although maternity leave, usually unpaid, may be provided, you must return to your job almost immediately thereafter or forfeit your career as a serious academic professional. (Farnsworth, 1974, p. 106)

Little has changed in 30 years. The rigidity of the academic career model means that the practice of "sequencing" (Rossen Cardozo, 1986)—temporarily drawing back from full engagement in the workforce during especially demanding periods, providing time to nurture infants and toddlers and care for elders—remains unavailable for women in academia. Those who enter graduate school with the popular notion that academic careers can easily accommodate caregiving find out too late that they may be professionally punished for any deviation from the accepted pattern. The tight job market makes this tendency even more pronounced. Graduate students hear comments about the "shelf life" of a PhD—that is, if you don't have a tenure-track position within five years, you have "expired" and are unlikely ever to get on the tenure track—and new faculty perceive the real possibility that if a professor leaves a tenure-track job, another one may never materialize again.

Role Hierarchies

The rigidity of the academic career model follows from the assumption that people organize their many roles hierarchically, and this leads to the expectation that faculty members must choose to prioritize either work or family (see Callero, 1985, for a summary of theories on hierarchical role organization). Women who highly value their careers often respond to the clear message that variations from the norm are unacceptable by engaging in "discrimination avoidance," that is, "behaviors intended to minimize any apparent or actual intrusions of family life on academic commitments" (Drago, Crouter, Wardell, & Willits, 2001, p. 4). Such behaviors can include opting out of partnering and children altogether, delaying childbearing or limiting the number of children, and attempting to hide one's caregiver status by not taking advantage of family-friendly policies (Drago et al.). To the extent that such strategies help a professor/mother to appear as an "ideal worker" (Williams, 2000), women with children can have successful academic careers. The disparate rates of career success between male and female academics, however, suggest the difficulty of combining caregiving with ideal-worker behavior.

Some women, however, are not willing or able to render their caregiving work invisible. Those who wish to devote a substantial amount of time to child rearing while still maintaining a commitment to academic work may find that others perceive them as having unequivocally prioritized motherhood, and such a perception can close off women's career options. Too many women with strong commitments to having children either leave the profession altogether, often before attaining a tenure-track position (Mason & Goulden, 2002; Menges & Exum, 1983), or become marginalized in part-time and non-tenure-track positions (Benjamin, 1998). Evidence suggests that women who "choose" marginalized academic work often do so because of their family commitments (Perna, 2001).

Many academic parents seek—and find—ways to honor and give equal expression to their varied roles in life, but they do so against the prevailing ethos of the academic culture and often with concern for how these choices will affect their careers. In a study of 124 female assistant professors' perceptions of barriers to tenure, Kolker Finkel and Olswang (1996) found evidence of women's awareness of bias against mothers: 30% of their sample had decided never to have children, and 49% had decided to postpone childbearing. Many study participants saw "Time required by children" as a serious impediment to achieving tenure: 40% of the sample cited this as a concern, including fully 82% of the subsample of women with at least one child under the age of six (Kolker Finkel & Olswang).

Perceptions and Attitudes

The perceptions of faculty parents and the attitudes of their colleagues may affect work-family balance in the academic workplace as much as the policies on the books. Despite growing support for and implementation of family-friendly policies in academia, attitudes change more slowly than policies, and the bias in academia against "special treatment" for parents has a long history. There has even been disagreement among feminists about whether policies that could be perceived as preferential to women would lead to fewer women being hired. This attitude was expressed in 1988 by Mary W. Gray, the head of Committee W on the Status of Women, in her support for the AAUP's position at that time, which favored stopping the tenure clock only when a parent took a leave of absence. Gray argued, "If you're being paid full-time, you should be working full-time. This could be seen as asking for special favors" (quoted in Mangan, 1988, p. A17). Although the AAUP has since changed its position and now favors policies to stop the tenure clock even when new parents do not take leaves of absence (see AAUP, 2001), the bias against family-friendly initiatives still persists among some senior faculty, the very professors who will participate in the tenure decisions of their younger colleagues.

Awareness of departmental bias against mothers who request "special favors" leads many women to attempt discrimination avoidance (Drago et al., 2001), trying to fly under the radar by, for example, scheduling their childbirth for the summer months (Wilson, 1999b) or not using the leaves or parental supports that policies allow. In a study of almost 1,400 professors of both sexes, Kolker Finkel, Olswang, and She (1994) found wide support for family-friendly policies such as paid parental leaves, flexible schedules, and tenure-clock stoppage, yet most of the professors did not use these policies when they were available: Parents seem to expect that departmental attitudes will penalize them, even if institutional policies appear to support them. In this, we see parents' awareness of what Anita Ilta Garey (1999) terms the "orientation model" of work and family: Our culture perceives work-family balance as a zero-sum game, such that an "orientation" to work or family necessarily implies a corresponding deficit of attention to the other sphere. In a workplace governed by this model, any utilization of family-friendly policies will be perceived as signaling a lack of scholarly seriousness.

Possibilities

Despite the challenges of combining academic work and parenting, evidence suggests that doing so can have distinct benefits, not only for individuals, but for the academy as well. Rejecting the emphasis on living one's roles hierarchically and instead seeking balance among one's varied roles in life can lead to a ripple effect of positives, leading out from the individual to the academy and the larger society.

Benefits for Individuals and Children

Studying a sample of working mothers, Marks and MacDermid (1996) found that *positive role balance*—"the tendency to become fully engaged in the performance of every role in one's total role system, to approach every typical role and role partner with an attitude of attentiveness and care" (p. 421)—was associated with lower measures of depression and higher measures of self-esteem and general well-being. Researchers have found correlations between participation in multiple roles and increased physical (Verbrugge, 1986) and psychological (Baruch & Barnett, 1986) health. Many academic parents provide anecdotal support for these data. Joanne S. Frye (2003) reports her seven-year-old daughter's demand, "Which do you love more—me or your work?" and her honest, though unpopular, answer: "You can't make me choose. I have to do my work, not just for money but for me. But I have to be with you too. I love you and I love my work" (p. 21). Frye's insistent *and* when faced with an either-or question subverts the dualistic thinking behind demands for hierarchical prioritizing of roles—demands placed on women not only by the academy, but by family members as well.

Though the effects of a parent's academic career on children will depend on multiple factors, including age of child, quality of child care, family income, and institutional support for parenting, some positive general conclusions seem warranted. For older children, increased housework and self-care responsibilities due to parental workplace involvement can lead to a greater sense of self-reliance and mastery than children acquire when parents subscribe to cultural images of children as primarily passive and economically dependent (Thorne, 1999). Additionally, parents who model active commitment to intellectual life will communicate this enthusiasm for knowledge to their children. The disproportionately high number of children of academics who themselves pursue academic careers suggests how enduring this method of values transmission can be. For example,

Simone Davis, the daughter of mathematician Chandler Davis and historian Natalie Zemon Davis, explains her parents' influence on her choice to become an academic herself: "The values they instilled in me left me ill-suited for much else beyond academics. I was taught to lust after books, to respect the notion of service, to distrust both high salaries and business sense ... to honor wide-flung curiosity, and to grab at thought bubbles if they aimlessly rose and squirrel them away for harvesting" (Booth et al., 1999, p. 25).

How Academia Benefits from Welcoming Mothers

Academia can also benefit by welcoming the contributions and perspectives of mothers. Following Tillie Olsen's (1978) comment that the lack of writers who are mothers has led to significant "silences" in literature, Nancy Hensel (1990) asks, "Would a biologist who is also a mother ask different research questions from a biologist who is not a mother? Or a sociologist, historian, or psychologist?" (p. 4). Personal accounts of mothers in academia suggest the many ways that the maternal role can directly affect one's research program: For example, Suzan Banoub-Baddour's (2002) personal experience with breastfeeding inspired her to make breastfeeding a central topic for her research and teaching in nursing. Andrea O'Reilly (2002) describes how becoming a mother gave direction to her feminism; this led eventually to her founding of the Association for Research on Mothering.

Nurturing work can also positively affect the way professors interact with students and with each other. Spore, Harrison, and Haggerson (2002) listened to academics' stories of their experiences with people who embodied for them the "Good Mother" archetype in academia. The stories reveal the importance of nurture from colleagues, both female and male, in developing confidence and competence as academics. Students need mothering, too, and Rebecca Mark explains the political dimension of the mothering she offers gay and lesbian students who seek her help: "Mothering students is not the touchy-feely-cookies-'n'-tea pampering that so many of my colleagues conjure up. . . . It is instead strong guidance, respect, willingness to listen to and support a student through . . . any number of difficult life passages. It is political action in its most important manifestation. When I parent [young people], I am teaching them to parent themselves" (Mark, 1998, p. 81). Welcoming not just mothers, but maternal ways of relating, can make the academy a more welcoming place for many students and faculty members from groups that still struggle for full recognition within the academy.

Egalitarian Marriages

In general, fathers in academia have different experiences than mothers in academia. For example, male academics are more likely than female academics to have spouses who work less than full time (43.8% versus 11.5%) (Jacobs, 2004). Perhaps because of this extra support, the "early baby" effect does not apply for male professors; in fact, having a child within five years of completing the PhD actually gives male professors a slight edge in attaining tenure (Mason & Goulden, 2002). However, data that examine the aggregate of men cannot deepen our understanding of those male academics who do participate or wish to participate as fully engaged parents. The concerns and experiences of such men are rendered invisible by aggregate-level studies, but qualitative research (e.g., Coltrane, 1996) suggests that men who attempt to become fully involved parents face not only the same institutional difficulties that women face but also added pressure from cultural expectations that nurturing children is women's work. Nevertheless, more men are taking responsibility for family work, and academic institutions can help facilitate coparenting.

Some dual-academic-career couples are using the flexible scheduling of academic work to practice egalitarian coparenting, with neither partner acting as "ideal worker" and neither serving as the sole caregiver. This practice should receive more institutional support, as it has the potential to improve not just families and not just academia, but the larger culture as well. As of 1989, among married or partnered faculty members, 35% of male and 40% of female professors indicated that their spouses or partners were in academia as well (Astin & Milem, 1997). Currently, presumably because of cultural expectations of the man as breadwinner, the women in such academic couples are more likely than the men to become "trailing spouses" (i.e., those who seek employment accommodation when their spouse obtains a tenure-track job; estimates suggest that the male partner is the primary hire in two thirds to three quarters of spousal-hire situations [Loeb, 1997]).

There is growing interest in sharing or splitting positions, with each partner expected to perform one half to three quarters of a regular load of research, teaching, and service. Tenure decisions are made either jointly or separately, depending on institution. Wolf-Wendel, Twombly, and Rice (2003) cite benefits of shared and split positions, including the avoidance of the stigma experienced by many women perceived as "secondary hires." About 20% of all institutions had job-sharing policies in effect in 1991 (Hutton Raabe, 1997), and the numbers have certainly risen since then.

Shared positions are no panacea—the most obvious potential problem occurs when a couple sharing a position divorce, and a half-time income is no longer enough (Trubek, 2004). Further, those applying to share a position because of discouragement about job prospects may become quite frustrated with a half-time appointment. But for couples who would prefer a more egalitarian distribution of labor than generally occurs, such arrangements can benefit the whole family and can provide an alternative to the "ideal worker"/full-time homemaker model.

Change

Change will not occur at the individual level, and change will not occur by waiting patiently for the university to change spontaneously. Tenured women, working together, can bring about change; thus, more women achieving tenure is a first step to bringing about systemic change to make academia a more welcoming place for mothers (Farley, 1990). But getting to tenure is discouraging, especially given how inhospitable the environment sometimes is, the increased difficulty for women of achieving tenure, and the sense that one may be shortchanging one's family. For pretenure women, sisterhood may sometimes seem too abstract a goal to fight for.

Mentoring

Many tenured women have recognized the special importance of mentoring in helping more female junior faculty to achieve tenure. Certainly, change will come in part through mentoring, both one-on-one mentoring and the advice contained in books such as *Ms. Mentor's Impeccable Advice for Women in Academia* (Toth, 1997) and *Career Strategies for Women in Academe: Arming Athena* (Collins, Chrisler, & Quina, 1998). To be maximally effective, however, mentoring must begin much earlier, in graduate school. Mason and Goulden (2002) note that "a large proportion of women drop away before taking on a tenure-track job. They need to be counseled and supported much earlier, as graduate students, when they are making difficult decisions." As it is now, most women make their decisions by looking around and seeing the facts: Women with children often have a hard time gaining the respect of others in academia, and women without children seem considerably more successful. So they either decide to delay childbearing, with the attendant risks (Varner, 2000), or they revise their career aspirations, sometimes becoming Aisenberg and Harrington's (1988) "deflected" women, off the tenure track permanently despite having the same qualifications and apparent talent as those who succeed in gaining tenure.

But although mentoring can help graduate students and junior faculty to understand and succeed within academia, mentoring alone cannot effect systemic change. Senior female faculty who focus on the broader goal of increasing the numbers of tenured women often advise junior women to fit in at all costs until they get tenure. In this advice we see a conflict between the mentor's goals of increasing the number of tenured women faculty and, sometimes, the quality of life an individual woman experiences for some six years of her life. Mentoring focuses on pragmatic, achievable goals within the context of the academic culture as it is; activism, policy changes, and paradigm shifts can actually change that culture.

Policy

Increasingly, college and university administrators are implementing family-friendly policies, and faculty activists are becoming more educated about how to achieve policy victories. Surveys conducted in 1991 and in 1995 show a definite trend, with policies such as employment assistance for spouses, stopping the tenure clock, and job sharing in place at many more colleges and universities in 1995 than just four years earlier (Wilson, 1996; Hutton Raabe, 1997). As previously radical ideas such as tenure-clock stoppage become commonplace, work-family theorists and activists continue to press for even more fundamental changes: for example, changes that recognize that child rearing takes close to two decades, not the one year of a stopped tenure clock, or changes that reconceptualize our understanding of gender roles and family structure. Robert Drago and Joan Williams (2000) provide a rationale and model language for a half-time tenure track, under which policy a parent could work half time for up to 12 years before coming up for tenure. Annette Kolodny (1998) provides a checklist of ideal family-friendly policies and calls on universities to address changing family structures and the needs of *all* members of the university community, rather than focusing family-friendly policies to benefit only the most privileged members of the university workforce. She notes that "the difficulties in creating a family-friendly campus do not derive entirely from a paucity of financial resources. Instead, the real problem is our long-term failure of commitment and imagination, a failure that we can no longer tolerate" (Kolodny, 1998, p. 304).

As helpful as policy ideals are, however, in stimulating imagination and pushing the limits of what parents in the academy can hope for, Kathy

Bischoping (2003) points out that university negotiators are likely to dismiss model clauses as utopian and without precedent. To combat this objection, she assembled a summary of "best practices" in Canadian universities, so that Canadian faculty representatives could cite precedents in lobbying for family-friendly policies. The Association for Women in Science (2002) provides a similar list of best practices for colleges and universities in the United States.

According to Jerry A. Jacobs (2004), however, current efforts at policy change do not go far enough. He believes that part-time tenure-track positions will merely reinstitutionalize gender inequity in another form and that tenure-clock stoppage, by focusing on allowing parents to "catch up," ignores the larger problem of the ever-increasing demands on professors' time. The pace and demands of academic careers continue to increase: At an average of 54.8 hours for men and 52.8 hours for women, professorial workweeks in 1998 were roughly two hours longer than they had been only six years earlier (Jacobs, p. 14). Jacobs proposes policy changes to limit the workweeks of all professors, thus addressing the cause, rather than the symptoms, of work-family balance difficulties in the academy.

Culture

Unfortunately, the low rates of utilization for family-friendly policies (Hutton Raabe, 1997; Kolker Finkel, Olswang, & She, 1994; Drago & Colbeck, 2003) indicate that policy implementation is not enough. Low utilization rates in academia mirror the nonacademic world. For example, though many have praised the family-friendly policy initiatives of Sweden (e.g., Crittenden, 2001), Williams (2000) points out that these very egalitarian policy measures have nevertheless not led to equality in Sweden: Women still take the majority of leaves and do the majority of child care; men don't take leaves because they fear being marginalized at work. We require changes in perceptions—changes in how we conceptualize work and in how employers structure work, such that women and men with significant caregiving responsibilities can be recognized as valuable and effective workers. Such cultural changes in the academy will embolden larger numbers of parents to feel safe in taking advantage of the family-friendly policies that have been instituted. Thus, efforts for change cannot stop with the institution of family-friendly policies: Administrators must follow up such initiatives with concrete measures to shift attitudes of the senior faculty who actually decide the fates of junior faculty members. Joan Williams (2002) recommends that universities follow the example of the corporate world by designing training programs to make faculty members aware of the messages they send colleagues about work and family. The limited use of sensitivity training for employees, even at universities showing leadership on family-friendly policy implementation (Wilson, 1996), suggests that concrete measures to change attitudes and ideals within departments are an important area for change.

THE ESSAYS IN THIS COLLECTION touch on a number of topics and concerns covered in this introduction, and the collection contributes to the conversation begun by the many recent collections of personal essays by women in academia (Hannah, Paul, & Vethamany-Globus, 2002; Keahey & Schnitzer, 2003) and by parents in academia (Coiner & Hume George, 1998; O'Reilly, 2003). Such stories play an important role in changing others' perceptions of parenting in academia and serve as well to broaden academic parents' own understandings of their situations. Recognizing the similar struggles and rewards of others combining motherwork with academic work can provide a deeper context, a sociological imagination that sees the political in the personal, the communal in the private.

REFERENCES

Aisenberg, N., & Harrington, M. (1988). *Women of academe: Outsiders in the sacred grove*. Amherst: University of Massachusetts Press.

American Association of University Professors. (2001). *Statement of principles on family responsibilities and academic work*. Retrieved May 20, 2004, from www.aaup.org/statements/REPORTS/re01fam.htm

American Association of University Professors. (2004). Don't blame faculty for high tuition: Annual report on the economic status of the profession, 2003–04. *Academe, 90* (2). Retrieved May 13, 2004, from www.aaup.org/surveys/zrep.htm

Association for Women in Science. (2002). Model programs and policies. *Academic climate: Addressing the climate for women in academia*. Retrieved June 10, 2004, from www.chillyclimate.org/examples.asp

Astin, H. S., & Milem, J. F. (1997). The status of academic couples in U.S. institutions. In M. A. Ferber & J. W. Loeb (Eds.), *Academic couples: Problems and promises* (pp. 128–155). Urbana: University of Illinois Press.

Banoub-Baddour, S. (2002). A nurse educator's experience in academia. In E. Hannah, L. Paul, & S. Vethamany-Globus (Eds.), *Women in the Canadian academic tundra: Challenging the chill* (pp. 22–25). Montreal, Quebec: McGill-Queen's University Press.

Baruch, G. K., & Barnett, R. C. (1986). Role quality, multiple role involvement, and psychological well-being in midlife women. *Journal of Personality and Social Psychology, 51*, 578–585.

Benjamin, E. (1998). *Disparities in the salaries and appointments of academic women and men: An update of a 1988 report on Committee W on the Status of Women in the Academic Profession.* Retrieved May 20, 2004, from www.aaup. org/Issues/WomeninHE/Wrepup.htm

Bischoping, K. (2003). The best you can expect when you're expecting . . . and beyond: A review of contract language for mothers in the Canadian academy. *Journal of the Association for Research on Mothering, 5*(2), 77–86.

Booth, W. C., Booth, A. D., Davis, C., Zemon Davis, N., Davis, S., Davis Taieb, H., et al. (1999). Going into the family business: Academic parents, academic children. *Academe, 85*(3), 20–27.

Callero, P. L. (1985). Role-identity salience. *Social Psychology Quarterly, 48*, 203–215.

Coiner, C., & Hume George, D. (Eds.). (1998). *The family track: Keeping your faculties while you mentor, nurture, teach, and serve.* Urbana: University of Illinois Press.

Collins, L. H., Chrisler, J. C., & Quina, K. (Eds.). (1998). *Career strategies for women in academe: Arming Athena.* Thousand Oaks, CA: Sage.

Coltrane, S. (1996). *Family man: Fatherhood, housework, and gender equity.* New York: Oxford University Press.

Crittenden, A. (2001). *The price of motherhood: Why motherhood is the most important—and least valued—job in America.* New York: Henry Holt.

Drago, R., & Colbeck, C. (2003). *The Mapping Project: Exploring the terrain of U.S. colleges and universities for faculty and families* (Final report). Retrieved May 20, 2004, from http://lsir.la.psu.edu/workfam/mappingproject.htm

Drago, R., Crouter, A. C., Wardell, M., & Willits, B. S. (2001). *Final report of the Faculty and Families Project.* University Park: Pennsylvania State University. Retrieved June 9, 2004, from http://lsir.la.psu.edu/workfam/facultyfamilies.htm

Drago, R., & Williams, J. (2000). A half-time tenure-track proposal. *Change, 32*(6), 46–51.

Farber, S. (1977). The earnings and promotion of women faculty: Comment. *American Economic Review, 67*, 199–206.

Farley, J. (1990). Women professors in the USA: Where are they? In S. Stiver Lie & V. E. O'Leary (Eds.), *Storming the tower: Women in the academic world* (pp. 194–207). New York: Nichols/GP Publishing.

Farnsworth, M. W. (1974). *The young woman's guide to an academic career.* New York: Richards Rosen Press.

Frye, J. S. (2003). Making a living, making a life. *Journal of the Association for Research on Mothering, 5*(2), 21–28.

Garey, A. I. (1999). *Weaving work and motherhood*. Philadelphia: Temple University Press.

Hannah, E., Paul, L., & Vethamany-Globus, S. (Eds.). (2002). *Women in the Canadian academic tundra: Challenging the chill*. Montreal, Quebec: McGill-Queen's University Press.

Hensel, N. (1990). Maternity, promotion, and tenure: Are they compatible? In L. B. Welch (Ed.), *Women in higher education: Changes and challenges* (pp. 3–11). New York: Praeger.

Hewlett, S. A. (2002). *Creating a life: Professional women and the quest for children*. New York: Miramax.

Hutton Raabe, P. (1997). Work-family policies for faculty: How "career-and-family-friendly" is academe? In M. A. Ferber & J. W. Loeb (Eds.), *Academic couples: Problems and promises* (pp. 208–225). Urbana: University of Illinois Press.

Jacobs, J. A. (2004). The faculty time divide. *Sociological Forum, 19*, 3–27.

Keahey, D., & Schnitzer, D. (Eds.). (2003). *The madwoman in the academy: 43 women boldly take on the Ivory Tower*. Calgary, Alberta: University of Calgary Press.

Kolker Finkel, S., & Olswang, S. G. (1996). Child rearing as a career impediment to women assistant professors. *Review of Higher Education, 19*, 123–139.

Kolker Finkel, S., Olswang, S. G., & She, N. (1994). Childbirth, tenure, and promotion for women faculty. *Review of Higher Education, 17*, 259–270.

Kolodny, A. (1998). Creating the family-friendly campus. In C. Coiner & D. Hume George (Eds.), *The family track: Keeping your faculties while you mentor, nurture, teach, and serve* (pp. 284–310). Urbana: University of Illinois Press.

Loeb, J. W. (1997). Programs for academic partners: How well can they work? In M. A. Ferber & J. W. Loeb (Eds.), *Academic couples: Problems and promises* (pp. 270–298). Urbana: University of Illinois Press.

Mangan, K. S. (1988, February 3). Women seek time off to bear children without jeopardizing academic careers. *Chronicle of Higher Education*, pp. A1, A16–A17.

Mark, R. (1998). Lavender labors and activist mothering. In C. Coiner & D. Hume George (Eds.), *The family track: Keeping your faculties while you mentor, nurture, teach, and serve* (pp. 80–85). Urbana: University of Illinois Press.

Marks, S. R., & MacDermid, S. M. (1996). Multiple roles and the self: A theory of role balance. *Journal of Marriage and the Family, 58*, 417–432.

Mason, M. A., & Goulden, M. (2002). Do babies matter? The effect of family formation on the lifelong careers of academic men and women. *Academe, 88* (6), 21–27.

Menges, R. J., & Exum, W. H. (1983). Barriers to the progress of women and minority faculty. *Journal of Higher Education, 54*, 123–144.

Olsen, T. (1978). *Silences*. New York: Delacorte.

O'Reilly, A. (2002). What's a girl like you doing in a nice place like this? Mothering in the academy. In E. Hannah, L. Paul, & S. Vethamany-Globus (Eds.), *Women in the Canadian academic tundra: Challenging the chill* (pp. 183–188). Montreal: McGill-Queen's University Press.

O'Reilly, A. (Ed.). (2003). Mothering in the academy [Special issue]. *Journal of the Association for Research on Mothering, 5*(2).

Perna, L. (2001). The relationship between family responsibilities and employment status among college and university faculty. *Journal of Higher Education, 72,* 584–611.

Radcliffe College Committee on Graduate Education for Women. (1956). *Graduate education for women: The Radcliffe Ph.D.* Cambridge: Harvard University Press.

Rossen Cardozo, A. (1986). *Sequencing.* New York: Atheneum.

Sandler, B., & Hall, R. M. (1986). *The campus climate revisited: Chilly for women faculty, administrators, and graduate students.* Washington, DC: Project on the Status and Education of Women.

Sorcinelli, M. D. (1992). New and junior faculty stress: Research and responses. In M. D. Sorcinelli & A. E. Austen (Eds.), *Developing new and junior faculty* (pp. 27–37). San Francisco: Jossey-Bass.

Spore, M. B., Harrison, M. D., & Haggerson, N. L., Jr. (2002). *Stories of the academy: Learning from the Good Mother.* New York: Peter Lang.

Thorne, B. (1999). *Pick-up time at Oakdale Elementary School: Work and family from the vantage points of children* (Working Paper No. 2). Berkeley: Center for Working Families, University of California.

Toth, E. (1997). *Ms. Mentor's impeccable advice for women in academia.* Philadelphia: University of Pennsylvania Press.

Trubek, A. (2004, February 20). From spousal hire to single mom. *Chronicle of Higher Education,* pp. C1, C4.

Varner, A. (2000). *The consequences and costs of delaying attempted childbirth for women faculty.* Background Paper for the Faculty and Families Project. University Park: Department of Labor Studies and Industrial Relations, Pennsylania State University. Retrieved May 20, 2004, from http://lsir.la.psu.edu/workfam/delaykids.pdf

Verbrugge, L. M. (1986). Role burdens and physical health of women and men. *Women and Health, 11,* 47–77.

Williams, J. (2000). *Unbending gender: Why family and work conflict and what to do about it.* New York: Oxford University Press.

Williams, J. (2002, June 17). How academe treats mothers. *Chronicle of Higher Education.* Retrieved June 26, 2002, from http://chronicle.com/jobs/2002/06/2002061701c.htm

Wilson, R. (1996, October 11). A report praises 29 colleges for family friendly policies: But other institutions are faulted for failing to help employees with child care and aid for sick relatives. *Chronicle of Higher Education,* pp. A13–A15.

Wilson, R. (1999a, March 10). Scheduling motherhood: Women on the tenure track have trouble fitting children into career timetables. *Chronicle of Higher Education,* pp. A14–A15.

Wilson, R. (1999b, June 25). Timing is everything: Academe's annual baby boom: Female professors say they feel pressure to plan childbirth for the summer. *Chronicle of Higher Education,* pp. A13–A15.

Wolf-Wendel, L., Twombly, S. B., & Rice, S. (2003). *The two-body problem: Dual-career-couple hiring policies in higher education.* Baltimore: Johns Hopkins University Press.

PART I

Challenges

Anita Ilta Garey (1999) describes the many types of resources that women must take into account in considering how they will "weave" together their work and family lives, including income, class background, education, occupational field, job security, marital or relationship status, support from other family members, racial-ethnic privilege, public social support, neighborhood, transportation, family size and ages of children, and the mother's own physical health. For a specifically academic context, we might add institutional support for parenting to this list. A lack of resources or an excessive burden in even one of these areas can greatly increase the challenges involved in creating a satisfying combination of work and family.

Shimberlee Jirón-King describes the poverty in which both she and her spouse grew up and how the chaos and pain of her life made success in college impossible initially. Her struggle to attain an education has made her an activist, and she continues in academia not solely for her own intellectual pleasure, but so that she can effect change in the system for other girls like her and for Mayra, the 10-year-old girl she tutored who said, "It doesn't matter if I don't read. I'll never go to college. I'm a Mexicangirl." Jirón-King's essay explores the many ways she had to learn to "pass" within the privileged institutions where she attended graduate school, not only attempting to hide her class background but learning as well to avoid drawing on her experience as a mother to support points in class. Throughout, she emphasizes the importance of community to her life as an intellectual, implicitly rejecting the image of the scholar as loner; she describes the mentors who supported her and took chances on her, her academic work's activism on behalf of Chicana/o children, and especially the support she has received from her spouse and sons.

In her essay in this collection, Lynn Z. Bloom describes learning to work in the minutes stolen between parenting tasks. Marc Christensen, recounting his three years as the primary, at-home caregiver of his young children, explains the drawbacks of working in this way, how his engagement with "the language of parenting" affected his access to academic language. During his time at home, though he still viewed himself as belonging to the academic community, the lack of reinforcement from the world of academia, including the physical space of the campus itself, made academic work difficult or impossible. Christensen's essay focuses our attention on the social interactions that feed individuals' intellectual lives; without such interactions and support, maintaining one's identity as an academic and continuing to perform academic work can come to seem pointless.

Janice Rieman explores the meaning of these institutional social supports, narrating her continuing struggle to understand her identity as an intellectual in the context of her life as a former tenure-track professor who now works as an adjunct lecturer and is primarily focused on raising her daughter. Resisting the academic yardstick that measures intellectual merit by one's position in the academic hierarchy, Rieman describes her changing self-concept as she shifts from considering herself an *academic* to viewing herself as a *scholar*, a valuable part of her identity regardless of whether she achieves institutional validation through another tenure-track job. Rieman's story provides a personal angle to an institutional problem: the growing numbers of dual-career academic couples combined with geographical isolation and limited job prospects at many colleges and universities. Research on the topic has demonstrated the need for more policy solutions (Ferber & Loeb, 1997; Wolf-Wendel, Twombly, & Rice, 2003), but as long as policy lags behind reality, couples will be faced with the choice of whose career should come first.

Katherine Lane Antolini, Donna J. Nelson, and Kathryn Jacobs all engage with the issue of how cultural expectations of motherhood shape the experience of individual mothers negotiating careers within specific departments. Sharon Hays (1996), in her analysis of our culture's ideology of mothering, asserts that the ideology of "intensive mothering"—the idea that good mothering requires women "to expend a tremendous amount of time, energy, and money in raising their children" (p. x)—pervades not only an individual mother's consciousness, but the ideas and structures of the institutions with which women come into contact. For Lane Antolini, her own internalization of societal expectations of mothers was mirrored by the health care and social service workers who criticized her decision to continue with graduate studies despite her son's diagnosis of autism. But although she struggles with guilt, she knows that her ability to "escape" into scholarly work makes her a better and more emotionally available mother. Donna J. Nelson expresses no guilt for her decision not to scale back her work as an academic chemist following the birth of her son; nevertheless, her tenure case was nearly derailed by the department chair's assertion that they didn't want people like her in the department, because she should have been home with her son.

A similar paternalism characterized Kathryn Jacobs's experience at her first tenure-track job. As a woman with one child, she wasn't taken very seriously, but the situation didn't become unbearable until after she gave birth prematurely to twins, one with extensive special needs. For her colleagues, mothering three children apparently precluded her being considered a serious scholar, so Jacobs's teaching schedule shifted from literature courses to "service" courses in areas in which she had no expertise. Both Nelson's and Jacobs's experiences happened in the late 1980s; a lot has changed since then, but it's still possible to find similar stories (see, e.g., Cohen, 2002). Facing the reality of possible bias against mothers in the academic job market, Gale Walden attempted to "hide the baby" while searching for a tenure-track job. Her experiences suggested to her that not only potential colleagues, but graduate students as well, had a difficult time imagining a mother "fitting" with a department. Not surprising, given that Fiske, Cuddy, Glick, and Xu (2002) found that a sample of students rated "housewives" as similar in competence to "elderly," "blind," "retarded," and "disabled" people.

As much as weak family policies and overwhelming workload, perceptions such as these—which fellow professors and students alike share, since they are drawn from the larger culture—have the ability to derail a parent's academic career. Tarshia Stanley began her graduate career in the early 1990s, just before giving birth to her daughter, confident in her ability to combine single motherhood with graduate studies. She was right, but her success continually amazed the professors who had laid bets on how long she would last in graduate school, sure that a single African American mother could never make it as a scholar.

In the face of this type of bias and judgment, the safest course is to put the best face possible on the situation, to go on record only with positive stories in an attempt to change people's perceptions. Cindy Patey Brewer's husband advised such a course upon hearing part of her essay for this collection, the part about her fantasies of escaping her academic career. He counseled, "I want you to get tenure, and talking about your desire to commit career suicide makes you seem flaky." But she had to narrate the desire to escape, which appeared temporarily during her sixth pregnancy and constituted part of the ebb and flow of her shifting allegiances: Sometimes mothering her six sons pulls her toward exclusive devotion to family life, whereas other times the delight of scholarly life pulls her to deepened commitment to her academic career. Describing the real difficulties of parenting within academia is not the safest course, but it is a necessary one.

Both families and academic institutions, as they are constituted at this point in history, are "greedy institutions," demanding great investments of energy and commitment. Given this, we can expect real challenges to arise from attempting to combine parenting with academic work, but honest stories from people living with these challenges can let others dealing with the same problems know that they are not alone. Additionally, such stories can contribute to our understanding of the sociology of academia and of the family, becoming, we can hope, impetus for change in both institutions.

REFERENCES

Cohen, H. (2002, August 4). The baby bias. *New York Times,* Education Life supplement, p. 25.

Ferber, M. A., & Loeb, J. W. (Eds.). (1997). *Academic couples: Problems and promises.* Urbana: University of Illinois Press.

Fiske, S. T., Cuddy, A. J. C., Glick, P., & Xu, J. (2002). A model of (often mixed) stereotype content: Competence and warmth respectively follow from perceived status and competition. *Journal of Personality and Social Psychology, 82,* 878–902.

Garey, A. I. (1999). *Weaving work and motherhood.* Philadelphia: Temple University Press.

Hays, S. (1996). *The cultural contradictions of motherhood.* New Haven, CT: Yale University Press.

Wolf-Wendel, L., Twombly, S. B., & Rice, S. (2003). *The two-body problem: Dual-career-couple hiring policies in higher education.* Baltimore: Johns Hopkins University Press.

1

La estudiante caminante: My Motherwork Is Here, My Otherwork Is There

Shimberlee Jirón-King

> Caminante, no hay puentes, se hace puentes al andar.
> [*Voyager, there are no bridges, one builds them as one walks.*]
> —Moraga & Anzaldúa, *This Bridge Called My Back*

In order to understand the difficulty of this sojourn, my readers must understand that my spouse and I do not come from the working class. Working-class children grow up with more stability than we did, for their parents work steadily, and the children usually stay in the same schools and spend most of their childhoods in one place. Adam has lived in more than 30 different places, and he spent his childhood unsupervised, fatherless, playing on the streets in the Bronx, always on welfare until he left home. I had little more stability. When I was nine, my parents divorced; my father left the house and moved into a camping trailer. He lived there until he committed suicide two years later. My mother struggled; she did her best, drawing on the few resources she had. My grandparents helped her financially, but not one of my many relatives took any interest in my life. A quiet, introverted girl, I survived by retreating into my room and my books, awaiting the day I would leave. There is not enough space here to explain the agony that Adam and I endured; it is enough, I think, to say that we experienced comparable versions of poverty, violence, madness, substance abuse, illness, disappointment, rejection, neglect, and alienation.

We found each other at Colorado State University—one refugee can always recognize another. Adam had graduated with a BA in social work, but I flailed about, not knowing what to do because I could not pass the basic math requirements to graduate. People in this much psychic pain cannot study—it is enough if they can continue to breathe. I didn't know how anyway: I dropped out.

After we married, we discovered that Adam's BA meant that he didn't have to do manual labor, but this particular degree does not raise one much above minimum wage. I found myself at jobs that kept me on my feet all day, miserable. It took only a few years for us to realize that old-fashioned diligence, hard work, and teamwork would make it barely possible for us to pay rent and bills. We would never save anything; we could dream of nothing.

I was so frustrated by my condition. I couldn't make enough money, but I knew I was better than this. I knew I had potential. I had worked as a waitress, hotel maid, clerk. I worked in a supermarket deli, I worked as a cashier, and it was becoming extremely clear that without any education I was doomed to a lifetime of mindless, manual labor. So, when I was hired as a private nanny and discovered I could earn twice as much money, I was elated. I took care of four children and loved them immensely. It was so good to be off of my feet all of the time and to be doing something that had some meaning to me. Instead of working in a dull, hostile environment all day long, I was in a well-furnished, middle-class home taking care of beautiful children. I loved it. We read books, we went to the park, we took walks; I made their meals, played games, devised art projects, taught them their alphabet. I took my job seriously, and I was good at it, but when my employers found out I was pregnant, I was fired. It seems these people wanted the type of person who was willing to love their children but never to have her own.

Even though I was fired, I still wanted to be a nanny because I loved children so much. I found employment again right away, and these families assured me they wouldn't mind their nanny having children of her own, so things seemed to have worked out all right. However, as soon as I began to show, life got difficult, and I could tell that my pregnancy did bother them. One mother began verbally abusing me, hoping I would quit so that the agency would send a replacement. It was impossible to make me quit, though; I had dealt with so much verbal abuse in the past, I knew how to cope. But when I got home, my spouse began recognizing the change in me. I was forlorn, and tired. When I told him I was being harassed because I was pregnant, I saw the despair in his eyes, and I think it was at that moment that we both realized that we would have to take a new direction in our lives, that something would have to change, that the American Dream was out of our reach. I was a good, honest, hard worker, but these were the real conditions of our existence.

Eventually this woman fired me because I used a sick day to go to an OB appointment. Soon after this, Adam pointed out the obvious: We were both going to have to go back to school, and one of us would have to repay our defaulted student loans. Most people don't understand the pragmatics of poverty and college funding. It is not unusual for the working poor to find that they cannot repay their previous student loans, and in many cases those loans go into default. As a result, they become ineligible for all student aid—including scholarships and programs designed to help those who cannot pay tuition. Without the help of Pell grants and other forms of student aid (such as Stafford loans and other federal programs), neither of us could afford to go back to school. For us, the problem was that we had both defaulted on our previous student loans, because we had not found occupations that would make it possible to repay our former student debts and also meet our present financial needs. Adam's debt was $10,000; mine was only $4,000. Because we were both longing to return to school, we used the amount of our debt as the deciding factor—with less debt, I went back first. It is much easier to raise $4,000 than to raise $10,000. (It has taken several years and a lot of hard work to bring Adam out of default. But what is worse, I think, is that despite all of my education, I will probably always remain an indentured servant to the government for the student loans that I have required in order to earn my doctorate. I hope that some day, the poor in this country will be able to go to college without such burdens. As it is now, higher education remains class-based and economically prohibitive.) But I think, also, that because Adam actually had a BA, he knew he could earn a little more money than I could, and he had more flexibility regarding his hours. Besides this, I think he felt it was his duty.

"Do you think you can do well in school?" he asked.

"Yes—I know I can." I knew I could—especially after I had tasted what the world has for those who can't, or won't. I was determined to succeed. And besides, now I had 10 times the psychic energy I had when I was at CSU. I loved school as a child. I had been identified as "gifted and talented." Besides my room, school had been my only refuge. The smell of new crayons, pencils, and the crackling pages of new books excited me.

As Adam and I spoke, I began to feel some of that excitement again.

"Go as far as you can. Maybe you can become a school teacher, or maybe you can get into a graduate program. Who knows? When you're done, you can put me through school, and maybe I can become a writer."

After we made the decision, I was elated. I was still pregnant and unemployed, but I couldn't have felt better. We had a battle plan. We were in such bad condition that I had a mental picture of Adam and myself standing at the bottom of a high wall. On one side was our poverty, and on the other side was the promise. One of us had to get to the top while the other boosted, and then the one at the top would have to reach back and pull the other up. I enrolled at the Metropolitan State College of Denver. Now the pressure was on me to succeed in school. I was determined not to repeat history. I went to the Denver Public Library and checked out and read every book I could find on study skills.

I learned that it doesn't matter how gifted or how much potential a student has if she does not have mental discipline, the ability to concentrate, to organize, to understand, and to absorb material. Students fall victim to the bell curve because the educational system is designed to sift students—putatively separating the talented from the mediocre, the average from the slow. I learned how to master the material I was studying, no matter how much time it took, no matter what the subject, no matter what the effort; I learned that preparation is key.

As we waited for the baby to be born, I studied prealgebra and algebra every day, preparing for the math placement test at Metro. I avoided a year's worth of remediation and passed out of the basic requirements. This was my first academic victory; I gave birth a few weeks later. After the first year, I began winning awards and scholarships, so we didn't have to pay tuition with loans. And we found that with financial aid and the student loans I was now eligible for, we had just as much money—if not more—than when we were both employed. We began to have some hope about using education to climb out of poverty.

I HAVE BEEN IN SCHOOL almost as long as I have been a mother; I resumed my BA six weeks after my oldest was born in 1995, and we've all been in school since. I'm proud of my spouse and three little boys who can turn any campus into a playground, a Star Wars scene, a racetrack, the site of an epic battle, or even a quiet place to take a nap. They have vicariously attended three different institutions. They have enjoyed the attention of friendly college kids who think they're cute, and they have wandered the campus grounds, seeing museums, sculptures, exhibits, and sights that I never have time to see. They associate me with books, libraries, writing long papers in a short time, and perpetual reading. They already know that just because Mommy is home, it doesn't mean she isn't at work, and they take for granted that Daddy will wipe their tears, change their diapers, prepare their meals, and take care of them when I study. We've traveled across the country twice, following the best possible opportunities, leaving possessions behind and starting from nothing—but we had nothing to lose.

The academic space bends with enough imagination, but it is most versatile when imagined in terms of its relationship to other spaces that are always already a part of life, and in our case, it overlaps with and redefines the family space as well. This seems obvious to me, but when people discover that I have three children, ages two, five, and eight, there are only a few basic responses: (1) *"Are you CRAZY??!!"* This response is rarely articulated, but easy to read because everyone responds this way at first. These open people are actually the easiest to win over. So far, only other graduate students say it this way—professors will not because of its inflammatory potential. (2) *"How do you do it?!"* This is the polite version of "Are you CRAZY??!!" If I wait, this response has an important follow-up. If the person expresses admiration, then there is hope that I will convince her that motherwork in the academy is possible, even if it is not easy. If the person says something like, "You must be soooo busy . . . ," she is often saying that I must be shortchanging something because "You can't do it all, dear." If she smiles and silently wags her head from side to side, I don't waste any more time. Men usually nod up and down. It means just about the same thing. (3) *"So, how are your kids? What are you working on right now?"* Rare. This person is unusual—he or she already takes for granted that female intellectuals *can* have both families and successful academic futures. If my director did not respond to me in this way, I'd be in big trouble.

THE GREATEST CHALLENGE of being a mother and a graduate student is convincing my peers that I am a serious and committed scholar. I find it's usually easier not to remind professionals around me that I am a mother in order to convince them that I, too, am a professional. For instance, when I introduce myself at the beginning of a seminar, I never say, "Hi—I'm a mother of three." If I can avoid letting people know about my motherhood right away, I get a chance to demonstrate that I should be taken seriously without having to explain myself. I never have to explain why I, as a Chicana, wish to focus on minority literature, but I am so often questioned about my family role, and yet *familia* is an important part of Chicana identity, even if one chooses not to raise a family or makes choices different than my own. The world is changing, and the Chicana mother is changing. She will no longer be defined as unschooled or housebound. We are educating our children, and we are educating ourselves—aggressively. It's the only way.

How will I be understood *en el otro lado?* I want acceptance by my peers as a worthwhile member of an intellectual community; I want the esteem of my professors as a promising scholar; I want respect from undergraduates as a knowledgeable and qualified teacher. Evaluation is subtle and not always explicit—I sense opinions formed behind closed doors and expressed in a cabalistic code that I cannot decipher until I cross to the other side. When I do, I hope I will see clearly, looking back as well as forward. I will cross. *Mira*.

I HAD ORIGINALLY PLANNED to become an elementary school teacher, because I do enjoy kids, but when I studied literature, and met some wonderfully inspiring teachers, such as Stacey Coyle, who taught American literature, and Elizabeth Holtze, who directed my honors thesis, my intellectual perspective began to change. When I was introduced to Chicana/o literature such as Lorna Dee Cervantes's *Emplumada,* Ana Castillo's *So Far From God,* Sandra Cisneros's *House on Mango Street,* Tomás Rivera's *. . . y no se lo tragó la tierra/and the earth did not part . . . ,* I was inspired.

Chicana/o literature, however, is not being taught in the schools. Even though Metro was at least 50% Chicana/o, there were no courses available at that time. I am happy to say things have changed at Metro in the last five years, and it now awards more degrees to Hispanics than any other institution in the state ("College earns national ranking," 2002). Metro has developed a major in Chicana/o studies when many schools across the country have made budget cuts and postponed or eliminated offering a major. Many public schools in the Denver area have large Chicana/o populations, but Chicana/o literature is rarely, if ever, taught there. Even though I had grown up as a Chicana in the Denver area myself, I had never had a Chicana/o teacher, nor had I ever encountered Chicana/o texts in school. I began to understand that there is a growing need to show teachers at every level the importance of Chicana/o literature in teaching children to read and take interest in school.

As my intellectual interests were being reshaped, an amazing thing occurred. I was assigned to a practicum in West Denver as a tutor to a Chicana child who could not read. She was a beautiful, intelligent little girl—wide-eyed and curious—but something negative had already been planted in her mind. Whether it was society at large, her family, her school, her neighborhood, or maybe all, these powers had already placed formidable boundaries around her. I was stunned and broken-hearted when she told me she believed that going to college was out of the question:

"It doesn't matter if I don't read. I'll never go to college. I'm a Mexican-girl."

"*Mira*, Mayra. You can go—look at me!" I wanted to hold her in my arms and read *House on Mango Street* to her. She was only 10, already responsible for younger siblings after school, helping her hard-working mother at home, staying out of trouble for herself while her parents worked, starting dinner so the family didn't eat too late at night. Perhaps she will someday look up and see her own intelligence in the mirror; maybe she will catch the sparkle I saw as she connected images and ideas with those abstract symbols on the page. What do the schwa and the digraph signify? Nothing, if they don't help a Mexicangirl with dreams but few opportunities; nothing, if they won't open doors. At the very least, I taught her to read and exposed her to a little Chicana literature. After a while, she seemed to enjoy it. Give her *Emplumada*.

Chicana/o children in Denver (and too many other places) aren't exposed to successful Chicana/o role models. Chicana/o texts are usually unavailable and unknown in these schools. Even as the body of these texts has grown in print, they are still left out of circulation. Children cannot access texts that their teachers ignore. Moreover, teachers are often willfully ignorant. While they could inspire their students to read by providing literature through which students could identify with the protagonist, the teachers instead protest that they must raise test scores. As it is, a Chicana/o student who wants an education must eschew her language and her culture and become entirely immersed in a curriculum that is completely unsympathetic and uninspiring to her. Give her *Dew on the Thorn, Who Would Have Thought It?, Caballero*. Schools with high populations of Chicana/o students must serve those populations; Chicana/o students require a curriculum that inspires and challenges them but doesn't alienate them.

The Chicana/o canon has been established, but little has been done to disseminate it into the American public school system, even though the Chicana/o population has continued to rise. These texts are available, and elementary and secondary school teachers who teach Chicana/o students have a responsibility to know and read them. First, because if they are not Chicana/os, then they need to understand something of their students' histories and worlds, but also because their knowledge of these texts will enable them to address important issues as they develop curricula, design lesson plans, and select materials. Educators have long recognized the importance of teaching about Martin Luther King Jr., Harriet Tubman, and George Washington Carver. Students who attend school in predominantly African American communities read Ralph Ellison, Richard Wright, and Toni Morrison. So too should Chicana/o students learn about César Chávez, the consequences of the Treaty of Guadalupe Hidalgo, the history of El Movimiento, and they should read Tomás Rivera, Lorna Dee Cervantes, and Jovita Gonzalez, among others. There should be no fear that educators are leading students to a dead end. These texts have the potential to open Chicana/o children to a universe of learning and knowledge that affirms their identity and their potential to make significant intellectual contributions to their worlds.

"I'M NOT SURE I WANT TO BE an elementary school teacher. I think I want to go to graduate school and study literature."

"Well, you're getting straight As. I think you could do just about anything you want. Why? What's the matter?"

"I'm never going to change the system as a teacher, and besides, I love Chicana/o literature, and I know I can teach other people its importance, and maybe even get a few of them to love it too—maybe even influence the curriculum in a few schools. That's what will help change things."

"You should always do what you like—don't get stuck in a job you hate. Believe me—just keep going until you've gone as far as you can. We'll make it. Remember, you'll send me later."

WHEN I WALKED INTO THE examination room to take the Graduate Record Exam (GRE) and the Literature in English Subject Exam in 1997, the room had more than a hundred people in it, and I was the only one pregnant. Our second child. I pretended not to hear any of the comments of the examinees as I gave my identification to the proctor; I only thought about English literature. Bede, Beowulf, Shakespeare, Donne, Dryden, Johnson, Swift, Hawthorne, cummings, Pound, Bishop, Eliot, Jarrell, Joyce, Toomer, Johnson, Walker, Williams, Cervantes, Cisneros, Castillo, Anzaldúa, Moraga, Rivera, Gonzales. . . .

The proctor said, "None of these seats was intended for a woman in your condition."

The Educational Testing Service (ETS) does not take into account that some bodies might be shaped differently than others, except for advance notice of handicap—pregnancy is not a handicap. I squeezed into the flip-top desk, facing forward as much as possible in order to comply with the proctor's insistence that examinees should keep their heads turned toward the front of the room at all times. I smiled as she watched me, hoping to assure her of my goodwill, my integrity.

Many more women were in that examination room than men, yet most were younger than me, single, and childless. Unlike me, they fit into the desks. My shape was more apparent than my race, and I felt their eyes as I entered the room, as the proctor watched me take that test, as I rose to hand in my bubble sheet.

These were not the peers with whom I studied at Metro—this was a different set. They came from the universities; I came from a commuter college. My BA in English had an emphasis in elementary education, but my outside studies had been geared toward this exam. I spent my senior year studying, reading, sitting in a cubicle at Denver University where I could read books but not borrow them. Adam spent afternoons and evenings caring for our son and slept only four hours a day. I aspired to this new future, this new set of peers, and I felt I was breaking certain conventions by attempting to enter graduate study.

If I had tried this a generation ago, I'm not sure I would have made it, so I count myself fortunate and celebrate the transformations effected by my predecessors. Those brave women. Yet, much remains for my own generation. Women have had to struggle for their space in the academy; women continue to struggle for a space in the academy that allows us the same rights to family life as those given to male academics. Even now, I find that male graduate students who are expecting a baby gain congratulations whereas I myself have been questioned.

In graduate school, one professor wrote on my file, "She is not sure of her intellectual commitment." I was spending 10 hours a day studying, hardly spending any time with my children; we had traveled back and forth across the entire country twice, each time selling all of our possessions in order to afford the crossings, and because I was pregnant, this man was questioning my intellectual commitment?! He rarely gave me more than 15 minutes when I visited his office hours. He was always "too busy," he almost never let me speak in his seminar, he made virtually no comments on my final project. He saw only my motherhood, but never understood that pregnancy is not a handicap. ETS does not consider pregnancy a handicap and thus does not afford enough space to comfortably take a crucial test; a professor *does* consider pregnancy a handicap and thus does not afford enough space to make a fair judgment. Fortunately, however, my experience in academia is not about the judgment of one person or one test, but about persistently appealing to the judgment of a number of people, most of whom have enough sense, grace, and wisdom to understand that the mind and the body can be in harmony. One of the professors on my orals committee at Stanford, Jay Fliegelman, told me the first time he met me that he thought it a great advantage for me to have children, to watch them grow and develop linguistically, to be able to witness and test theories of language and psychology as I study. One narrow gate closes, a wider one opens: I cross the boundary where I fit through.

IN MY PENULTIMATE SEMESTER of undergraduate work, I went to class three days after my second child was born because I didn't want a B for poor attendance in a senior seminar that allowed only one absence. I appealed, but the instructor insisted she would make no exception for me. It was the last term that would show on my transcript for applications to graduate schools, and I had a 4.0 to defend. I will never forget the moment when my classmates gave me a standing ovation for coming to class. I earned an A, but more important to me, at that time, I got the GRE scores I thought I needed to get into graduate school for English literature. Three years later, John Bender, the director of graduate studies at Stanford at that time, informed me that my subject score was one of the highest of my cohort, and his initial concern that my educational background would be inadequate had dissipated when he witnessed my determination firsthand, even though I was pregnant at the time. His encouragement and support meant a great deal to me.

Maryland offered me a fellowship in early March. Adam and I celebrated and wept with joy as we replayed the voice-mail message over and over to make sure we weren't dreaming. Later, Georgetown, Boston College, Notre Dame, Denver University, and University of Colorado made offers, but we chose Penn State because it had the most reputable English department, and they offered the most generous fellowship.

Few people outside of my cluster of cubicles at Penn State ever saw my boys, but some graduate students openly expressed their dislike for children and avoided me. With practice, I came to look and sound like the other graduate students except when I mentioned my experiences as a parent, but I quickly learned not to mention those experiences. A female professor laughed at me and said I'd better speed up on the learning curve. I learned that there is clearly a bias in graduate school against bringing personal experience as an example or as evidence for an argument in theoretical discussions, especially if that experience is *maternal*.

It wasn't until after I had almost completed my MA and was considering PhD programs that I came into contact with Paula Moya, who affirmed that my experiences were indeed valid. She sent me a copy of an essay from her forthcoming book, *Learning from Experience,* where I was at last comforted to see someone expose and critique the idea that "appeals to 'experience' or 'identity' may cause [the feminist scholar] to be dismissed as dangerously reactionary or hopelessly naïve" (Moya, 2002, p. 25). When Moya's first book came out, she dedicated it to her daughters—many academics dedicate their work to their children, and some even say that their works *are* their children, but it was very meaningful to me because her daughters had been young while she attended graduate school, too, and I saw that although one female professor had disdained my position and my experiences, there was another somewhere else who would support me. I learned that it is a grievous error to believe that the ovum precludes the oeuvre—academic mothers know much more of labor than is understood. Learn that curve.

I USED WHAT I HAD LEARNED at Penn State to make myself a more attractive candidate when I applied outside. I had been granted early acceptance to the PhD program there, but now that I had greater cultural capital, I wanted to study Chicana/o literature where I could have a director who knew the field. I did have teachers at Penn State who helped me. Nicholas Joukovsky and Djelal Kadir taught me a lot about writing and careful attention to detail. Their seminars had an air of scholarship I had never experienced before. Robert Hume trenchantly advised me to be certain I found a good teacher when I made my choice. He said that academics who won't give prospective students their time aren't worth traveling across the country to study with. I knew I would need the most supportive possible director, so the summer before I applied, I researched possible schools and sent e-mails to professors whose work I admired. The only person who sent back an encouraging e-mail was Stanford's Ramón Saldívar. I was elated because *Chicano Narrative* is such an outstanding text, and he had no way of knowing whether I would be accepted or not. Other professors simply ignored me.

Berkeley made the first offer by e-mail in February, and I ran down the stairs of our apartment yelling the news and crying. Adam could not believe what I was saying, and the boys did not understand, but they began to celebrate by jumping up and down and yelling with us. We read and reread the e-mail, looking for some flaw, some sign that it was a mistake; finding none, we rejoiced.

The next few weeks were phenomenal. We couldn't believe how many offers I was receiving. It was like Christmas. Finally, we could begin to see that the difficulties of coming to Penn State were paying off. We had sacrificed so much in coming to State College. When the movers arrived to take our furniture from Colorado to Pennsylvania, they demanded double the price they had quoted us before, and we didn't have the money. We had one night to decide what we would take—only what fit in the trunk of our car, what we could send through the mail; we gave or threw the rest away. When we arrived at our apartment in State College, we had no furniture and slept on the floor. My spouse worked overnights at a job he hated and hardly slept for those two years, and we desperately needed this confirmation that all that we had endured had been worthwhile.

Berkeley's offer was followed by offers from Chicago, Rutgers, UCLA, University of Texas at Austin, and Indiana, but Stanford's offer made me the happiest because I knew I wanted to work with Ramón Saldívar. When I told my professors at Penn State the news, they were happy for me. James Rambeau, who had recommended me, went around bragging about me, asking friends which school they thought I should choose and offering a continuous stream of advice. In the end he recommended Stanford.

IT'S BEEN MORE THAN HARD—and we barely scrape by on this stipend, these loans, and my spouse's overnight job, but we've been doing it for years. Sometimes we make the utility companies wait, but I turn projects in on time. I have never taken an Incomplete—that's a big deal at Stanford with the quarter system. *Never.* But I need other *nevers.* I should never have to justify my family life or the fact that I struggle against disadvantages I might not have suffered if I had come from the middle class with a "proper academic upbringing." Poor Chicanas don't attend prep school, and we often get excluded from college-track education in the first place. Private education is rare and therefore precious. Yet, I don't want people to believe in exceptionalism—I'm not an example of that. I want people to know that this is no easy road, that we have paid dearly, and that it shouldn't be this way for me, for any other woman of color, or for any woman with children who would be an intellectual if only she had the opportunity. Not all scholars come from privilege, and not all serious academics postpone or forgo family life for the sake of scholarship, nor should we have to.

Even when intellectuals and administrative officials from within the academy find themselves in agreement with me, and most say they do, the structure of the university itself is simply not friendly to aspiring female academics with families. Individual attitudes can be bad enough some-times, and I've experienced the awful sting, but the material conditions have just as much potential to make or break a working-class mother's academic career. The truth is that it's one thing to sympathize with the left, to align oneself with women of color and those suffering poverty on an intellectual level, but it's something entirely different to actually *do something* that mat-ters to those on the outside. Someone will ask how I define substantive and effective activism, but those who act don't have to ask or theorize because they're not afraid to get their hands dirty. If you write about the subaltern, third-world women, and minority discourse, if you base your career on discussing the pain and agony of Others, if you make claims of radicalism and align yourself with the left, I want you to know that it is not just enough to "expose" material conditions and "restore the voice of the silenced." It's not. Poverty is humiliating; marginalization kills people; hunger is physical: I am not being metaphorical.

REFERENCES

Moraga, C., & Anzaldúa, G. (Eds.). (1983). *This bridge called my back: Writings by radical women of color* (2nd ed.). New York: Kitchen Table, Women of Color Press.

Moya, P. M. L. (2002). *Learning from experience: Minority identities, multicultural struggles.* Berkeley: University of California Press.

College earns national ranking. (2002). *Metropolis Magazine: For the Alumni and Friends of Metropolitan State College of Denver, 13*(2), 5.

2

The Language of Parenting

Marc Christensen

On the morning my youngest child began her first regular, scheduled, away-from-dad care, I picked up a book of poetry my wife had brought home the night before. I skimmed the pages quickly, and my sense was that these were poems I could enjoy, though the rushed experience of skimming them was almost completely without pleasure. The single magnificent thing was this: I knew that my sense of poetry, and my ability to critically measure and judge against my own likes and dislikes, was still with me. This may be an easy thing for most graduate students in literature to know, but after spending three of the last four years as a full-time dad, without regular access to child care, my critical faculties were no longer something I could take for granted.

Later that same day, I read all of that slim poetry collection. Though the poems were perhaps relatively unremarkable in the grand scheme of literature, that night I was the book's ideal reader: rapt, and receptive. The difference between *skimming* and *savoring* was not merely the time away from my two children. True, I'd had seven hours' break from child care and housework, but more significant was the sense of freedom and patience I'd acquired knowing that another day to continue my work was just a few days away.

During the three years I'd spent trying to work on various writing projects while staying at home and raising my kids, I'd lost plenty of ground. I took every moment I could spend reading or writing seriously, but the pressurized effort, formed of time stolen away from the routines of housework and child rearing, hadn't done much but keep me feeling faintly aware of my subjects. Even literature had become problematic. With limitations on comfortable reading time, I didn't feel as if I could afford to linger over poetry or novels. Time had shut down my options even to enjoy literature.

One thing that dawned on me, far beyond my own small experience, was that some of the blank looks I'd seen on my students' faces when I'd introduced poetry into a class could perhaps be attributable to their *own* sense of time's passage. Could it be that hurried students (like hurried parents, or hurried children) don't feel the time to dawdle over—or even really fully consider—some of the literature we put before them? That day, it seemed obvious to me, as something I'd *felt,* rather than just thought about in the abstract. Of course there are many other mitigating factors, other things that keep us, and our students, from the life of the mind that academic culture offers. But for more than a year prior to that day, the only poetry I'd enjoyed had been work I was already familiar with, which I visited for comfort. To stretch my mind toward a *new* piece of poetry seemed far outside the realm of possibility. And coming back from that limited state, I had a different sense of the enormous effort we ask our students to make on a daily basis.

It's not just students who are asked to perform Herculean tasks, of course. There is a certain truth in the commonly held belief that mothers must be superwomen, even without the pressures of holding a job. But women (and male caregivers) who are also academics may be in particular jeopardy, as they must be super-capable both at work and at home. A recent Education Life supplement to the *New York Times* suggests that the conflict between tenure clocks and biological clocks is so embedded as to be nearly intractable:

> It would seem that a university—with its ability to allow teachers to work from home, its paid sabbatical semester and its famously liberal thinking— would be an ideal place to balance career and family. But by all accounts, the intense competition, the long hours and the unspoken expectations of the academy's traditionally male culture conspire to make it really, really hard to have a baby and be a professor. (Cohen, 2002, p. 25)

The sobering fact is that untenured faculty members place themselves in jeopardy by having other significant interests and distractions, like children. And the article suggested that a solution wasn't just a matter of tenure review boards, or administrative extensions of the tenure clock. Underneath, the competitive nature of the academy not only relies on total preoccupation but also enforces it through fairly competitive tenure review. It seems like a simple case of labor market mechanisms, distasteful as that may sound.

The real problem is that both roles, professor and caregiver, presuppose total preoccupation and total commitment, making them feel like mutually exclusive domains. Little seems to have changed about this problem in the 40 years since Tillie Olsen wrote about the multiple demands of family and scholarship in *Silences*. Using as examples those writers who failed to maintain what Paul Valéry called the "undistracted center of being" to serve their writing, Olsen presents a long list of material circumstances that impede creativity. Time lost from reading and writing, either to the economic demands of a nonliterary job or to the emotional demands of child rearing, can be debilitating for a writer. Starting with the conflict between writing and other careers, she states:

> A few (I think of the doctors, the incomparables: Chekhov and William Carlos Williams) for special reasons sometimes manage both. But the actuality testifies: substantial creative work demands time, and with rare exceptions only full-time workers have achieved it. Where the claims of creation cannot be primary, the results are atrophy; unfinished work; minor effort and accomplishment; silences. (Olsen, 1978, p. 13)

Olsen declares openly the truth we always knew: that only with a huge degree of preoccupation can one be a writer or an academic. The stated job requirements may be far less than 40 hours per week, depending on teaching load, but the fact remains that only those who take their work home with them, as part of their person, survive. We work in our fields, in a broad sense, far more than 50 or even 60 hours per week. Academic workers are expected to identify with our fields of study, and our expertise, well beyond the lecture hall or the research lab. And for the most part, we may even happily do so. But in a world that puts so much of the social burden for raising children on parents, and usually on mothers, children pose a serious threat to our academic preoccupations.

I love my children dearly, and, by a combination of circumstance and choice, I stayed at home to raise them. But just as three years away from my children would be a terrible hardship for me now, years spent with only sporadic and inconsistent contact with the world of ideas presented painful tests of patience. Not really knowing when I'd get back to a particular idea or book acted as a weight that slowed my progress, not like a ticking clock that made me move faster or with more determination. Moreover, time spent away from the cultural environment of the university brought me to reckon with my own ideas of academic behavior.

Though it may be a simple truism—like the observation that hurried students aren't often good students—the campus environment helps to create the illusion that when away from that setting we'd still all be studying, reading, or writing about many of the same things we study on campus if only we had time away from day-to-day routines that aren't central to our purpose. But, cases of true genius notwithstanding, the campus environment does an amazing amount of work, and it organizes us to do research and teaching in ways that I, at least, found more and more difficult to mimic when removed from the university setting. My academic work came to a complete and full stop. Knowing that I was still the same person, with many of the same ideas, didn't seem to help. I felt as useless and out of touch with myself as with the academic culture, simply because I *identified* myself as belonging inside it. Like the worst nightmare of the research professor constantly interrupted by teaching and administrative duties, when I was removed from the university, I found that I was unable to write or even to juggle the intellectual categories of my projects in full.

It's true, of course, that the constant attention required to raise children doesn't help. We rarely imagine workaholic professors pining away for free time to play with or raise children. Children leave academics and intellectuals of all sorts caught between Bill Cosby's version of parenthood and Tillie Olsen's, comically struggling to find time and a clear enough sense of person to complete a sentence.

In what is probably the most influential standup routine of his career, Cosby told audiences in 1981, "Before we had children, my wife and I were intellectuals." Threading this commentary through the better part of his *Bill Cosby, Himself* performance, Cosby tells us that it started with that very first child: "My wife and I have not been intellectuals since" (Cosby, 1981). Assured of a good laugh, Cosby revisits this proposition, and its comic corollaries, in his best-selling book *Fatherhood*, endlessly reproducing the drama of normally well-collected and intelligent people brought to their behavioral and intellectual knees by the challenges of parenting. And though its points may be humorous, the ring of truth is there: As parents, we are not often called into the position of the intellectual. Sometimes it's hard to remember that you have a mind of your own.

The responsibilities of child rearing openly compete with the prerequisites of academic duties. But where Cosby's effect may be light, Tillie Olsen's remarks are sobering:

More than in any other human relationship, overwhelmingly more, motherhood means being instantly interruptible, responsive, responsible.

Children need one *now* (and remember, in our society, the family must often try to be the center for love and health the outside world is not). The very fact that these are real needs, that one feels them as one's own (love, not duty); *that there is no one else responsible for these needs,* gives them primacy. It is distraction, not meditation, that becomes habitual; interruption, not continuity; spasmodic, not constant toil. . . . Work interrupted, deferred, relinquished, makes blockage—at best, lesser accomplishment. Unused capacities atrophy, cease to be. (Olsen, 1978, pp. 18–19)

In a very narrow way, the tenure review boards that have questioned granting tenure to mothers (or other caregivers) for wavering in their dedication to their departments or fields may have a point. The total commitment to another human being demanded of caregivers does bump up against the totalizing demand of "being an academic." But this version of *being* leaves little room for being anything *but* an academic, like our scapegoat figure of the workaholic professor who would rather not have to teach at all.

Moreover, the bond of love between parent and child is *exactly* the force that makes the position of the academic parent so difficult. Both writing and child rearing are, at their best, not merely *responsibilities,* but *drives.* The ferocity with which Olsen rejects an either/or choice between writing and child rearing shows her as both parent and intellectual, struggling to make the two coexist.

Many people in and around the academy may point to the dilemma of motherwork as a terribly imperfect solution to social atomization, a solution that gives one parent almost total responsibility for raising a fragile little person. But providing a critique of parenting in a complex, modern society doesn't necessarily produce any better solutions, either. The big choice, between career and child rearing, is not so different for academics than it is for any other sort of professional. At best, academic training and enculturation might provide some ground to help challenge the all-encompassing presuppositions of motherwork. If we accept the basic premise that "it takes a village," rather than one supermom, to raise a child, then why do we sometimes resist or feel guilty for even thinking about finding child care for our children?

What if the culture of super-responsibility that marks motherwork is also at work in the academy itself? Single individuals take on superhuman tasks—book projects, primary research—which they are expected to complete more or less alone. And most professors take to these tasks, like parents to children, with both love and occasional frustration. The multi-faceted challenge of nurturing research and book projects while teaching four, five, or six courses each academic year, all the while serving as a kind of embodiment of expertise in your field of specialization, seems more and more like the complicated juggling act of parenthood. But both fields are marked also by the single-mindedness required of those who do these multiple sets of tasks *well*. If the academy expects us to be driven and committed to our work, so too does the task of the parent—especially, perhaps, the parent who is trained by the academy to be an overachiever.

Even the humorous stereotypes are reversible. The example of the absent-minded professor suggests that the world of ideas makes for its own kind of perpetual distraction, and, like the part of a parent's mind that needs to know where children are at all times, so, too, the professor must constantly look around to see where his or her field might be dawdling, playing with rocks beside the road, and not looking where it's going. Bill Cosby, without putting his wit directly to the professoriat, hits the flip side of the coin as well. Enmeshed in the parenting skit of *Bill Cosby, Himself* is a jab at intellectuals (as he and his wife once were) for distractedly reading about things that are, of course, "only natural." In the Cosby mythology, inarticulateness apparently comes in two varieties: the spluttering speech of the parent desperately trying to cope with children, and the disembodied eloquence of the intellectual, who might not really know what to do either but has read quite a bit about what one might do if one were ever faced with reality.

If parents, as Cosby's routine suggests, can easily be reduced to monosyllabic nincompoops, then mixing parents and academics might make for an even more comic effect. Cosby puts on physical display the way that the immediacy of a situation (and, as Olsen reminds us, *all* child-related situations are immediate) can reduce a parent's access to words. The familiar trope of the parent who calls out every name but the name of the child he or she means is a perfect example. Recently, with my young niece approaching the edge of a tall staircase, I called out nearly every family name between us, except hers or mine, finally relying on an almost-incoherent collage of hand gesture and intonation to draw her away from the edge. Is this any different than the spluttering of a professor asked to explain deconstruction or a complex mathematical algorithm in ordinary language? Just as primary caregivers help to establish language for their children only to find that their own access to language can falter and blunder, so too our academic culture produces its own share of instances where access to "ordinary" language seems impossible. Although this trait may supply plenty of opportunity for humorists, the stuttering remainder of parental incomprehensibility isn't any more amusing during a job talk or dissertation defense than the difficulty of explaining basic presuppositions about research methodologies is for professors who are deeply embedded in their own studies. Just as every young child has words that are only heard and understood properly by caregivers, so too every academic discourse has specialized terms that aren't clearly understood when used in a colloquial setting. The implications of psychoanalytic "transference" are just as specialized and indecipherable as the urgent "TAH-ter!" that my niece uses to demand a soda cracker.

Diminished access to ordinary language seems to come with parenting, as part of the job. When I began staying at home with my first child, I was a pretty normal graduate student; complicated and involved books and essays filled me with excitement and challenge. I remember reading some of French psychoanalyst Jacques Lacan's seminars out loud to my son when he was two or three months old. (One assumes only crazed grad students subject their poor children to such things.) I even went so far as to dictate papers to him (with a tape recorder nearby), as if delivering a lecture. And although I'm sure he liked the babble of language, I knew that after about 20 minutes, he would get cranky.

Despite the narrow daily window of opportunity for these readings, two good things came of them. I discovered that there is something incomparable about the ventriloquism of speaking someone else's ideas aloud that enhances one's understanding of it. And, depending on your source material, you may gain something from the context of your own children. When I read Lacan aloud to my son, it was the Russian theorist Lev Vygotsky who quarreled with him inside my head, almost on behalf of my son, challenging Lacan's explanation of the development of language and the role of infirmity versus ability. As two sides of the same coin, Lacan, through my mouth, struggled with Vygotsky, a ghost voice in my brain, to come up with an explanation that made sense of my son's simultaneous development of personality and language acquisition. Was it a rejection of frailty and fragility that would draw my son into competence, or was it the constructive and elaborative accretion of positive social positions, drawing him first into a community of the family and then into a wider *socius?* Would my son acquire language and personality through my own bumbling, from the internal contradictions of his social position, or from the breadth and diversity of his experience with the social fabric?

Of course, my son did indeed learn to talk, though neither Lacan nor Vygotsky can claim him as an exemplar. But as he grew and acquired the ability to gurgle, and complain, and demand (all of which children can do well before they say their first proper word), the length and complexity of essays and articles I could read in his company diminished. My access to language, even just for reading, was falling away. In the stolen moments of his naps, or commuting to school, walking to class, and holding my single office hour each week, I plotted a composition curriculum built not on textbooks, but on newspapers and magazines. By my son's sixth month, I could trust myself to read nothing longer than a *Harper's* or *New Yorker* article. And necessity, the ... er ... caregiver of invention, drove me to teach articles that I could be energetic about, that my students could be engaged by, and that I could quickly describe, diagram, and have time to read with a baby slung over my shoulder. With magazines for lesson plans, I could read my source material walking down the sidewalk with my son in a stroller, which I found impossible to do with full-size books.[1]

And it wasn't just the reading. Even before my son learned to talk, I found myself unable to complete long thoughts in his presence. I don't think I'm unusual in this regard. Put two parents of toddlers in a room and challenge them to have 20 minutes' conversation without interruption. Even without direct interference, a significant portion of a parent's brain is often focused on his or her children, if they are playing nearby. Indeed, parenting skill may perhaps even be measured by how far away one can be while still maintaining contact with one's child. If you can hear your sleeping child wake, upstairs and down the hall, without a radio-transmitting child monitor, then you're a skilled and seasoned parent. This doesn't make a comfortable condition for intellectual work, however. You're always *listening*, aware, distracted, already half-interrupted.

More than simply being constantly available to a child, though, the primary caregiver also serves as auditor to the budding conversationalist. And this does nothing to extend a parent's already taxed resources for reading, reflection, and deliberation. After spending three years as confidant to my talkative son, my ability to get a word in edgewise—whether audibly or internally—has been severely compromised. It seems that the more he speaks, the less able I am to say anything worthwhile. I clearly shouldn't have read so much Lacan to him, as he's learned the lesson of Lacan's seminar performance well, keeping his audience suspended in the belief that there's dialogue just around the bend in the monologue. Often, I can barely even punctuate his discourse with a simple affirmative "that's right" before he's moved on to the next sentence. My son, whose conversation can oscillate for 30 minutes at a time between an endless stream of monologue and almost-dialogue, requires my *attention,* whether or not he makes room in the conversation for my words. And it's not just *me,* either. In perfect Cosby-esque form, at only four years old, my child can handily immobilize any adult who even so much as *begins* to listen to his conversation.

Though most adults eventually do find other conversations to participate in, parents have little choice in the matter. When our children begin to converse, we're in by default. And as grateful as I am that my son expresses himself so well, there is something about the parental connection that doesn't allow me to turn off my ears when he speaks, or even to think far beyond his choice of topics. Removing myself from that constant availability has been, at least for me, a prerequisite for almost all written work. I can write with loud music around me, but not with my children speaking to me. After several years as full-time caregiver, it's been extremely hard to step out of that frame of reference and back into the academy. What is the language of a parent? The sea of language flows around—interrupts us, punctuates our thought—but how we come back to words is as essential today as it was for Tillie Olsen: why we write, how we guess our audience, and how we find the time and clarity to do the work, with hands on keyboards, pens on pads of paper.

An eight-hour-day solution was around the corner for me. Late in August, I was hired to teach a section of English at a local college. It was a crazy whirlwind of preparation, much like the change in lifestyle I experienced after having children, only this time it was all in reverse. The shock of *not* having children around is significant, once you've spent years constantly with them. In comparison, the adult world can be eerily quiet, empty and lifeless. It takes a while to readjust.

It also took a frantic week of searching before we found full-time child care, so that I could reorient myself to the adult world. We found a really exceptional situation, and I'm thankful beyond belief for it. But by all indications, it takes the exceptional case to make academe and parenthood coexist: access to good, meaningful child care while one is either studying or teaching. This is by no means the rule, but it ought to be.

Access to child care isn't likely to change the rules of the steep climb for tenure, and perhaps it shouldn't. But by making decent child care available, colleges and universities can help ensure that scholars don't have to abandon their career paths for having children. I feel like a better parent when I have child care, because I can focus my energy and attention on my children when I'm with them without also feeling that their presence seriously impinges on my ability to do work that's important to me. When I have the time and freedom of attention to pursue my academic interests, not only am I more like the person I want to be, I can be more like the kind of *parent* I want to be, knowing there will be time to do the other things, too.

REFERENCES

Cohen, H. (2002, August 4). The baby bias. *New York Times,* Education Life supplement, p. 25.

Cosby, B. (1981). *Bill Cosby, himself.* Twentieth Century Fox.

Olsen, T. (1978). *Silences.* New York: Delacorte Press.

NOTES

1. I don't wish to belittle this curriculum, because necessity aside, I've developed a serious commitment to using magazines and newspapers as source material for composition instruction. But the world of longer argument dropped away from me for almost two years, until child care intervened.

3

Escaping Autism: Balancing Motherhood and Academia

Katharine Lane Antolini

Two years ago, I sat in a small examining room with my son, John. I watched him play with the toys a nurse had seductively laid out for him, happily unaware of the doctors who observed through a two-way mirror. Eventually a doctor emerged from behind the glass to tell me that my son was autistic. John would never live a normal life, he told me, but would demand an intensive regimen of behavioral therapy and a complete devotion of our economic, physical, and emotional resources. He recommended that I postpone "indefinitely" my plans to complete a doctorate in history and "think twice" before having more children. He then left the room with the perfunctory, "Don't hesitate to call if you have any questions," while his assistant handed me a folder of general information on autism. Then it was over. I swear that doctor shattered the dreams I had for my son and the dreams I had for myself without even blinking. My mother-in-law, who had accompanied me to the pediatric clinic in Morgantown, West Virginia, is still amazed how one man could forever alter the lives of an entire family in less than 15 minutes.

We knew that autism was a possible diagnosis, one of many suggested to us by various therapists, doctors, and social workers. Of all the possible diagnoses, autism was certainly the most frightening and hardest to accept. We recognized that "something" was different about John. At two years old, his language and social skills lagged behind normal levels of development, and seemingly innocuous noises and images sent him crying from the room. At the same time, however, John understood the alphabet, both verbal and written, counted to 10, easily operated the computer, and read simple words. One speech therapist did not believe me when I bragged of John's ability to draw all the basic shapes. She jokingly bet me 50 bucks to prove it; I should have deducted the money from her bill. For a year, we wrapped ourselves in the comfort of denial and waited anxiously for John's skills to balance themselves out with a little help. Someday I want to write an essay entitled "Albert Einstein Didn't Speak until He Was Four Years Old." Not only was it the most commonly used expression by others to alleviate our fears, but it also summed up our year of hoping against hope. Two weeks before John's third birthday, however, we found ourselves in that little examining room, sobbing over the brutal end of that hope and denial.

I was numb at first. I knew that whatever treatment my son needed could not be done alone. Nonetheless, I pictured myself carrying most of the responsibility. My husband was less emotionally prepared for John's diagnosis than I was. I knew he would view his primary role in John's care as an economic one and channel his energy to earning the most he could in a small-town economy. Thus the intimate management of John's needs would lie the heaviest on my shoulders. If I were a good mother, I thought, I would quit school and devote myself to my son. I would strive to be just like the heroine in the typical Lifetime Channel movie who selflessly nurses her child through everything from eating disorders to devastating cancer. Thanks to the dedication of the child's mother, the movie always has a happy ending. Yet, the thought simply overwhelmed me, and I felt emotionally bankrupt by the end of the day. After reliving the entire clinic visit with every family member who called to ask of the doctor's diagnosis, I was just empty.

When the house was finally silent, I picked up one of my history books and began to study. After all, I had a midterm to take the next day. And for those quiet hours, I stopped obsessing about autism and my family's future; I stopped crying. I did not think about our lack of health insurance or our tenuous finances. I did not think of the obstacles my son will always face. I pondered the development of the late 19th-century American metropolis instead. The next morning I again heard the psychologist's voice in my head, and I cried the entire commute to the university. During the hour midterm, however, two well-written essays on urban America during its Gilded Age silenced that damned voice. I eagerly concentrated on anything else but autism. I escaped, if just briefly. Moreover, I understood that I was not taking the doctor's advice to postpone "indefinitely" my graduate career.

Autism, Academia, and Motherwork

Although my reasons to continue as a student are stronger than other people's reasons to stop, it has not been an easy choice. I struggle with the disapproval I see in the eyes of other parents, school officials, and the occasional medical authority for attempting to be both a mother of a "special-needs child" and a graduate student. But I could not be an emotionally available mother without being a student. It is still so easy to become lost in an irrational disorder that enables my handsome five-year-old son to read on a second-grade level but not express himself to the people around him. Two years after John's diagnosis, I am still craving the escape from the autism. I continue to seek a place that offers order, a space that represents knowledge and reason.

Ironically, escapism is a powerful part of my son's life as well. Medical professionals generally describe autism as a child locked in his own world, unable to fully connect with the "real" world around him physically, emotionally, or socially. Some autistic children never leave their world. Imagine being a mother and looking into the eyes of a child you desperately love and having that child look straight past you. He does not acknowledge your presence or desire your comfort. On the other end of the spectrum, "high-functioning" autistic children (I truly hate that label) learn to negotiate between the two worlds and only periodically escape into a place that makes sense just to them. To outside observers, they may appear simply quirky or eccentric. John falls somewhere in between. We know that John has the skills to bridge the gap between his world and ours, but he needs extensive therapy to draw on them. It remains easier for him to sit on my lap and read aloud this paragraph, which he has, than answer basic questions such as, "How old are you?" or "What is your name?"

On some level, John and I share a similar need to have a world that provides order and, therefore, comfort. When frustrated or overwhelmed, I retreat into the study of American history, whereas he retreats into his mind. There is a painfully obvious difference in our escapism, of course—mine is a conscious choice. I am defying the maternal mystique that demands the complete submission of my needs to those of my child. My decision to balance motherhood and academia reflects a degree of selfishness, even if I rationalize it as self-preservation. I feel the guilt. On the applications for the government programs I fill out for my son, I stumble over the "total years of education" question. (It is the politically correct way the government ascertains if you have at least a high school diploma.) I pause for a moment, recount in my head, and then sheepishly fill in 22 years: high school diploma, bachelor's degree, two master's degrees, and two years into a doctoral program. It is startling to see the extent of my education written in raw numbers, particularly the 10 years spent in higher education. Old college roommates tease me and ask how much longer I intend to remain a student. "Until I learn to do something else," I answer.

But until I learn to do what? "Motherhood and Autism 101" does not appear on my formal semester schedule. How does course work in 19th-century American history really benefit my son? Last year I had an odd conversation with an administrator from the county's special education office. We were trying to hash out the total numbers of hours the school system would be responsible for my son's care and what behaviors I needed to correct at home. Both his preschool schedule and home routine had to fit around his private therapy appointments and, of course, my course load. During the conversation about balancing my graduate semester and John, the administrator casually remarked that she was among the generation of women who had fought for the luxury of a graduate career for women today. I was not sure how to respond to the comment; I guess I should have politely thanked her on behalf of my generation. Yet her usage of the word *luxury* has stuck with me ever since. I wonder how many people, directly involved in John's care or not, see *my* graduate career as self-indulgent.

I understand the outsider's perspective of my choices as self-indulgent. On my list of "pros and cons of a continual graduate career," topping the list of the "cons" column are the comparatively few immediate and tangible rewards that graduate school offers my son and the rest of my family. The hours of reading, researching, writing, and teaching are hours of lost "quality time" with John. Financially, I earn only the university minimum plus tuition remission as a graduate instructor, and although my earning potential will theoretically increase once I complete the program, I have to be honest with myself: Historians are not a rare commodity. Meanwhile, my husband and I rely increasingly on our extended family. Without the financial safety net offered by my parents and the hours of free child care provided by his, I would not have the "luxury" of being a graduate student. Instead, I would be struggling to find a part-time job that paid enough to relieve the stress off my husband and flexible enough to handle John's demanding therapy schedule.

My son's diagnosis has obviously altered my perception of motherhood. My increasing sensitivity to criticism compels me to adamantly defend or rationalize my choices in ways that may not be necessary for other parents.

I am acutely aware of the gap between people's perception of our life and the reality of it, for other parents, his teachers, his doctors, and his therapists do not come home with us at the end of the day. When I return to my list of pros and cons, however, I know that my choice to continue my graduate career does benefit my son in ways not measurable by hours of "quality time" or financial gain. John gets a mother who is not entirely consumed by her feelings of fear and frustration when she thinks of his daily struggles and the obstacles that hinder his future. And although he has to spend some full days in preschool or at his grandparents' home and knows the familiar sight of me reading a book or sitting in front of my laptop computer, he may also recognize that mommy cries and scolds less when the season turns from summer to fall and she goes back to school.

Autism, Academia, and the Motherwork of Others

Once, during a women's studies course on motherhood, the professor admitted that she hated not being the center of her children's world. She wrestled with the thought of her children enjoying (or even preferring) the physical or emotional care of others. Most of the students in the room nodded in agreement; one was a young mother herself, and the others were women barely 20 years old. I realized that I did not feel the same way, at least not at that time—only four months after John's diagnosis. I simply felt unqualified to assume such an omniscient position; I was still reeling too much from the diagnosis of autism to even fathom it. For contrary to the popular belief of most school systems and parents of "normal" children, parents of special-needs children do not instantaneously become medical experts and licensed therapists. The more I thought about it, the more I wondered if any mother could truly be the center of her child's life and whether she should even want to be. In a perfect world, women would be perfect mothers. The needs of a mother and her child would be indistinguishable. Not only would she be all things to her child, but also all things to herself. But in a perfect world, my son would not be autistic.

As John's mother, I have surrendered a degree of power in order to provide John with the best possible foundation on which to build his future. Unlike many other mothers, who may take this for granted, I do not make autonomous decisions about how my son is raised. Constructing a life around autism and academia has required deference, not only to various medical authorities, but also to the motherwork of others. To meet all my son's needs—and protect my emotional health—demands the expansion of motherwork to include an array of teachers, therapists, and extended family members. I am but one among many surrogate mothers in John's life. I may be the only "Mommy" to John, the one he seeks out for emotional comfort and protection, but I also serve to support his emotional and social connection with other women who can address specific needs in his life that I cannot alone.

In my supporting role, I attend all the public school meetings, schedule all the medical and therapy appointments, manage his small social security insurance benefits, and battle our archenemy, the West Virginia Department of Health and Human Resources. I scramble behind the scenes to ensure John's access to the direction and care of other women. For example, John receives approximately four hours a week of speech and occupational therapy: one hour of speech therapy from the school system and the rest from a private speech and occupational service. The young women who spend a couple hours a week with him are essential to his development (despite what the Department of Health and Human Resources and Medicaid believe). Their motherwork provides John and our family with the skills to live with the strange and potentially debilitating realities of autism. And John has taken to these young women who diligently work each week to pull him further out of his own world to tackle new skills.

As educators and therapists help my son learn to interact with other children at school and develop techniques to address his behavioral delays, I work toward my academic goals. Not surprisingly, balancing both our schedules has been a crash course in time management. Although the public school services are set in stone, the hours of private therapy fluctuate with my course load. The commuting time required between home, the therapy offices, and the university, however, means I cannot accomplish trips to both therapy and the university in one day. To attempt both trips means a total of three and a half hours spent in transit between the three locations. Thus, each semester I must design a schedule that leaves at least one day free from university obligations; this, of course, can be a feat in itself. But it is important to me to take John to his weekly therapy sessions. Somehow, asking my mother-in-law to accompany him to his occupational or speech therapy, regardless of how routine, feels as if I have crossed some invisible line of mothering misconduct—as if I must always be just one person removed from the one who cares for John in my place. A part of me continually gauges how closely I approach that invisible line. For although I respect and depend on the motherwork of teachers, therapists, and other family members, I grapple with that nagging guilt that questions what right I have to rely on them so much.

In our lives, then, autism and academia have adapted to each other. It has been a bizarre independent study for us: 50% trial and error, 40% professional behavioral therapy, and 10% assistance from the public school system and the state. Slowly, my son and I are subtly adjusting to each other's needs. I can now read and concentrate in noisy waiting rooms, for example, and John prefers to fall asleep at night with someone in his room quietly doing work. Or, as I type this essay, I sit forward on my chair so John can stand on the seat behind me. He looks over my shoulder, occasionally reading a few words that cross the computer screen, and strokes his fingers through my hair. It is an arrangement that seems to calm us both. I cannot deny that the balance between the two worlds is a tenuous one, but it is one we will continue to maintain. Those who recognize my academic accomplishments may admire my honest dedication to trying to reach my goals, whereas others concerned for my "special-needs child" may simply see my lack of courage or "maternal fortitude." Nonetheless, it is our reality and so far the only way we have found to start rebuilding the dreams that were shattered two years ago in that small examination room.

Postscript

John is now six years old and a graduate of kindergarten. In the past year, I have had real conversations with my son and discovered that my son has the same twisted sense of humor as his mother. I attribute his gains to the new group of public school educators that now surrounds him. (I realize that many parents of special-needs children cannot claim the same.) Since we lost our last battle with the Department of Health and Human Resources and can no longer provide John with private therapy, the public school system struggles to take on the added responsibility. They have accepted the reality that although John is the first autistic child to come through the system, he will not be the last.

His first year of school was a trial. It was the school's first experience with an autistic student, so John served as a sort of test case for his teachers, principal, and aide. During the first four months of the academic year, the school called home an average of three times a month requesting that we pick John up because he was too disruptive to remain in class. I know it was not a coincidence that school officials insisted that he needed to be picked up on the days they knew I was not teaching. John also grew familiar with the school's "choice room," a room where students go during recess when they make bad choices, and he can describe the decor of the principal's office. It has been a challenge for the public school system to view John as a student with autism and not simply a student with behavioral problems. But for every setback, there has been substantial progress, and I am grateful.

As for me, I passed my comprehensive exams and am currently teaching and researching my dissertation. Combining motherhood and academia is still a balancing act, but it has gotten easier as John and I have both matured emotionally. My graduate work continues to serve as an important escape for me in the same ways that my son's world of books, routines, and private games provides him comfort. Today, however, we can bridge our two worlds with less difficulty. Instead of standing on my desk chair as I work, he now prefers to sit at his own desk next to mine doing his own "schoolwork." (So much for the doctor who told me John would never have the capability of imaginary play). After a short period, he typically *announces* that homework time is over for both of us and that it is time to play. For parents of "normal" children, the interruption of children demanding their attention may seem commonplace if not sometimes frustrating. Three years ago, however, I could not imagine a time when my son would crave my attention in meaningful ways or openly express the sound reasoning that play is always more fun than homework.

4

Choosing Motherhood as a Female Chemist

Donna J. Nelson

More times than I can count, I recall my mother telling me, "Don't ever have a baby; they are too much trouble." Because I was an only child, there was no doubt about whom she was speaking. And I didn't understand that. I rarely disobeyed her, and I was a typical overachiever. I won statewide contests in math, sat first-chair saxophone in band and stage band, played oboe during concert season, sang in glee club, was a majorette, was a cheerleader, made straight As, and was elected to class offices. My senior year, I became feature twirler, was selected to be senior attendant to the football queen, and was voted most popular. It's a good thing I established a habit of being very active, because I believe even moderately successful female professors of chemistry in research universities must work constantly and be able to understand and interface with a wide variety of personalities in order to overcome and avoid the obstacles and disincentives in that discipline.

I paid great attention to my mother, and initially I decided against having children. I was extremely serious about a career and wanted to devote all my attention to it, anyway. However, as I grew older and married, I gathered additional information on the subject. At one point I was part of a women-in-science faculty lunch group, which had a couple of older women who had also decided not to have children. I recall them expressing concern about growing older without children and grandchildren; each wondered if she had made a mistake. Their friends all seemed to enjoy their families. I made a rare decision to go against my mother's advice.

I decided to schedule having my child during my postdoctorate. It seemed the most logical time. My goal was to be a professor, and I knew I would lose some flexibility when I gained teaching responsibilities. I thoroughly enjoyed my research, so I planned to minimize the time I took off to give birth. I was working in the lab of Nobel Laureate H. C. Brown at Purdue, so there was a fast pace in the research. In order to avoid pressure to take leave from some older women I knew, I decided to hide the fact that I was pregnant as long as possible. I got an assortment of large, thin jackets to hide my size, and most people didn't notice because lab coats were common. By the second week of December, Dr. Brown hadn't asked me anything about my plans, so I decided to write him a memo. I told him that I was scheduled to have a baby in the second half of January and that I planned to take a week off. After a day or so, he called me into his office; he said he had had no idea I was pregnant but that he had thought I was putting on a little weight. He also said I should determine the time off I was allowed and take it. I told him I didn't want to take off very long because I enjoyed my research so much, but he insisted that I at least determine what my benefits were.

At the benefits office, I was told the standard leave time was six months. I guess horror was obvious on my face, because the secretary apologized, "You don't have to take all of it; most women don't." I told her, "I don't intend to take any of it." And she replied, "Well, you're going to have to take some of it, because you can't have your baby in the lab, and if you take just one day, you'll have to complete leave paperwork." There was the 15-page application for up to six months, and there was the half-page application for up to two weeks. I completed the latter. My husband and I decided to split caring for our baby until the child was eligible for day care. We found a day-care center that specialized in small babies, but they did not accept babies younger than about two weeks.

Our son, Christopher Nelson Brammer, was born Thursday night at 8 P.M. January 21, 1982. That morning, when my water broke, I stuffed hand towels into my maternity pants and went into the lab to tell everyone I was going to the hospital and to make sure there was nothing that needed my attention before I left for the hospital. The next week, I stayed home with Christopher mornings, and his father stayed home with him afternoons; my first half-day back at work was the Monday after he was born. The following week, the day-care center accepted him; I recall them remarking that he was the first baby left there with its umbilical cord intact. I also recall one older woman in the chemistry department telling me I was a bad mother for leaving him at day care that early, but I still believe each woman must make the decisions that are right for her. I tried to make up for leaving my child in day care by always keeping him with me at other times. We took him when we went out to eat and when we went to the movies; he was quiet and caused no trouble. When I went to the lab, I put him in a playpen in the middle of the room. When I went to professional meetings to speak, I took him with me, and he watched as I gave my presentations. At the University of Oklahoma, I put a refrigerator in my office for milk, juice, and baby food. He went with me when I had to work in the office at night or on weekends. When he had a fever and couldn't go to day care, he slept on blankets and a foam mattress on my office floor. As a result, we are very close, and he is now a chemistry major in college.

I think it was a good choice to have my child during my postdoctorate; things do not always work out so well as they did for me. One tenure-track professor, in my department for about four years, became pregnant and was scheduled to give birth at the beginning of a fall semester during which she was scheduled to teach a large section (about 200 students) of general chemistry, without a teaching assistant. It seems to me that a woman cannot be expected to teach in the classroom on the same day she gives birth, so it seems reasonable to me that she tried to make some alternate arrangements for a couple of weeks. In spite of the fact that she had a mild disability (scoliosis), which might cause complications in pregnancy and childbirth, she didn't want to ask for time off; she requested that a teaching assistant be designated to help out while she was in the hospital by doing things such as administering quizzes that she would write in advance. The chair refused. Her husband, a tenured professor of physics at the University of Oklahoma, took over her classes, in addition to teaching his own, while she was in the hospital having their baby. Thank goodness she had no complications and was able to return to her teaching as she had intended. At the end of the year, she was given a poor evaluation for low productivity, with no mention of her pregnancy. She and her husband left the university together shortly afterward.

To my knowledge, bringing my son to my office never caused any problems for anyone. Shortly after being tenured, I was told by one member of my tenure committee, the group responsible for presenting my tenure case before the department, that the chair had said they didn't want people like me in the department, that I should be at home with my young son. I would have thought it would be an asset to have in the department an example of a woman balancing work and family, but we don't all see the same values in things. I did have many female students tell me they were glad they had the opportunity to see how I handled having a career and a family. They said it gave them confidence that they would be able to balance it similarly. Each woman is different, so each woman will need to make the decisions that are right for her, but it does help to have a large number of role models, so she will have more ideas from which to draw when deciding what she wants to do.

5

Tenure-Track to Mommy-Track: In Search of My Scholarly Self

Janice Rieman

"There is never only one, of anyone," or so claims the narrator of Margaret Atwood's 1988 novel *Cat's Eye*. As a mother and an academic, I've never felt this statement so truly. Maintaining my identity as an academic these days is a challenge. Frequently, the academic piece of myself feels illegitimate, tenuous, a part of my past instead of the ingrained fabric of my being that I know it to be. My task of late has been to integrate my academic self with my Mama self and to know that these two selves are not mutually exclusive. An important part of this process has involved the (not so) simple act of renaming, of seeing myself as a scholar instead of an academic.

Nearly two years ago, I left a much-desired tenure-track job at a school that was a great fit to relocate to the city where my partner had begun his much-desired tenure-track job at a great-fit school for him. We were a not-so-atypical academic couple in diverse disciplines whose respective ambitions led us through a four-year long-distance relationship. Although we'd hoped eventually to acquire desired academic positions in the same state, we were resigned to making an eight-hour drive to see each other for short weekends and during academic breaks. The catalyst for my departure from my position was an unplanned pregnancy that occurred over the first summer after my first full academic year as a tenure-track assistant professor. I was no longer a graduate assistant, an adjunct, a postdoctoral fellow; I was an assistant professor who was thrilled finally to feel "legitimized" by the academy in my new role. Unfortunately, my impending motherhood necessitated my making some difficult decisions regarding my career. Because my partner's job was in the state where both of our families lived, we decided that I would leave my position and relocate to where we had roots and a good deal of family support. Giving a semester's notice and revealing my reasons behind the huge decision to leave a tenure-tack position at a school I loved and with which I fit very well was bittersweet.

Fortunately, I didn't have to give up my academic identity as quickly as I'd feared. The serendipitous opening of a position at a university near where my partner worked lessened my sense of loss and provided a buoy for my scholarly self. In my mind, as long as I had this application in the works, I was still an academic. I made the first cut of applicants and completed a phone interview when I was eight months pregnant. When chosen for an on-campus interview to be scheduled at some indeterminate date (when the state budget lifted its interviewing freeze), I still felt a part of the academy and felt as if I could, with little difficulty, step back into the world I had worked so hard to join. Meanwhile, while waiting for my academic job interview, I enjoyed spending time with my newborn daughter, wrote two textbook articles, completed some freelance writing, and still felt like I could call myself an English professor.

After a year of waiting, the on-campus interview finally took place. It felt good to be back in the academic community, to step into the classroom, to field questions about research plans and pedagogy. It also felt good to have my companion, Bill, bring our daughter, Emerson, to campus during lunch so that she could nurse. As the week passed and I still hadn't heard any news about the job, I started to worry more and more about what I would do, how I would feel, if I actually didn't have a position come fall. Over the past decade, a new academic year hadn't passed that I hadn't had to prep for classes, that I hadn't been able to enjoy the excitement of facing a new semester. How would I feel if fall came and went and I had no place to teach?

I soon found out.

I found out when the department chair called to tell me what a difficult committee decision it was, but that they had offered the position to another candidate who had accepted the job. The good news was that the chair encouraged me to reapply next year, when the department anticipated more openings that I might be qualified to fill. So, in a sense, I'm still holding onto the hope that I will, perhaps next year, restart my quest for tenure, but until then, I am in academic limbo.

When I hung up the phone after news of my "rejection," I sobbed my disappointed little nonacademic heart out. I felt deeply sad. Having been rejected by a school or two after an on-campus interview before,

I knew the tenor of lost-job grief—the imagined world of grand potential suddenly ripped away, leaving only a non-me in that enviable place. This time, however, I knew that this might be *it;* this might have been my last chance at a tenure-track job, because I had committed to living in this city with my partner and our daughter. I had no plans for a national search the next year, no sense of the optimistic "Maybe I'd like to live in Oklahoma" when applying for future jobs. I had committed myself to living in North Carolina with my family, and, tenure-track job or not, here I am to stay.

Not getting the job chipped away at yet another portion of my academic self. At the time, I was scared there would not be much of that self left when the job-search season rolled around again the next year, but then, quite suddenly, the immediate and intense grief lifted, only to be replaced by an odd sense of freedom and relief. I began to feel liberated from confining notions about what it is to be an academic: Just because I wasn't currently affiliated with an institution and in a tenure-track job didn't mean I wasn't still a trained academic. The true epiphany solidified itself one day while I was reading *Good Night, Gorilla* to my one-year-old. In the middle of sharing this book with a preliterate child, in my head I was doing all sorts of literary analysis. The process came as second nature to me. I couldn't help myself. That moment marked my redefinition of myself as a scholar as opposed to an academic. In my mind, being an academic apparently means external validation and designation, whereas identifying myself as a scholar requires no more than my own recognition of that part of myself, no institutional seal of approval necessary.

I'd like to say that this revelation was instantaneously life-altering, that it propelled me into a state of mental contentment. But it didn't. I still carry around a slight chip on my shoulder about not having a tenure-track job, not being a current professor absorbed with important teaching and scholarship. However, the chip is smaller than it was a year ago. These days I feel less compelled to blurt out, "That's Dr. Jan, to you," at playgroup or to preface introductions of myself with "I left a tenure-track job. . . ." Leaving my job is becoming less of a defining moment in my life, and having such a job is becoming less of a definer of my identity.

What I've learned while traveling through this newer world of mommydom is that every mother has a story similar to mine. Every woman with a child was a woman without a child at some point, and all have vestiges of that past life within them. Although I may know Andrea as James's and

Amanda's mom, she's also an MD who works part time. And whereas Lynn is a parent to Franklin, she's also a former Microsoft worker who does freelance work building databases for companies in the wee hours of the morning when she has some time to work. Everyone has a story. Every woman who has chosen to be a mother, whether leaving her profession for a little while, forever, or never, has made decisions that deeply affect who she is and how she parents. And finding one's self within mamahood is not always easy. Obviously, I orbit largely in the galaxy of mothers who have, for the time being, forgone full-time careers. I'm certain that an entirely different world of full-time career moms has its own set of stories. One day I shall add such a narrative to my life as well. Right now, though, my main focus is motherhood.

It's so very easy to lose myself in being a mother. Though some days at this stage of my life have me believing that my role as a mother transcends everything else—which on one level it does—I know that there is a time beyond these early, all-encompassing years when I will want my full profession back, when I will desire the trajectory to the tenured position I studied so hard to obtain. I fear that if I don't try to get back in the game this year, it will be too late. Despite this knowledge, there remains a constant vacillation between caring deeply about my career and feeling how unimportant it is in comparison to motherhood, all while knowing this isn't entirely true, because there is a me before motherhood, a me as the mother of a toddler, and undoubtedly several incarnations of me after these days of deep dependence. What then of me, I ask? It feels safe to believe falsely that my career doesn't matter so much with a toddler in my life, but what of when she's a preoccupied preteen, an independent adolescent, a departing young adult? I do not want to leave myself behind.

This fall I began an adjunct position at the university where my partner teaches and thus have continued the psychic and self-defined evolution from academic to scholar that began as I reconciled myself to a life temporarily outside of the academy. Had I not been solicited for the course, had the class not been interesting to me, had the time not been right, I would not have placed myself in the often unenviable position of an adjunct academic. As I hesitatingly expected, the part-time work has provided a nice segue for me, both professionally and emotionally. I am returning to the classroom with a new sense of myself as a teacher and a scholar, one who has accepted the internalization of my identity as a scholar and who is less reliant on the academy for any sense of "legitimacy." Motherhood has allowed me that. Because I feel so secure in my role as Emerson's mom, I am more able to embrace the scholarly side of myself and know for certain that it is just one of my many selves, for "There is never only one, of anyone."

Reference

Atwood, M. (1988). *Cat's eye.* New York: Bantam.

6

Madonna with Child: Untenured, but Not Undone

Cindy Patey Brewer

My son, Nicholas, was born August 1 of this year, 2002. The last two months of pregnancy coincided with one of the hottest summers on record in Utah, and I spent it contemplating various methods for committing career suicide. "Honey," I whispered in bed at night, "I could quit my job and we could move to Africa." Earlier in the week I might have whispered Australia . . . or Austria. For this essay, I started with the countries at the beginning of the alphabet, because the country I chose on any given night was completely arbitrary. I know that now, as I am writing, but at night in the dark, when I was plotting my escape, the destination was carefully selected, weighed against a dozen others. I have been doing this for months now. These contemplations have given me moments of rebellious pleasure, a fantasy of freedom. These fantasies grew in frequency as my belly grew in size. The destinations, at first specific to my profession as a professor of German literature (Germany, Austria, Switzerland) or somehow connected to our family's past (Israel and New Zealand), grew to include virtually every country known to me. It was no longer important where I escaped to, only that I should escape.

I read the preceding paragraph to my husband over the phone, thinking he would be pleased with how I managed to capture briefly what we have spent hours discussing. He responded with silence. I had to coax a response out of him.

"It's okay," he said blandly.

"What do you mean, 'OK'?" I responded with irritation. "What's wrong with it?"

"I don't think you should write that," he said. "I want you to get tenure, and talking about your desire to commit career suicide makes you seem flaky. I just don't think you should publicly expose yourself to that risk."

"But my experience is real," I protested. "What purpose is a personal essay if it can't be real, if I have to put on another front?"

We briefly debated the risks of varying degrees of honesty, each of us becoming more animated and frustrated.

"Can't you just tone it down?" he asked.

But I felt adamant. "If I cannot write honestly, I cannot write at all!" I was hurt and angry, and after a long period of silence, I hung up the phone.

But perhaps I was unfair in my reaction. Perhaps his silence reflects an all-too-clear understanding of my quandary. How do you talk about a very personal, very emotional struggle to juggle work and motherhood when you were hired for your cool intellect, your seeming ability to step back from emotionally charged issues and view them with analytical objectivity?

The intense heat of that summer dragged on, and I confined myself to the office, where the air-conditioning provided a brief reprieve. Regrettably, I couldn't work. I tried to write but found myself unable to keep a train of thought. I reminded myself that my lack of intellectual productivity was adequately counterbalanced by my increased physical productivity, but that did little to assuage my guilt at not being able to finish my article on Friederike Unger, a 19th-century author I had been working on for over a year. I got dizzy often, slept on a mat on the floor, and finally surrendered to tasks that required only brief periods of concentration: e-mail, grading, and other tedious paperwork. I told myself that when the term ended, I would then focus on my research. What energy and mental alertness I could muster went into teaching the one class I had on my docket for the spring term.

But I felt inadequate for this task as well. When, for the third time in one class period, I had to stop midsentence because I couldn't remember how it was supposed to end, I began to wonder if there were such a thing as pregnancy-induced Alzheimer's. One morning I stood in front of my office door with its conventional lock, and as I repeatedly pressed the button on my automobile key fob, I wondered why my office door wouldn't open. When the fog cleared, I slipped red-faced into my office. I thought of science fiction movies I had seen, and I felt as though the essence of who I am had been transplanted into a body I did not recognize, one whose shape and limitations were foreign to me. The most troubling thing about it was my inability to feel at home in the new body. I could still remember having been someone different, someone capable of the tasks that daunted me now, someone who could speak and write.

Humor became one method of coping. Instead of writing essays, a task that eluded me anyway, I wrote lists. Remembering Jeff Foxworthy's "You know you're a redneck when . . . ," I began my own list entitled, "You know you're pregnant when . . ." in which I documented my key-fob experience and other pregnancy moments. This method of coping expanded to include multiple lists. My favorite list was born in the bedroom one night when neither of us could sleep. My husband, more interested in me than in what I was saying, patiently endured a long and tedious list of my complaints, frustrations, and regrets.

As I neared the end, he suddenly interjected, "You're not going to have a midlife crisis on me, are you?"

I paused, taking in the various implications of his lighthearted question and responded gleefully. "That's perfect! A midlife crisis might be just the thing I need."

Thirty-six is not too young for a midlife crisis, and I decided I would plan mine. I solicited suggestions from my friends and colleagues. The most important criteria on the list were that (1) it had to be something I would otherwise never do, and (2) it could have no lasting negative consequences, because, in spite of my current frustrations, I love my job and my family, and I didn't want to put either of those in jeopardy. And so I contemplated taking a long girls-only road trip in a rented convertible, tattooing ivy leaves around my belly button, or starting up a faculty-and-staff conga line in the hallways of the Jesse Knight Humanities building. Pasted to my office door was a magazine photo of a woman in a Madonna outfit complete with pointy aluminum breasts conversing with Prince Charles at a breast cancer awareness event. I imagined going grocery shopping in such an outfit, a vision of myself contrary to my conservative upbringing and one that conveniently omitted the current size of my belly. Top on my list was purchasing the $6,000 bedroom set I had been drooling over and putting it all on my credit card. In truth, this is the one my husband worried about most and the one I was most likely to do. But all these things, besides being generally harmless, were only a means to get my mind from one day to the next, a temporary distraction.

Now that Nicholas has been born, I don't need these distractions. I feel good. I can think more clearly, and I am regaining my confidence. But there are still some residual effects of pregnancy trauma. I still, for example, think about quitting my job. I feel no connection to it right now. This, of course, is not surprising. In the last 10 months my only satisfying accomplishment has been the birth of this child. With Nicholas in my arms, I feel amply rewarded for months of mothering efforts. Work has strained me, too, but has offered no tangible rewards. Success at work, measured by the number of pages written about my research, has been virtually nonexistent. It is no wonder, then, that I might want to abandon one disappointing arena of my life for another arena where I have found such brilliant success. But I try to keep this in perspective, too. Two months after the birth of a baby is the wrong time to make career decisions. I know from experience that this is a transitional phase and a far cry from how I will feel once I have gained some distance from it. For now, in order to keep my perspective, I have to call up in my mind other phases of life, times when I felt differently about my roles as mother and academic. Whereas right now, it is work that seems to intrude on my happiness, at other times, it is parenthood.

I cringe when I look at that last sentence. It seems harsh and cold, even blasphemous in the context of my Mormon upbringing. (Even worse is feeling as though this thought somehow betrays my children's innocent devotion.) Here in a culture that applauds women who stay home with their children, I have ventured to have a career. Never mind the fact that 60% of women in Utah work, I still feel like an anomaly. On the other hand, in a profession where most of my colleagues nationwide have only one or two children, if they have any at all, I feel out of place as well. At least at Brigham Young University, none of my colleagues questions my desire to have more than two children. They understand and, I believe, welcome my decision without resentment, even when I want to have children prior to tenure. Although institutional support for pregnant faculty is limited to a single one-year delay in the tenure review process, my department has been generous, arranging the course schedule and hiring extra teaching assistants in order to give me an unofficial semester leave.

But no matter how generous institutions or departments might be in regard to faculty who choose motherhood as well, striking a healthy and functional balance between the two often conflicting sides is difficult. The most stressful years of our profession, those prior to tenure, coincide with a woman's biological clock. Postponing children is to risk not having any at all; having them is to risk your chances for tenure. Those with children quickly learn that no matter how you arrange your routine, and no matter how involved your spouse is in child rearing, work and motherhood are bound to encroach upon each other in a myriad of uncomfortable ways.

In April 2001, my sons and three of their friends sat beside me as we watched an amateur juggler doing elementary math. He started with one ball; looking somewhat bored, he tossed it leisurely into the air. It returned securely to his well-trained hand. One plus one is two, two plus one is three, three plus one is four. Soon five, six, seven . . . *ten* balls were spinning, flying above the now-insecure movements of his blurred hands and whizzing past his face, strained with painful concentration and delight. I was intrigued that he had placed a bag of spare balls on the floor in front of him for the occasion when he inadvertently dropped a ball and it rolled out of reach. Was this an open admission of his imperfect talent?

I find myself wanting to conceal my imperfections. An open admission of my shortcomings seems against reason for one yet untenured and anxious to satisfy colleagues and review committees. I can't help but compare myself to my more experienced colleagues, and I often wonder if I would have been better off had my path to academia been different.

I married in 1989. In 1990 I graduated with a bachelor's degree and had our first son, Kenneth. I finished my master's degree in 1991, and Jacob arrived two months later. I started my PhD in 1993 and gave birth to Josh in 1994. Andy wasn't planned like the others, and he arrived to completely overwhelm us in 1995. I might have suspended my education had a generous scholarship not provided timely relief. I worked at home in the mornings and Saturdays when my husband, Bruce, was home. In 1997, when I received a Fulbright grant, Bruce took administrative leave from his job at Weber State University, and we all left for Berlin. As a chaplain in the Utah National Guard, Bruce made special arrangements for assignments in Europe to supplement the Fulbright stipend, which was not intended for a family of six. We continued to juggle as before, but in new roles. When he was not away on a military assignment, Bruce took care of the kids and the house. In 1998, Brigham Young University offered me a tenure-track job, and Bruce was accepted to the Counseling Psychology PhD program at the same university. Overwhelmed with the pressure to finish my dissertation before I started teaching and insecure about the holes in my education, I was jealous of many cohorts who pursued their education and careers more single-heartedly. At least, I perceived them to be at a great advantage.

As the fall semester approached and my dissertation was not yet complete, Bruce and I hatched a plan to liberate me from all responsibilities so that I could pursue my scholarship with one mind. He left Berlin seven weeks early, taking all four children with him. He would move to Provo, find an apartment, set up shop, and await my return. I would stay and devote myself solely to my writing. I delighted in the prospect, rejoiced over the many pages I could write, and planned on returning with the dissertation finished well ahead of schedule.

I approached my first week alone with new vigor. I was continually astonished at how little I had to do to complete household tasks. Laundry was reduced to a mere tenth, and I was at leisure to write 8 or 10 hours a day. But this euphoria soon vanished. Weighted so heavily on the scholarship side of the scale, I sank to a new low. I worked poorly, laughed weakly, slept restlessly in an empty bed, and pined for my smudged and sweaty litter to come in from the playground. After three weeks of mediocre work, I surrendered and took the first available flight to Utah, where I could go back to juggling.

July and August 1998 were my most productive months ever. The job deadline of August 31 kept me motivated. My husband and, yes, even the children helped keep me sane. For the first time in my academic career, I ceased to see my sons as a burden to my intellectual progress. I realized that at the very least, they gave me as much as they took. It is true that I had fewer hours to work in a day, and I slept fewer hours at night, but I, for one, had become dependent upon that daily dose of physical exertion coupled with heartily administered affection.

I still think the childless academic has a greater time advantage, but I have ceased to view the differences between us as an unbridgeable chasm. Children have slowed the pace of my academic career with time constraints, maternity leave, and delays in the tenure process. They continue to check my speed even when we move out of that strenuous and demanding baby phase, but they have not brought my progress to a standstill.

In January 1999 I was pregnant again. Yes, it was planned. Our son Logan arrived in the middle of the fall semester. When Logan was two years old, our juggling act reached a peak. It looked like this: I worked 9 to 5 (except on Mondays), alternating teaching and research days. Sometimes I managed to write, but since students and children don't restrict their crises to my office hours or even my teaching days, success was somewhat limited. Bruce worked as a counseling psychology intern at Wasatch Mental Health from 8 to 6 except on Wednesdays. My friend Jenifer, who lives with her two boys in our basement apartment, took Kid #1 to school at 7:30. At 8:15 Kids #2 through #4 were dropped off at school by me, Bruce, or Lisette, depending on the day of the week. Lisette is a university student who lived with us and helped out with the kids in exchange for room and board. Either Bruce or I dropped Kid #5 off at the babysitter on the way to work. Kid #4, a first grader, got out of school an hour earlier than the rest. He was picked up by my friend Dru, who babysat him until 3, when the others were picked up—except on Wednesday, when Bruce picked up Kid #4 and Dru's daughter and watched them till 6:00. I picked up the kids on Mondays. Misty, another student who lived with us, picked them up on Tuesdays and Thursdays. Once a week she also cleaned house. All the kids got out early on Friday. Lisette picked them up and watched them the rest of the evening so Bruce and I could go out. Kid #1 had Spanish at 5:00 every weekday evening except Friday. Kid #2 had Spanish Monday and Wednesday evenings. Piano lessons were on Mondays. We don't play soccer.

This plan ran smoothly until after September 11, 2001, when the National Guard was called up in the wake of the World Trade Center attacks. Then I became a single parent on the weekends, and we had one fewer car on Thursdays. Luckily, Bruce wasn't called to go overseas. Instead, he worked irregular hours at the base in Salt Lake, comforting the families affected by overseas deployments.

It is times like these that I have to remind myself to breathe. Then we sit down together—Bruce, the two students living with us, and I—and we rethink and rejuggle the schedule. Sometimes, when the planning gets especially complex, I am reminded of the analytical section of the GRE. I thought of submitting a question based on my children's routine, the girls' school schedule, my and my husband's work schedules, and the three automobiles shared between four drivers.

Over the years, I have had to make hard choices about which balls to juggle and which to let fall. I limit myself to juggling the ones I feel most passionately about, but, in the process, some very valuable and meaningful projects have been indefinitely delayed. When I started working full time, I had to abandon my children's scrapbooks. I thought, at first, that I could work on them Sundays after church, but I never managed to do it. I lamented that loss many times, realizing how quickly we forget the details and how instantaneously the children grow and change. I juggle the balls that remain with imperfect talent. That is the price I pay for wanting more than just a career (like some of my colleagues around the country) or just a family (like my neighbors across the street and next door). I fault none of these women for their choices. I admire their determination, their potential for excellence, and their willingness to sacrifice. Now, I believe that living the full life is not so much about squeezing more into an already bulging schedule, but about learning to make peace with your best effort, valuing it for what it is instead of mourning what it is not. I, for one, will never be the perfect mother, perfect wife, perfect scholar, or perfect teacher, but I am passionate about all of these things. And I rejoice in these things that bring me both anguish and joy.

I have one lover, with his two jobs, two incompletes in his course work, and one unfinished dissertation. I have one article published and two articles unfinished on my desk. I have three classes to teach and four teaching assistants to train. I have six sons ranging from two months to 12 years. I have 12 people living in my house. I have 10 siblings and 49 nieces and nephews. I have 70 students per semester, thousands past and future. Each day when I go to work, I try to teach well, read well, and write well, but inevitably I spend my fair share of time staring with frustration at a still unrevised page on my computer screen and secretly lamenting that class today was not quite as exciting as I had envisioned. Then I go home to submerge myself in that occasionally soul-replenishing sea of diapers and disasters, fights and forays, housework and homework, and a young son who tells me he loves me one-hundred-and-one and insists that is the biggest number there is.

Today, two months after Nicholas's birth, I recognize that I am still too close to pregnancy trauma to consider myself "back to normal." I have had no time to absorb the cost, no time to reclaim myself, no time to rebalance the scale. It will be a while, I think, until I feel comfortable again in my professional mindset. But it will come. I know, because I have done this five times previously. Time heals the physical and mental wounds of childbirth, and the child heals my professional wounds. My roles as scholar and mother encroach upon each other, demand from each other, but also give to each other in ways I never imagined.

I remember one particularly healing moment. In my sixth month of pregnancy, I had gone to a conference in Georgia on German women writers of the 18th and 19th centuries. I wasn't presenting a paper. I simply felt a need to stay as connected as possible to my profession at a time when I was most tempted to withdraw into my cave. I met up with a well-respected colleague from Notre Dame at the airport in Atlanta. We chatted briefly about travel logistics and the weather as she swayed back and forth quieting her six-month-old daughter in the stroller. Then she asked about my pregnancy and began calculating the months till birth and a couple more on top of that. "That means," she concluded, "that come October you ought to have your brain back." I was stunned at first, then laughed heartily. I was relieved to know that I am not the only one whose mental capabilities seemed blunted by the physical and emotional exertion of pregnancy. Her empathy was reassuring. She understood my insecurity and was matter-of-factly confident in my eventual recovery. I clung to this glimmer of hope as best I could, but I still had several months to go.

In July, when I was no longer teaching, I tried once again to write my article and went home each day feeling like a failure. After agonizing over lost research time, I decided not to try any more until after the baby came. This required a radical shift in my thinking: How could I simply not worry about my research? Then I began a project that I found to be both rewarding and manageable for my circumstances, and I dove in with complete abandon. I caught up on all five years' worth of family scrapbooks that I had neglected since the day I was hired. In my office, no books or journal articles lay splayed open and overlapping across my desk and table top. Instead, the office was strewn with colored paper, photos and their cropped-off edges, vinyl sheet protectors, sport-camp certificates, grade reports, and vacation memorabilia. The project was liberating, satisfying, and, most important, it kept me sane. When asked by a colleague if I was trying to finish my article before the baby came, I cackled brightly. "Are you kidding? I'm not working. I'm nesting!"

Looking back on those roasting days of summer in my last month of pregnancy, I now view them as somehow paradisiacal in their noncon-flictedness. The truth is, I was completely miserable on the physical front, tortured by lack of sleep and a myriad of other ailments, which I am loath to discuss publicly. But, miraculously and unlike during other pregnancies, I had managed to banish the reprimanding inner voice that usually pontificates throughout every activity not related to my research. July 2002 was a month of blissful quiet in my mind. I forgot what was before and what would be later. There was nothing but today only, and my thoughts focused on making it through that one day, carrying our sixth son inside me and pasting yet another snapshot into the albums on my desk.

No, I'm not so naive as to think that such an existence, no matter how blissful in the short term, would satisfy me indefinitely. I know that I need the professional side of me as much as I need the mothering side. And in fact, I later discovered that on the professional front, things weren't as bleak as I had imagined. That spring term class I taught while pregnant didn't turn out as poorly as I thought. One month after my son's birth, I received the results of the student evaluations. It took me two days to get the courage to open the envelope. To my astonishment, I received some of my highest course ratings. Only one student commented on a weakness I could attribute to my pregnancy. That student wrote: "The class was a mix of the topic and some unrelated tangents." Two thoughts occurred to me. First, I wondered if the student's comment might not better reflect my life rather than my lecture style, although I would have attributed more meaningfulness to the "tangents." Second, if that is the worst my students had to say, then perhaps that overwhelming feeling of inadequacy that accompanies my pregnancies is more debilitating than the pregnancy itself.

I am now contemplating a new scrapbook, though I am not sure when I will work on it. It will comprise not family photos, but instead memorabilia from my profession. Published articles, photos of my colleagues, news clips about the department, wedding announcements from my students, thank-you notes from the ones whose lives have changed. I especially treasure those from the women who have hopes for their own careers and families that are, though not perfectly, at least meaningfully, combined.

This month, as I ease my way back into the rigors of my profession, I have mixed feelings. I am overwhelmed, revived, and overwhelmed again. We all have limits. I am forced to respect mine. And I also try to remember. One ball was no feat and no pleasure to the juggler; only in the whirling, sometimes dizzying, sometimes falling, sometimes overwhelming blur of balls did the juggler's art have its meaning, and my life its chaotic, perilous balance.

7

Twins and the Academic Career

Kathryn Jacobs

IT STILL AMAZES ME that I managed to prosper in academia after the disaster of my second birth: twins, eight weeks premature and (in one case) seriously handicapped. Child care was impossible for medical reasons, yet I could not afford to stay at home, and (thanks to the mobility of modern academic life) I had no family within a thousand miles of me. Research was out of the question, my department became hostile, and I could not have done a worse job at department politics. And yet somehow here I am, a full professor with one book out, another on the way, dozens of articles and poems in print, and three healthy teenagers to welcome me back each evening. This is a story, then, of what went wrong and how I recovered—or, if you prefer, what I did when motherhood and academia collided. It is also a story that almost did not get written, simply because I did not wish to face again that endless question of divided responsibility. How many pages for motherhood, how many for academia, and how do I link the two? Which do I spend more time on? And most important of all, will I lose an academic audience if I dare to begin with something as "unprofessional" as motherhood? There is great power in that dreaded word *unprofessional*. Even now, in their efforts to avoid it, a majority of academic mothers struggle with the inflexible demands of their profession for the most part in silence. In fact, it is to break that silence, finally, that I write this at all—to provide some kind of support to parents who, stretched in two directions, nevertheless manage to accomplish something on the very edge of impossible.

ALMOST EVERYTHING ABOUT my second pregnancy made normal academic work impossible. I had intended, for instance, to work until the last moment, but I was barely five months pregnant when I went into premature labor and spent the next eight weeks in the hospital, trying to stave off delivery. Walking, visiting the bathroom, even sitting up in bed trig-gered contractions, so I was forbidden to indulge in any of these privileges. Meals were a hit-and-miss affair, depending on how many contractions I was having and which experimental drugs I was taking on any given day. I was forbidden to stand on a scale, so I had no idea how much weight and muscle I had lost. I did, however, notice the gradual disappearance of my thighs. Four days before delivery I asked for a tape measure and discovered that my knees were now distinctly larger around than the leg above them, even at midpoint. By the time I returned home I could not even climb stairs without sitting down to rest halfway. Rest and recuperation, however, were out of the question. When I first became pregnant in 1987 I was an assistant professor with classes and colleagues, savings, and, I thought, some stamina. Now, on unpaid leave, I felt like a housewife, but I did have something to show for it all: two three-pound babies and a four-year-old. I also had that immense asset, a supportive husband. This did not mean, however, that Doug was prepared for twins with medical problems. He was also temporarily unemployed, writing for publishers who might someday pay but had not yet done so. And when the children cried at night, he woke *me*. This was not a light matter, given that one baby had lung damage and both were decidedly underweight. To make it worse, I had been thoroughly indoctrinated about the benefits of nursing by the professionals at the intensive care unit where my children lived for five weeks. Until the twins came home, therefore, we drove two and a half hours a day to the hospital and back, to deliver milk and help teach them to suck. Born without this reflex, they had to be tube-fed for weeks. They were also on monitors, in a noisy room full of alarms, wires, and babies. I was scared to touch them. In-deed, the first time I tried to hold one of my hand-sized mummies (trailing wires), she instantly stopped breathing. After that—and the lecture given to us by the nurse, who emphasized the extreme fragility of preemies—it was weeks before my husband dared to do the same.

The babies I took home were larger, of course—almost five pounds in the case of my son, not counting the monitors that went everywhere he did. These monitors were essential, because both children suffered periodic apneas (meaning that their hearts stopped beating periodically, shutting down the lungs in the process). Driving in the car was particularly hazard-ous. One memorably awful journey—on the way to the doctor's office—I will never forget. Both twins were in the back, car seats faced backward as recommended for newborns, so that I could not actually touch them while driving. During that one 20-minute drive, Ray's monitor went off *three* times—and they were not false alarms. Twice I pulled to the side of the road—monitor screeching urgently all the while—and touched him into breathing again. Hearts with apneas "forget" to beat, so a few pats are usually all that it takes to "remind" them again. Once, however, in a busy section, there was no place to pull off, and I was forced to block traffic, hoping no one would hit us, before he turned blue. After that I refused to travel with them unless my four-year-old was seated between the two car seats, one hand on each baby to keep them alive.

Night posed different sorts of problems. I became accustomed, during those first months, to the idea that every now and then my children stopped breathing. The difficulty was in figuring out in the dark *which* baby needed me. The machines had red alert lights, but I often found both lights on, since they routinely suffered apneas too brief to set off the alarm. Once I anxiously poked and prodded poor Ray, only to find that Lizzy had not been breathing all that time. In those first days, then, I stayed home almost around the clock, watching them. No day-care center, obviously, would take the responsibility for children in this condition, and because (like so many academic couples) we had moved across the country for my job, we had no relatives to call upon. It was up to us.

The nadir of this sudden immersion in housewifery occurred when the twins were about seven weeks old—not yet due to be born. Since the day Ray came home he had cried weakly every 30 to 45 minutes—all night, every night. Ray was only hungry, but he had difficulty breathing and so could not suck for more than a few seconds without resting. At my doctor's suggestion I served him breast milk from a bottle with an enlarged opening (I pumped) and even mixed a few spoonfuls of rice cereal into it in an effort to build up his calories. Almost invariably, however, he stopped sucking not because he was full, but because he was exhausted—and woke up as soon as he had rested enough to try again. Lately, he had started coughing, too, so on this particular night I set him up, monitor and all, beside my bed. Still, the night began propitiously, for he slept much longer than usual—two, perhaps even three hours straight. When the monitor went off I touched him almost without waking. It was perhaps 10 seconds later before I realized that the alarm was still ringing. I touched, patted, even shook him slightly, all to no avail. By this time I was full of adrenaline—not to say terrified. Only after I began CPR did he finally start breathing again. For the rest of the night I paced the room with him, waiting for the doctor's office to open and thinking how chilly he was. The nurse who took his temperature refused to believe her reading the first time round: 96 degrees flat. Then she sent us to the emergency room. At the hospital they said he had pneumonia. It is a measure of how bad things were at home that, when told he would be in intensive care, I felt nothing but relief. He would be well cared for, and I would get some sleep at last.

He was in the hospital again, under an oxygen tent, when I returned to teaching the next semester. When home, he and Lizzy stayed with my husband and my four-year-old. But the responsibility for medication and monitors, not to mention twins, worried my husband, so he made me promise to spend the absolute minimum number of hours at the office— teach, and then leave whenever possible. Given my colleagues' reaction to this, it would have been better, perhaps, if I had taken another semester's leave. There was no question, however, that I had to teach as soon as possible, whatever the consequences: We simply could not pay the bills without it.

WHEN MY DEPARTMENT FIRST HIRED ME, I was its first new member in 12 years and the only woman. The youngest man there was in his 40s, and he was a commuter who taught just two days a week. All the rest were over 50. At the time, I thought relatively little about this except to assume that the department had been "tenured up," with too many faculty to justify a new hire. Nor was it surprising to find that a department hired almost entirely in the 1960s was composed of Caucasian males. Frankly, I was not inclined to dwell on such things; gender had never been an issue in graduate school, and I planned to keep it that way.

So it was something of a shock to discover, at the interview reception given by the eldest member of the department, that this was about to change. The first inkling of change arrived via my hostess, an earnest woman of the sort that we say "means well." I had only just met her, and we had scarcely gone beyond preliminaries when she began to confide in me the various difficulties thrust upon the hiring committee that year. It seems that my position had been funded only provisionally: They *had* to hire a woman. In fact, she soon waxed quite fluent on the grief this had caused the department. "So the first thing they did when the applications came in was sort them in two piles . . ." (gesturing to show me the handsome proportions of the stack composed by male applicants). "So many *wonderful* men, so well qualified, but they had to send rejection letters to *every one* of them." Years have passed since this particular conversation took place. The feeling in her voice, however—the emphasis on the tall stack of brilliantly qualified and sadly neglected men, plus the pain at having to limit themselves to the small pile of women that remained—this I will never forget. I had no idea what to say. If she had merely mentioned it and then gone on, doubtless I would have let it slide. Barely 26 at the time and with a brand-new doctorate, I had as little experience of department politics as is possible in this world, and none at all of the sort of half-suppressed resentment that I was now facing. But when she went so far as to expatiate on the difficult job market today and the advantages this gave women like myself, I felt obliged to speak. With a diffidence that had its ironic side, I declared myself arrogant enough to think that, even without such favorable hiring practices, I would still manage to find employment. She looked shocked but mercifully changed the subject. My practical education had begun.

LOOKING BACK, I FIND MYSELF WONDERING not why that job went wrong after I confessed my pregnancy, but why it did not go wrong long before, or what they wanted in the first place. Others who interviewed me—usually for the sake of my Harvard degree—wanted the publications I did not yet possess. But these colleagues actively discouraged my first efforts to remedy this deficiency. This was a service-oriented department, they said—and it was true that only two members of the department ever published. Perhaps, indeed, they found my limitations reassuring. Here I was with a fancy degree to my name, no publications to speak of, and woefully little teaching experience. I spent inordinate amounts of time on class prep, while they looked on indulgently and invited me to bring my 18-month-old daughter into the office. I had admitted the existence of this daughter in my interview (I was later told by a friend how unwise this was, but it did not occur to me at the time), and they had definitely beamed. It gave us something in common, and we talked children as if we were at a church get-together instead of a professional interview. In short, they were very kind to me those first two years, with the one small proviso that they never took me the least bit seriously.

I noticed all this from the beginning, of course, but I generally thought about it as little as possible. Perhaps I was simply used to playing graduate student. Certainly, I wanted a job. I did resent it, however, when the secretary took her cue from them. A grandmotherly woman who had been in the department as long as they had, she nevertheless never failed to address everyone in the department with a respectful "doctor"—except me. I was always "dear" and was once scolded by her for leaving the drawer under the coffeepot ajar.

There was, in short, only one advantage that I could see to all the gender stereotyping—it was, I thought, the ideal department in which to announce that I wished to take a semester's unpaid leave for reasons of pregnancy. Knowing them, I suspected that they would probably be secretly delighted, and I was more than a little chagrined at the prospect. So, although their reaction was more subdued than I expected, it was not until I answered a polite inquiry with a blithe, "everything's fine; in fact, I am having twins!" that I realized what I was in for. The next day they were all but rubbing their hands together. My department head told me how difficult things would be for me, in a "wash my hands of you" way that did not bode well. Within days he informed me that I would no longer be teaching many of my literature courses when I returned from leave. From now on they wanted me to teach other courses—courses that had not been taught in our department in years. I could begin, however, with grammar (sounding as if I should be grateful for the concession). And to reinforce the "we," my department head made the announcement in public, while several of my senior colleagues were watching to see how I would take it. Protests, even on grounds of competency, were dealt with summarily. When, for instance, I pointed out that I had never so much as *taken* a grammar course in my life and had no idea how to teach one, I was promptly (and rather smugly) told that I had better get the textbook and start prepping. The message was clear: I had been indulged too long and was now going to assume my proper place. There was also a pervasive assumption: You are in no position, now, to go elsewhere.

Such were my relations within the department when I disappeared on leave. By the time I returned, grammar book in hand, Ray was in the hospital, and I was grappling with my son's cerebral palsy (later, dyslexia and Tourette's syndrome would be added to the list). I had already been told that, when he returned home, he would need daily intervention and therapists if I wanted him to walk. *Intervention* meant tough love: It took hours, and I soon found that nobody but me would really make him do it. So every afternoon, while my colleagues were still making their presence known at the office, I was standing Ray against rolling carts and turning them around when he hit the wall—or, later, making him knock his left leg against stair after stair until he learned to lift it. (His twin Elizabeth came, too, running expertly up and down and calling for my admiration at frequent intervals.) For this early disappearance I was soon called to account. "You do *work* here, you know!" one colleague reminded me, oblivious to my four classes, four preps, and carefully fulfilled departmental obligations. It was as if I had committed some sin and had to be punished for it—or so I thought at the time. In fact, I had simply put myself in a vulnerable position, and they were not averse to taking advantage of it.

They were not even trying to drive me out, though to convince me of this took the palpable astonishment of my department head when I gave notice. In fact, in the months that followed my announcement I got the distinct impression that I had in some way hurt their feelings. They had given me a hard time because they thought they *could,* that's all—I wasn't supposed to *leave* because of it. Perhaps they saw me as some sort of spoilsport; perhaps they were a little ashamed. At any rate, they began to look down when I passed and to avoid speaking to me. It was as if I had a terminal illness, and we were all pretending that it wasn't true. When my last week arrived I waited in vain for some token acknowledgment of my imminent departure: a lunch, an impromptu party or reception, a card, even a simple farewell. Not one of them said a word to me. On the day I finished my last class I looked about—I was the only one in the office. Seeking closure, I scrawled a handwritten "Goodbye, everyone, and good luck!" signed it, and tacked it to the department bulletin board. I never heard from any of them again.

SO CLOSED MY FIRST ATTEMPT to mix motherhood and professorship. Looking back, it is apparent that my colleagues were not unusually malicious people, and I suspect that I would no longer have any difficulty handling them. At the time, however, I merely resolved never again to put myself in such a predicament. Why did my next job work so much better than my first one? I wish I could say that the world changed radically in those four years, but I do not believe it. Part of the credit, certainly, goes to my new department, which was larger and more varied. Instead of being the only untenured professor in 12 years, I was now one of six—four women (two of them mothers) and two dads. At campus events we generally arrived en masse. When we had information we shared it, and when we had counsel, we shared that, too. But the practical changes at home were probably even more important. For by now the twins were four, and the worst was over: The monitors were gone, my son walked, and I had no trouble finding child care. Finally, I was older too: I had taught, I had published, and I had at last learned something about office politics.

8

Hiding the Baby

Gale Walden

At first, I didn't consciously hide the baby as I looked for an academic job.

Everyone changes their answering machine messages for the job search. You remove that Elvis Costello refrain "I would rather be anywhere else but here today" or dump the line of dialogue from *Who's Afraid of Virginia Woolf?* So it didn't seem sinister to remove the lullaby from my answering machine and replace it with my phone number and a message that I would be happy to return the call.

We are, at least initially in the job search, called upon to be a blank slate for someone, a group, or several groups to project their illusions upon. The initial interview is like a first date, and a lot of the same rules apply: "Don't speak badly about the ex." "Don't chew gum." "Dress appropriately." "Don't lie." Just "be yourself." Here's where the first-date analogy breaks down: On any first date, giving the facts is a necessary step toward trust and fairness—you should say if you have a baby or if you are married (in which case, technically, you shouldn't be on the date).

On the job market, the unspoken protocol is to say as little about your personal life as possible. Everything is a possible hindrance: the spouse who will need a job, the relationship that will now be long distance, the children, the elderly parent who lives with you. These are all things that prove your humanity, but they also prove that you have a life outside the academy, a demanding life outside the academy.

Because people without children (a group I've been in for most of my life) don't tend to think a lot about the ins and outs of child rearing, it came as something of a surprise to me that a baby could be a large liability in a job search. My first inkling of this came through a friend who had headed a search committee and was complaining that the man the department had hired was due to become a father any day. "We would never have hired him if we knew that," my friend said. I was shocked. "We needed somebody young, with a lot of energy. You don't have any energy when you have a baby."

My friend was the father of a toddler, a late-in-life father, a tenured father, a father who, for his first year of sleepless nights, took a sabbatical. It occurred to me that the job candidate had successfully negotiated a job only by hiding his personal life—an option that would have been unavailable to his pregnant wife.

During my first round of job interviews, I was hiding only the *idea* of a baby. I was 38, had just published my first book, and had an idea that I should have both a real job and a baby by the time I was 40. I had simultaneously begun marital negotiations and filed adoption papers, in separate contingency plans, and my idea was this: I was going to bring a child into this world only if two people really wanted to, and if not, I'd raise a child already brought into the world.

On my only campus job interview that year, I asked about real estate prices in the area while silently thinking, *"Would he move here?"* and *"Would my adoption papers transfer to this state?"* "Are there any complications to your moving here?" the interviewers asked. And I said that there were always complications in any move, but none that I felt were overwhelming. Three weeks later I got a call from the department: "We just wanted to let you know we offered the job to someone who has accepted. I'm sorry. You were our first choice, but there was some reluctance coming from you that we couldn't figure out."

The next year on the job search I had a baby. By the time of the Modern Language Association convention, I had had a baby for four weeks. I had four interviews. The baby had pneumonia; I had pneumonia. This was not going to stop me from getting on a plane to San Francisco, and neither was motherhood. What did stop me, thankfully, was a fogged-in airport and canceled planes out of Chicago; this was the type of Mother Nature to which I would gladly defer.

After telephone interviews with the four departments, I landed two campus visits. At the first campus, I took my friend's dictum to heart and said absolutely nothing about my personal life. These hosts knew the rules; no one mentioned my wedding band, we talked about public schools via other people's children. There is ample opportunity for a person to reveal themselves over dinner and drinks, and I didn't deny my true political or philosophical nature. I also didn't lie, but when I returned, I felt deceitful.

I cringe when I say that at the second campus visit I not only looked at day-care facilities, I showed baby pictures. I wanted that job, and I wanted people to know me for who I was, baggage and all.

In the spirit of full disclosure, I announced that if I got the job, I would be arriving on campus alone with the child. "At least we won't have to find a job for your spouse," the head of the search committee remarked. I've had many graduate students on the market this year tell me they feel less hesitant bringing up the baby if there is no academic partner needing work in the picture. But a single-parenting situation can give a committee pause. Throughout the weekend the issue of the baby kept resurfacing. "We are worried you won't be as productive as before," said the head of the search committee during a private talk. I was offended. Another faculty member said, "We have a lot of evening programs you will be expected to attend. Will you feel comfortable leaving the baby? Have you thought about this?"

I was, at this point, learning my own hard lessons about the constraints of parenting, and having someone else project more on me made me livid, although I answered with reassuring phrases. Still, the head of the search committee told me, "I'd be more comfortable if the baby was three."

Here's whom else you might want to hide the baby from: graduate students. And here's why: A baby isn't sexy to grad students. If you are an aspiring writing professor and you are asked what you do in your spare time, here are the correct responses:

"I help edit *McSweeney's*. I throw dinner and dance parties for luminaries to which you are all invited. Enough about me. Tell me about your work."

Here is what not to say: "I hang out with my baby and write." For one thing, it's not true. It turns out hardly anyone hangs out with their baby and writes. It's more honest to say, "I hang out with the baby when the baby is awake. When the baby is asleep, I write. When the baby turns three, I will write even more." There has to be something in the mentor's life that makes the student desire that life a little. This is not it.

I wasn't offered the job I wanted, and because of the comments made, I felt trespassed upon and judged. For two weeks, I thought about seeking justice (which, by the way, hardly anyone who has a baby would have the time or energy to do), but even at that point I was aware that the faculty members who were (privately) making these comments to me were the ones with children. They were the professors who knew the demands of parenting.

Truth be told, I became a better teacher because of parenthood (another article), but I was less productive for at least two years. And truth be told, too, part of the reason I didn't get the job I wanted was that I didn't put enough time into preparing for the paper I was to give; it took at least a year for me to begin to balance time effectively again. I made several mistakes. I too am more comfortable now that the child is three, and I'm much more understanding of the comments, however improper, made to me at that campus visit.

I've learned how to balance things other than time. I was offered the job where I stayed mum about being a mom, but I didn't take it because of the heavy teaching load. I have remained at the institution where I have been "visiting," although I've been upgraded from lecturer to visiting assistant professor. One of my favorite students, given to understatement, says, "It's too bad you aren't really visiting, because then there would be a place to return." Yes.

Still, one of the reasons that I like the department I'm in is that it's child friendly, which doesn't mean everyone has children, just that everyone is welcome to.

I put a foot tentatively in the job market this year, but I study places well before I even apply; I still read work by the faculty, but I also look at school systems and clues for family compatibility. On one department's Web page, the chairwoman of the search committee is pictured with her 10-year-old, and I know immediately to apply. She isn't hiding her child.

9

The One with the Baby: Single-Mothering in Academia

Tarshia L. Stanley

In Search of Our Mothers' Gardens is a collection of Alice Walker's womanist wit and wisdom. Among her musings on life as a woman and a writer is a tiny section entitled "A Writer Because of, Not in Spite of, Her Children." Here Walker reflects on the dedication Nigerian writer Buchi Emecheta makes in her novel *Second Class Citizen,* "To my dear children . . . without whose sweet background noises this book would not have been written" (quoted in Walker, 1983, p. 67). Walker seems fascinated that Emecheta does not perceive motherhood as a deterrent to her writing, but rather sees her mothering as an enabler. Walker goes on to examine the way in which Western thought has wanted the woman to choose between her mothering and her art or her work, as if it were impossible for a woman to give herself to both. She counters those narratives with images of African women who worked the fields with babes strapped in rainbow rags to their backs—working and mothering were the same.

Particularly as an African-descended American and an academic, I want desperately to embrace Emecheta's mantra and boast that my mother-hood has not been juxtaposed to my work. I want to resist the notion that motherhood messes with my ability to produce cutting-edge, theoretically sound, peer-reviewed, well-received scholarship. The truth is I am tired in ways I cannot imagine my childless contemporaries to be—although they often assure me there is no difference. An even deeper truth is that the fatigue does not come from the physicality of juggling Senior English theses, virtual classrooms, and the tenure clock with my daughter's basket-ball, prealgebra, and hormonal surges. The truth is the guilt. Much of my decade of mothering has been shadowed by a gnawing guilt that I have not been an excellent mother because I was trying to be an excellent professor and that I have not been an excellent professor because . . . well, you know the rest. The irony of it all is that I only began to believe that I was failing because other people assumed I would fail.

Dear Thai,
We have officially arrived in our new home. We live in a tiny campus apartment here at the University of Florida. I thought things would be better when we actually arrived here. So many people told me I couldn't come to grad school pregnant that I somehow felt the battle would be partially over when I (or should I say we?) finally arrived. I am not nervous about school—though perhaps I should be. School is always what I've done best. I don't expect it will be all that different from undergraduate. I realize that you'll have to spend quite a bit of time with the babysitter during the week, but I promise I'll reserve the weekends for mommy/baby time. I've already figured out how I'll study at the library. I saw one of these baby backpack things, and once I have you on a schedule I'll just take you with me. I know this is going to be hard, but you and I can do this.
Love,
Your Mommy Very Soon

It is significant that I became a scholar and a mother at the same time. As I became responsible to humanity for the life I had added to it, I also became responsible to the profession I had chosen in ways I had not imagined when I was dreaming of becoming a professor with a Tuesday/Thursday teaching schedule. In much the same way I would nurture my daughter, I would have to cultivate an intellectual self. Every time my child has a birthday I take a mental inventory to see if the child of my mind is growing as fast and as fastidiously. I am always between my two offspring, trying desperately to perform a delicate balance between teacher/scholar and mother/mother.

I didn't think my being seven months pregnant was going to be a big deal in graduate school. I was 24 and had managed to win a full five-year fellowship, so I felt old enough and financially prepared enough to have the baby and continue my studies. I was determined not to let an unplanned pregnancy stop me from achieving my goal. I'd wanted to teach since I was in the fourth grade, standing at the blackboard demonstrating why Florida was a peninsula.

That's why I wasn't afraid to move to a new state where I didn't know a soul, with one suitcase and plenty of defiance. I had no idea that people would see me and judge my ability to survive both in school and in life by the fact that I was a single parent. It was the early 1990s and I thought sexism and racism were quite passé. I had for the most part been judged on the content of my character and thought my fellowship and my intellect would be all I would need. Not only was I naive, it was easier to plow ahead blindly than to wait for a moment and contemplate the journey to which I was committing myself.

Dear Thai,

Happy birthday—you're exactly 24 hours old. I have no idea how I have enough strength left to write in this journal. I don't even remember putting it in my bag. I am so tired and I hurt all over and I have a paper due tomorrow. I called my professor and told him I wouldn't be able to get my paper in on time because I'd gone into labor. He was nice enough. He told me to take my time and he would turn in an incomplete for me until I gave him the paper. I know I shouldn't be thinking about this now, but I don't want my professors to think I am using you as an excuse. You were there on our first visit to the department. Dr. X and I met in the elevator. I didn't know she was an English professor when I asked her for directions. I told her I was a new student. "But, aren't you pregnant?" she asked. It was my first indication that this might not be the cakewalk I had planned. I stammered what I am sure was a nearly incomprehensible affirmation, and she said, "Oh, you must have one heck of a husband." No, I didn't have a heck of a husband, but I was getting a heck of a headache. I smiled my synthetic smile [the one that would find its way to my face on many occasions during the next seven years] and followed her into the English department. So here I am writing to you when I should be finishing my paper. I wish I could hold you. I feel as if I've hardly had a chance to see you. They won't let you stay in the room with me until my temperature returns to normal. They say we should be together by the morning.

Love,

Your Brand New Mommy

I am from one of those Southern black communities where mothering is the reason you exist. You go to school and do well so you can get a good job, so you can take care of your children. I think they must have been whispering this to me from the time of my own cradle. Even before my daughter came into existence, I was achieving for her, living, in many ways, for her. I had always imagined what I would do for my hypothetical child, the music lessons, the dance lessons, the excellent schooling. I could achieve none of that on a graduate school fellowship. We could barely survive—and this child's life was supposed to be better because I would give her mine. There were days my life could hardly buy diapers and nights when I was so afraid to miss class that I left her with less-than-adequate babysitters. I would go to school and discuss the Marxist theory of economics and Chodorow's take on Freud's pleasure principle and come home and hold real life in hands that had begun to shake all the time. That's not good for a filmmaker. I was having difficulty reconciling Foucault and food stamps.

Dear Thai,
I am so tired of Dr. Y referring to me as "the one with the baby." First of all, when I arrived in this department I was only the third minority in residence. So to learn all three of our names isn't asking too much. Second, when she calls me "the one with the baby," she says it as if it were some kind of punishment. Sweetheart, you're three years old, and I'm almost finished writing my thesis. I want so badly to ask her why she does it and demand that she call me by my name if she has to address me at all—I wonder why I don't.
Love,
Tarshia, Your Mother

I reached a crisis situation the semester I took my first film theory course. Our assignment was to write a paper using pictures. They could be magazine photos, Polaroids, and the like. I thought long and hard before I made my daughter the subject of my project. She was four, and I had long since ceased to speak about her or to bring her to campus. Dr. "the one with the baby" had worn something in me down. I was almost afraid to mention my child, in a way bordering on insanity, I think. Anyone who hadn't come into the program about the same time I did and saw me pregnant or who hadn't heard about my going into labor two days before the end of the summer session wouldn't have known I had a child. I was finally feeling like I had earned some respect in the department and thought that maybe using pictures of my child wouldn't be seen as a weakness. As I watched her discover the world, I was so fascinated that I wanted to convey somehow, through a montage of her image, this sense of the incredible I felt. I was careful when I wrote the paper not to call her my daughter. It felt like some kind of covert operation as I talked about "this child." I thought I'd done an incredible job when I turned in my project. My professor's only comment was "I don't understand where you're trying to go with this." Even now I don't know if the project really was perplexing, or, if in testifying about myself as a mother, I spoke against myself as a scholar. I took it quite personally and spent a miserable semester in his class—listening to him talk about his own children—and wondering where this part of me that was a mother fit in my academic life.

> Dear Thai,
> You know Dr. Z told me that I had been the talk of the first faculty party the year I entered the department. He said they were all laying bets as to how long I'd be able to keep up in school with a new baby. They can't believe I just finished my qualifying exams. I probably looked so stupid, standing there with that fake, dazed smile plastered in place. I didn't think that was one bit funny. "Now," he said with his head thrown back and a twinkle in his eye, "we'll see how you do with the dissertation." Whatever joy I'd felt hadn't lasted long. I glanced down at my watch; I'd have to leave soon to pick you up from preschool.
> Love,
> Mommy

Mothering and guilt go hand in hand. There is always something you didn't do or that you did do that could cause your child to be a miscreant. I am sure many working mothers feel "motherguilt" in our society. In academia, however, we like to take guilt to new levels. Whereas, on the one hand, the flexible teaching schedules and the ability in many ways to determine your course loads are wonderful things, the tenure clock waits for no man and seems in a particular hurry to leave women with children behind. I find there is nothing like being compared to the boy or girl wonder in your office who just happens not to have children—especially when that comparison is made by women who've either never had children or have forgotten what is was like when theirs were young. I don't mean to suggest that the standards of evaluation should somehow be waived for academics with children, I just wish I could leave a late-afternoon committee meeting without the convener feeling an obligation, or perhaps a right, to ask everyone to excuse me because I have "day-care" issues. Better yet, I wish I didn't care.

Dearest Thai,

We have finally arrived, I think. I got the job at Spelman, and no one here seems to mind that I have a child. I was a bit worried during the hiring process. When they called Dr. X for a reference she recommended me quite highly and then proceeded to tell them, or maybe warn them, that I was a single parent. I really don't understand why that had to come up. It got even worse when Dr. A wrote my recommendation and my new chair told me he spent more time talking about the fact that I had a child than my work. Nevertheless, I am determined to do well here. It is strange to hear all these people call me "doctor." I couldn't have done it without you. I am sitting here in my very own office, having just introduced you to everyone, and I don't feel any guilt and I didn't have to apologize for having a child.

Love,

Dr. Mommy

I bring my daughter to work with me on Wednesdays. I have a late-evening class and have not found a sitter who could pick her up from school and stay with her until 8 or 9 P.M. So once a week we tumble into my office, backpack, blanket and pillow, dinner in Gladware (or a five-dollar bill so she can eat in the cafeteria). I am in a much better position than most working mothers. Still, I find myself urging her to stay close to my office. I am not implying that she should keep out of sight—just not be seen so easily.

Once I returned from class to find her lying on her stomach on the floor outside of my office reading a book. I nearly had a breakdown. Although it was late and the only other person on the hall was the cleaning lady, I rushed her into my office and gave her a good "talking to." "This is my place of work," I said in my most formal English professor tone. "I have to be seen as a professional at all times." As my voice got louder, I wasn't sure I was talking to my daughter anymore. Then she said, "But Mommy, what does me being in the hallway have to do with you teaching your class?" I stopped in midsentence, sat down at my desk, and waited for my hands to stop shaking. It was then I knew that I was afraid. I was halfway through the tenure process, had received excellent reviews, and was anticipating a publisher for my manuscript, but somehow I was scared that being a mother made me less-than in the eyes of my colleagues. Perhaps what I had called guilt all those years had been mostly fear.

Dear Thai,

I have finally filled up the first journal I have been keeping for you.
This begins a whole new book. I want to start by telling you about
an interesting conversation I had with one of my female colleagues
the other day. We were fantasizing about quitting our jobs and being
perfect, cookie-baking, stay-at-home moms. (It's easier for me to
fantasize about this because I can't actually do it.) We were whispering
in hushed tones about the kind of pressure we feel to be good teachers
and publish, and why we seem to be the only ones feeling this way.
We pondered this profession and how it was really patterned after the
monastic, single life—the male, monastic, single life. We ended our
conversation as we always do—with lamentations and encouragement. I
wonder if you'll have to face these feelings as a working mother. Maybe
something will be different by then.

Love,

Your Mother

I have a coworker who brings his child to work. This delightful child rushes
up and down the hallway, poking his head in all of our office doors. Even
at his age, he never fails to flash an endearing grin before he races back to
his father's office. My colleague intermittently looks up from the work on
his desk and smiles back at the little boy. That's all he does. He never checks
to see who's watching his son, never tells him to be quiet, never admon-
ishes him to stay near his office. I am jealous. That's probably what Buchi
Emecheta looked like when she was working. It's definitely what I want to
look like when I'm working.

REFERENCE

Walker, A. (1983). *In search of our mothers' gardens.* New York: Harcourt, Brace,
Jovanovich.

PART II
Possibilities

There are very real challenges to combining parenting with an academic career, but the rewards are equally significant. Women display higher self-esteem and greater well-being when they engage positively in a number of different roles (Marks & MacDermid, 1996). We gain a sense of this vibrancy and promise in the essays by Rachel Fink and Susan Jacobowitz, both of whom express delight in having lives that, although busy, are packed full of activities and commitments that make them deeply happy. Jacobowitz refuses the sympathy of those who pity her for being so busy, because she believes that "in some alchemical, synergistic way, one feeds the other—that my love for my work enhances what I bring to my children as a parent and that the love I bear for my children brings something extra to my work." Fink, a marine biologist, delights especially in sharing her work with her children: teaching them to identify male and female killifish, letting them help create killifish embryos for her to study. These essays suggest the potential richness of creating a satisfying balance between parenting and academic work.

But sometimes, creativity, flexibility, and a willingness to try "plan B" are necessary to achieve such a balance. Lynn Z. Bloom and Heather Bouwman both recount their experiences trying to find a way of working within the academy that allowed them to express both their maternal and scholarly selves. Bouwman left her job at a large research institution when she realized that her commitment to mothering lowered her status and value in the eyes of her colleagues. She now teaches at a university where she feels accepted as both a parent and a professor, but the difficult academic job market means that many professors are unable to find another job with a better "fit." For Bloom, pursuing an academic career meant doing something that had previously seemed incompatible with her ideas of good mothering: taking a job 1,000 miles away from her home, leaving her husband to provide all of the weekday care for their two teenaged sons. Without the freedom—and the support from her husband—to make this unconventional choice, Bloom believes that her career would have foundered from the lack of opportunities in her local area. The three years of commuting were complicated but amply rewarding both personally and professionally. The experience she gained in those three years made it possible for her and her husband to get jobs in the same place, proving that a commuter-marriage situation need not be permanent.

Those who succeed in expressing both their intellectual and maternal selves argue that their work benefits in multiple ways from their maternal perspective. Michelle M. Francl-Donnay sees no dichotomy in her dual roles as mother and chemist, and she resists the idea that the demands of academic science cannot be reconciled with the demands of mothering. She has found many ways in which parenting young children has strengthened in her the qualities she needs for success as a chemist and a teacher, recounting, for example, the ways that attention to small, apparently minor details, which her children help her to practice, has led to breakthroughs in her work as a chemist. Nancy Gerber reports similarly fruitful connections; she found upon her return to graduate school that her experience as a mother was becoming an important part of her understanding of feminist thought, and she decided to make mothering the focus of her doctoral research. Her goal was to legitimate motherhood as a serious focus of scholarly inquiry, to bring motherhood from the marginalized academic spaces of hallways and classroom breaks into the seminar room and, eventually, the dissertation defense. In this, she reminds us of the importance of having mothers fully represented in academia because of the different perspectives they can provide. As Nancy Hensel (1990) asks, "Would a biologist who is also a mother ask different research questions from a biologist who is not a mother? Or a sociologist, historian, or psychologist?" (p. 4). They would, and they do.

Experience with motherwork can also create benefits in the classroom. While not about literal motherwork, Norma Tilden's essay describes how a maternal perspective, in her case informed by a Catholic understanding of the nature of the Virgin Mary, can effect change in the college classroom. In explaining her comfort in the role of adjunct instructor—a position she held for 12 years before becoming a tenure-track professor—Tilden uses the stories of New Testament women that surrounded her in her Catholic girlhood as analogies for the kind of power that adjunct instructors have. Like these biblical women, adjunct instructors effect change in people's lives without receiving much credit. In their careful listening to students, Tilden and other teachers of introductory composition show the same kind of ability represented by the Virgin Mary: "the mother as *magnifying*—of making visible and tangible what had otherwise been only an idea, an abstract promise unfulfilled." In her emphasis on the connections between the quiet, hidden power of biblical women and that of the overworked, underpaid, largely female pool of adjunct instructors, Tilden expresses her vision of an "adjunct pedagogy" based on feminist pedagogical theory that emphasizes the importance of decentering classroom authority.

Lorretta Holloway's experience with her daughters' need for female African American role models helped her to understand and value her importance to black students as an African American professor—often the first her students have had. She started having her children watch the WNBA when she discovered that her older daughter thought that every black woman they saw was "Mama"—implicit in this observation is the idea that African American students deserve to see more than one or two black role models on their campuses. Perceiving her daughters' need helped Holloway to embrace her position as "role model," despite the extra pressure it put on her. Tilden's and Holloway's stories go beyond the simple idea that mothers can bring more to the classroom because of warm, fuzzy (and essentializing) qualities of nurturing. Any parent, male or female, who makes a serious commitment to nurturing the next generation will likely bring to the classroom a broader understanding of the personhood of students and a longer-range understanding of the purpose of education than they otherwise would. Surely these are perspectives that the academic community would wish to endorse and support.

REFERENCES

Hensel, N. (1990). Maternity, promotion, and tenure: Are they compatible? In L. B. Welch (Ed.), *Women in higher education: Changes and challenges* (pp. 3–11). New York: Praeger.

Marks, S. R., & MacDermid, S. M. (1996). Multiple roles and the self: A theory of role balance. *Journal of Marriage and the Family, 58,* 417–432.

10

Today, She's Just Mama

Lorretta Holloway

Instead of focusing on the perfect mother/scholar or complaining about the difficulties in combining the two, I would like to focus on the moments of crystal revelation that motherhood has brought to my academic career. Children, ours and others, are constantly telling us things about ourselves—often things we would rather not know. Barefaced honesty without equivocation remains rare in the academic world. Instead, we emphasize careful framing of messages to colleagues and not hurting students' feelings. But children are not necessarily interested in rhetorical niceties. They are trying to understand and to get everyone to make sense. This became painfully clear to me when I finished my dissertation. I had a friend watch my children during my defense, and while I was gone she prepped my then almost three-year-old to greet me upon my return with "Hello, Dr. Holloway." But the next day, when someone came by and called me Dr. Holloway, my toddler interrupted with a correction. "Oh, no," she said very seriously. "She isn't Dr. Holloway. That was yesterday. Today, she is just mama." Everyone laughed, but she was right. I wanted to bask in the glory of my successful defense. I wanted fanfare. (What I really wanted was a full-page ad in the newspaper and a gold medallion.) But in the real world, it really did not matter to anyone (outside of my family and my committee) that I was finished. In the real world, I was "just mama" until I used that PhD to do something. My toddler knew that. And she made me remember it. Children, in their messy honesty, make us remember.

Most interestingly, children can supplement our academic existence. My children have forced me to be stronger, nicer, meaner, and pushier than even I thought I could be. Yet, despite my penchant for sentimentality (I do specialize in the Victorian novel by choice), I quickly lose patience with the Hallmark Hall of Fame vision of motherhood, a view often reinforced—ironically enough—by my colleagues. When I take my children to campus (and this happened in graduate school as well), faculty and staff melt with wonder and are struck with a treacly gaze. Although I am pleased that other people like my children, I can only smile wanly. I am not empowered or soothed by motherhood. I do not feel young, relaxed, or spontaneous, and the only future I think about is what I can make for dinner and what I can possibly do with the children at the next conference. The only time I get that serene look attributed to mothers in Johnson & Johnson commercials is when my children are finally asleep or if I get to take a bath in an empty house.

Here I will focus on the other ways (I am tempted to say "real" ways) motherhood has made me a better student, teacher, and scholar. Parenting continually forces one to work through exhaustion, raises the ability to bounce back from embarrassment, and reminds one to always be humble. If you think about it, all of these are essential skills for surviving graduate school, academic job searches in the humanities, and doing research in a world where research seems to be distancing itself from pragmatic application.

In the Beginning: Exhaustion and Infection

I call my children the bookends to my dissertation. My first was born the day after I started drafting my first chapter. The second was born the day after I received the last chapter back from my committee chair. People often stop and wonder at this, but the reality was much less miraculous. After all, it took me three years to finish the document, and that first chapter was, in its initial stages, worse than some freshman essays I have graded. I managed basically because I never believed in any but individual versions of motherhood and because the purely physical exhaustion of pregnancy, childbirth, and toddlers pushed me from one day to the next. Parenting was merely an addition to the regular mental exhaustion required by graduate school and pretenure work. With almost every job, there is always the pressure to work, to work more hours, and to work harder than others work. Academia feeds into this by openly and voraciously encouraging competition and the idea that much of the "work" comes not from sweat and effort but from intellect or the more elusive talent. There is even another challenge, for the belief lurking underneath all of this is that the inspiration is finite and the judgments complete.

For anyone who is not independently wealthy, there is always the feeling that you must work. Children only increase the work. All parents know that parenting is like constantly being at work. So to do both, you must work all the time, perform, and pass tests constantly. I did research while the children slept, read while I cooked, and wrote on the floor while children played on top of me and around me. The understanding was that I had to work when I could, work "now" because later someone would be crying, someone would be vomiting, someone would be crying and vomiting, someone would be crying and vomiting on me. This might seem a gross idea, but parenting is not for the squeamish. Then again, neither is the academic world. Both are full of phlegm, phlegmatic personalities, and other bodily fluids literal and figurative that we have to sift, stomp, and wade through to finish degrees, receive appointments, publish, potty-train, and run school bake sales.

One might think that this kind of disgusting exhaustion would be conducive to neither parenting nor academic work. But there really is not a choice once one decides upon these endeavors. One could choose not to parent (as many do) or decide not to put up with the rules and games of academic life (as many more do), but after making the decision, parents should embrace the ways that the two can actually enhance each other. For example, the two endeavors lead to two very different kinds of exhaustion, which can balance each other out. The mental exhaustion of trying to decipher manuscripts, revise pages of your own work, or read literary criticism in code balances the mind-numbing exhaustion of cleaning the bathroom during toilet training or reading a book to a sick child for the 1,044th time. I have actually felt my brain cells dying when playing Candyland (an insipid board game created for children who haven't learned to read or count), but then I have had the same feeling in committee meetings. Both groups expect intense interest and enthusiasm. If you can manage enthusiasm for Candyland, you can manage alertness for the most petrifying committee meeting about copy machines.

The Importance of Snacks and Patience

Parenting is a matter of keeping patience with others and oneself while developing clear boundaries. These techniques come naturally to some, but it took me a while—and the added pressure of pregnancy—to achieve them. When I first began teaching as a graduate student, I spent proportionately far too much time on teaching, allowing my office hour to become an office day. This pattern reflected in my graduate work with professors as well: I showed up to office hours looking for answers to amorphous questions and left with notes that were not helpful, feeling silly and ignorant. But then I became pregnant, and the number of times I needed to snack or to go to the bathroom increased. Suddenly, I felt an urgency to utilize all the time and to get to the point sooner. I started telling students to come in with questions written down or specific goals for our meetings. I began doing that myself for meetings that I had with professors. It worked brilliantly. The meetings with students and professors became more worthwhile, and when they were over I felt that I had accomplished something and that everyone had a clear idea concerning what to do next. Sometimes students do need to come in just to talk without a preplanned agenda, but I found that with my new rules I actually had more time for those students. I also learned that if you have enough snacks to share, students (who are hungry most of the time themselves) do not mind if you have to eat *now*.

This qualified patience with self and others makes one understand the limits of the work of parenting and school and may help us to relax our perfectionism. Early in my master's work, the graduate coordinator warned us that we would not be successful unless we were completely focused on the perfection of every piece of work and every endeavor. We had to be. The competition was stiff. They let in 40 MA degree students in my year but then told us that they had only six spots in the PhD program. "If you can even imagine yourself doing anything else," he warned ominously, "you do not have the dedication required." But we all know that dedication is not the only marker of success. In fact, manic dedication almost makes things too important, so that the rejections and criticisms hurt too much for them to be helpful. Much (if not everything) depends on managing one's talent by picking the right projects, mentors, jobs, and conferences—those that match one's own interests and skills. Children remind us that everything does not have to perfect; anyone who has spent hours shopping for the perfect gift for a child only to watch the child play with the box instead knows this. Those cupcakes don't have to look like Martha Stewart decorated them as long as there is extra frosting. Some things are fine at "good enough." When not everything has to be perfect, it leaves time for extra effort on the special chosen things that usually need particular care, such as the special project that has been on the mind for years, or the costume for the recital, or that student who needs extra time.

Not Everybody Can Play, or the Rules for Embarrassment

Children know what they like and are not afraid to say so. Your children, especially when they are small, like you. Unconditionally. Because of this, they can be a great pick-me-up after being trampled by the often nasty atmosphere of graduate school or being verbally assaulted by a supposed mentor. They can bring you back to value yourself after what seems like the last unbearable rejection. They do not care if you got a form letter in that envelope. Your presence is enough for them to love you.

They also serve as a lesson in rejection. They reject and get rejected by others very often, and even if they suffer despairing tears for a brief time, five minutes later they have moved on, playing happily before the tears have even dried. I remember feeling sorry for my daughter because she found out that she wasn't invited to a classmate's birthday party. Later, I asked if she felt all right about it. She gave me the "I'm fine" look with the "Why are we still talking about this?" look mingled in for good measure. "After all," she said philosophically, "she can't invite everybody." Why couldn't I feel that way over my last rejected abstract? How come I stayed awake at night when the MLA rejected my special sessions proposal? The odds are that any conference or convention doesn't have room for everyone who qualifies to come. Maybe professional bodies and professional journals should utilize this philosophy when they reject people (which they should probably do with more care, since they reject more than they accept). Open convention notices with "After all, we can't invite everybody." Put it on the banner headline of the convention materials. At least include it in the letter. The *MLA Directory of Scholarly Presses in Language and Literature* helps by telling the average number of submissions and the average number of acceptances. This was the problem with my master's program: They invited everyone to the party, and once we were there, they told us we would need to leave. Soon.

My daughter got over her hurt feelings and what I thought would be embarrassment very quickly, but then that shouldn't surprise me, because children are excellent at embarrassment. I figure that the assault on the senses that parents cause teenagers is all payback for what they put us through when they were small. I remember having to meet a professor on my dissertation committee, and I had to bring my toddler. She behaved very well for a while, snacking on a lemon poppy-seed muffin, and then she tapped me on my leg. "Excuse me." "Just a minute," I told her (although

I do not know why I ever say that, because it is never a minute). She knew this even then. "Excuse me," she persisted. Of course I gave the look and another "just a minute." The next time she tapped me, I was all set to give her my "you are interrupting Mama" speech when her indignation trumped mine. "But Mama, I just farted!" I was mortified. There went my professional intellectual demeanor, although how much of that I really had with poppy seeds scattered over my feet I do not really know. My professor chortled until tears ran down his face. He was ready to pledge a marriage bond between my daughter and his grandson at that moment. I, however, mumbled apologies and thanks and retreated as quickly as was graciously possible.

So when I do something embarrassing, particularly in class, I'm rarely fazed. Once I fell on the floor in the middle of a lecture (thinking there was a seat behind me, but it had rolled away). I made a rather odd noise, and the bouncing was a bit jarring, but I never stopped talking. I even worked the fall into my lecture. I gestured at them from the floor behind my desk (I was in pain; there was no way I was going to pop back up), exclaiming that they needed to take even this as a lesson. Students talked about that for days: "She never stopped talking!" "I couldn't believe it." "I was more embarrassed than she was." Oh please. What was that compared to Kiana's intestinal comment? I saw a T-shirt once that sums it up: "You can't scare me. I've got kids."

Real Fear

Of course, this isn't completely true. I have kids, so I am in a constant state of fear. Parents have a murmuring underground fear all the time—wondering if they are doing the right thing, if the children are all right. But doesn't this sound like the underlying fear we have in academia? The academic world encourages hierarchy almost from the start. Instead of focusing on mere job performance, academics make a constant, public display of the hierarchy. Graduate students often behave as if only two or three As could be had in a course. They argue and fight in front of a seminar teacher as if they were gladiators trying to kill the lions, when really the behavior is much more like siblings vying for the fleeting attention of the parent. It is no better outside of the program; conferences sometimes become open season on the less fortunate (the graduate student, the unpublished, the scholar from a small school). I have seen people attend sessions just so they can argue a point in front of a crowd. I have seen people look first at your nametag to see what school you are from before they will even talk to you or constantly scan the room while they talk to you to see if someone better is coming in. This assault on self-esteem breeds constant fear.

Children get you used to the fear. Any honest parent will admit that most of the time we feel completely inadequate to the challenges facing us and are always questioning whether or not we are doing the right and the best things for our children. We also fear the outside world and, when our children are not directly in our sight, what that outside world is doing to them. Being a parent means always having a bit of fear for your children. This relegates those other fears to second place unless they directly affect the children. Losing a book deal, not getting a research grant, or being humiliated at a conference takes on any level of importance only if it will affect the way I can care for my children. I do not mean that these things no longer bother me, but they do not rank as high.

It is not just an issue of priorities, although parents, women in particular, have been accused of losing their intensity for the job (research, campus service, etc.) when they have children. This has been the excuse for not hiring women or people with young families. However, I do not think this is a completely accurate picture. I have seen people lose intensity for all sorts of reasons: death, divorce, illness, or, more often, fights within departments or with administration. Instead, I think that my children, or at least the image of them, shapes the decisions I make about the fights I choose to wage. I do not fight about everything, even when it is a fight I could win. Sometimes now I acquiesce in situations that I know I would not have relinquished years ago. Initially I started thinking that the stereotype was true—I was losing my edge—but I came to realize that I chose not to fight over things that just were not that important. I have particularly learned this through watching and refereeing my children's battles with each other. Their fights over turf, attention (see above), and toys are often so petty. They want things just because the other has them or because they do not want the other to have them. So much of this annoying and frustrating bickering mirrors the fights that I see in academia. I always have in the back of my mind the question of whether an argument that I am about to have with a colleague is something I would want my children to see. I want them to grow up to be strong women and to fight for what they think is right, but I also want them to be able to distinguish between being strong and being petty. I call this the role model challenge.

We Are the World?, or Thank Goodness for the WNBA

This is the challenge that has made me reevaluate my position in the academy. As a black woman in institutions with minority populations ranging from 4 to 10%, I had grown accustomed to being the only black person in class and the only minority in most. I have even gotten used to the startled look when I open my mouth and the second glance people who have talked to me on the phone give me when they meet me for the first time. Despite affirmative action, I still have been put in the situation where peers, instructors, and colleagues expect me to be able to speak for all black people. I have been in institutions where I could go an entire day and see only one other black person. Still, this contradictory nature of the "liberal" academy did not seem so startling until the children came. It is not that I didn't realize I was being watched. I had advised students about the burden of being the only or the first minority, knowing I was often the first black teacher many of my students had ever had. I have had parents of minority children come to me and thank me. But there is a notable lack of progress that gets pushed aside in the quest to achieve and prove achievement on one's own merits.

The world of academia and of most college towns—even when they are a bus ride away from big multiethnic cities—are typically very white, despite their multicultural opportunities. This is the world my children see. When my older daughter was very small, the only black women she had seen on a regular basis were my mother, one of the librarians in the public library, and myself. I did not realize the effect this had until my husband told me that my daughter thought another black woman they saw when they went out was me. The woman was coming across the street, and Kiana was disappointed and confused that she did not turn out to be me. A picture in the newspaper of a black woman—Mama. A black woman in the next aisle at the store—Mama. Initially, she did this when I was not with her, but then it became more like a name or label. They looked like me, so they must all be mamas. I started letting her watch the WNBA just so she could see large numbers of black women. It was a trying and an embarrassing time.

I have managed my own way in higher education without minority mentors, but when I note that I have only two minority students in my freshman classes and that I do not see many—or any—professors who look like me, I think of my daughters and wonder whether they will be freshman without mentors. I had a black student in her senior year who told me at the end of the semester that the first thing she did after our first class meeting was rush home and tell her friends that she had finally had a black professor. That kind of pressure is immense, and before having children, I took on the responsibility only reluctantly. My children shamed me into it. Now I embrace it. After all, we can't all be invited, but we can't all work for the WNBA either.

The End

I have had many different jobs—convenience store clerk, bakery assistant, fish gutter, among others—and working in academia is the only one that I would turn and have gladly turned into a career. The combining of family work and academic work can be straining, but it does not have to be stultifying. Someone asked me whether I thought that my children have held me back in my career. Perhaps, but I can't know that for sure. I would probably submit more things (articles, grant proposals, etc.), but there is no guarantee that in our highly competitive world, where even graduate students are expected to publish, I would have a string of publications. I feel very fortunate to be working in the field at all, when so many of my peers are still looking for full-time employment and many more have left the profession altogether.

But in any situation like this, where there is very little to be had and many highly intelligent and diligent people after the same "prizes," perspective and self-preservation are in order. My children have helped me to gain perspective and preserve myself, and they have improved my skills in the bargain. The graduate coordinator who expected blind devotion was wrong. I have noticed that the people who survive in this field with their humanity intact are those who have other interests—collectors, say, or sports fans or avid gardeners. Or parents. Real people like this can have real conversations with their students and with colleagues in other departments. People like this can recover very easily from department fights, labor disputes, or disagreements with administrative bodies. When parents have this kind of balance, they can see the connections between the one endeavor (parenting) and the other (academic work), even when the paths seem to be on contradictory if not conflicting trajectories. We have to laugh at these points of connection and contact, or we will spend too much time crying.

11

Mary Was an Adjunct

Norma Tilden

Some years ago, when I first decided to speak publicly and positively on my experience teaching as an adjunct, I began by writing my grandmother's name, "Mary DePascale," at the top of the page. It was an odd pseudonym for a writer to hide behind. As far as I know, the name "Mary DePascale" was all that my grandmother could write. On the few occasions when I saw her shape the letters, she took slow pains to form them round and clear, next to the X on the line. My grandmother would not have been pleased to see her name in print. She taught me to keep things close and quiet. She knew that to hold onto secrets conferred a kind of veiled authority. In this sense, like the Virgin for whom she was named, Mary DePascale was a powerful woman.

"BE-E-E CAREFUL," MY MOTHER WARNS, when I confide that I am interviewing for a tenure-track job at the same university where I have taught as an adjunct for many years. It is the day after Christmas, and she is anxiously following me around her house as I prepare to leave for the MLA convention.

My mother is a news junkie. From her kitchen in northeastern Ohio she tracks danger on many and remote fronts: tornadoes in Indiana, tainted hamburger in England, planes flying into Italian ski lifts. Today she lights on a new threat: "I saw a TV show. The colleges are replacing all of you professors with unqualified teachers. They're waiting in line to get your jobs. I can't remember what they're called."

"Adjuncts?" I venture.

"That's it. They're terrible. Watch out for them."

"Mom, I *am* them. I'm an adjunct."

"Oh no, don't tell me that."

Like my mother, we have all heard the bad news about adjuncts. Our professional organizations monitor the erosion of tenured ranks by the hiring of contract laborers, the "untenurables," as we grimly identify ourselves. On the adjunct side, the litany of grievances has become tedious to rehearse even among ourselves: last hired, first fired; teach more, paid less; no security, benefits, or paid leave; disproportionately female. And even as we wring our hands on both sides of the tenure divide, the adjunct "crisis" hardens into institutionalized despair. Last year, in the English department where I have taught for 17 years, more than 40% of the faculty were adjuncts, a situation that reflects the national average. A recent front-page article in our student newspaper speculated on factors that might threaten the university's standing in *U.S. News and World Report*'s annual college index. Apparently, my adjunct colleagues and I are partly to blame: "In the past," our own students write, the "high number of adjunct professors . . . has lowered the university's national ranking." No news here. We know these realities, as the phrase goes, "by heart."

What we fail to understand is why so many of us—again, predominantly women—are willing to settle for such positions. And why say "settle"? In fact, we compete for them. At one time or another every one of us has eagerly responded to some version of the adjunct job offer: "Sure it's unfair, but if you don't want this job, there are a hundred more PhDs out there who do." Pop open the champagne.

In many ways the adjunct question cannot be adequately addressed by the supply-and-demand statistics of the institutional job market. Despite very real inequities, some of us resist the temptation to internalize the power structures telling us that we should be angry or alienated—that we do not belong in the departments where we teach. In fact, there are secret satisfactions to our work that we seldom allow ourselves to admit, let alone speak about in professional contexts.

A few years ago I prepared a presentation on this issue for the biannual meeting of the National Association of Women in Catholic Higher Education. Between panels, I found myself in conversation with a woman who had noticed the title of my paper in the program and was eager to talk. We were both in our middle 40s. Like me, she was the only daughter of an Italian mother, raised in an extended Roman Catholic family, a PhD in English now teaching at a Catholic university. At that point our histories diverged. Her version of the up-from-the-immigrant-colony narrative had ended in a full professorship and election as the first woman chair of her department. I was a long-time adjunct, teaching three sections of first-year composition every semester. Still, despite the difference in our professional status, she had a peculiar confidence to share with me: "I fantasize about being an adjunct," she admitted. "If only I could afford it, I swear I'd take the cut in pay. It would be very fulfilling for me not to be a professor"—blowing out the word in a puff of smoke—"but to concentrate all my energies on teaching."

Her wistful comment begins to explain why, like the biblical poor, adjuncts may always be with us. Institutional economies aside, there are cultural reasons for our persistence. Her quiet admission bolstered the position I was about to argue in my paper: Just as a feminist pedagogy is based squarely on the experience of growing up female, so those of us who grew up in a tradition of ethnic Catholicism absorbed a particular way of teaching from the teachers we admired and the stories they passed on to us. For many women who teach as adjuncts there is a secret—because shameful—sufficiency, rarely voiced. Like the nuns in our first schoolrooms and the Virgin Mother whom they emulated, we long ago consigned ourselves to careers of hidden usefulness.

To reflect on such issues forces me to confront the manner in which my experience of the feminine has been constructed as an expectation of service and support rendered within a powerful hierarchical structure. In some ways, higher education has translated these subjective and ethical imperatives into academic ranks and salary scales. For better or worse (or, more aptly, "for richer, for poorer"), the subjectivity of Catholic women and the structure of the university make for an easy fit.

IN HER 1994 MEMOIR *Crossing Ocean Parkway,* Marianna Torgovnick describes the challenge of crossing cultural boundaries as she moved from an Italian American girlhood to a prominent position in academe. Although she and I started from similar places, my career traced a different trajectory, not so much "crossing" these boundaries as working within and at the margins of their powerful confines. Like a number of other Italian American scholars of my generation—Torgovnick, Sandra Gilbert, Linda Hutcheon, Josephine Hendin—I was born into a cultural tradition that posed contradictory expectations for its women. Unlike these academics, I have worked for most of my career as an "instructor," more teacher than professor, negotiating authority behind the classroom door. It would be easy—and tedious—to rail against the factors, both internal and external, that have contributed to my "nontraditional career," but that would leave out a big part of the story. The truth is, I have found myself oddly comfortable in an adjunct role.

For the two generations of Italian American women who raised me, the term "nontraditional career," whether in higher education or anywhere else, would have been redundant. Women should be mothers or, failing that, nuns. Because nuns were teachers, they, too, devoted themselves to "bringing up" children—a tidy equation of the mothering function. And for both these roles the Virgin Mary was the supreme, if somewhat paradoxical, model.

Torgovnick (1994) sees the Italian American family as "hostile"(p. 150) to its intellectual women. The word may be strong, but I know what she means, having been initiated early into a confining orthodoxy in which ignorance was equated with innocence, and both were expected of women. It was entirely possible for an otherwise good child to know too much.

Sometime before I started school, I was taken to a wake in the neighborhood by my grandmother, called Mary, and her friend, known to us as "Holy Mary from down the street." My playmate, the little brother of a friend, had died during what should have been routine surgery. Now the child was laid out in the parlor of his home in a tiny casket, dressed in his white First Communion suit. The warm room was filled with women and girls. My grandmother nudged me forward, urging me to kiss the rosary draped across his folded hands. As I stood there staring, Grandmother Mary keened to Holy Mary in that mournful sing-song of old Mediterranean women: "Aaah, *povero* [poor thing], so smart, God bless 'im . . . five years old and already he could read." In a similar cadence, Holy Mary picked up the dirge: "*Si, povero,* too smart. He was too smart, so God killed him."

If being too smart was risky, it posed particular dangers for girls, even those destined to become nuns and teachers. Still, by the time I was six, I knew I wanted to be a teacher—and not for the noblest of reasons. I took great pleasure in games of "school," administering tests and report cards to my boy cousins. In our world, there were only two kinds of authority available to women—motherhood and teaching—and they were seemingly interchangeable. Significantly, both gave you a secure place within a community of women, a tightly bound order in which any kind of standing out could be seen as a form of betrayal. If you stepped out of line, whether in a holy-day procession or by reading alone in your room, you could be marked as a bad girl. At home, however, with the aunts, great-aunts, and cousins, we were enveloped in a powerful maternal community. In her self-ironic essay "Portrait of the *Puttana* as a Middle-Aged Woolf Scholar," Louise De Salvo, another Italian American academic, describes this first sisterhood: "I come from a family, from a cultural heritage, where women ... sit around and wait for their men. Or they watch their children and wait for their men. . . . Or they make a sumptuous meal and they work very hard and watch their children and wait for their men. But they don't . . . do anything for themselves alone without their men. Except complain" (De Salvo, 1985, p. 94). Membership in this circle provided certain comforts, primarily a license to complain and protection from the curse of separation, of standing out. Here we had tenure.

A more positive form of authority came from teaching, and, as far as I could see, this power was reserved to nuns, whose work conferred another sort of motherhood, one modeled closely on the Virgin Mother. The order of nuns who taught in our school was called Sisters of the Holy Humility of Mary, and *all* the nuns were named Mary, followed by a saint's name to distinguish one from another: "Sister Mary Caroline, H.H.M." From membership within their "humble" community of Marys, these women derived the unquestioned authority they exerted over us and even over our mothers. Women, wimples, and power—I was in fourth grade before I realized that you could be a teacher without taking the veil.

Long before that, I came to recognize the link between the two sisterhoods. Lacking any real compass of authority, the women I admired formed communities of watchers and "minders," not so much submissive as attentive. These were formidable women. They looked out for one another and for us, teaching us an intimate, interdependent way of knowing our world.

In school and at home, the model of womanly perfection was always "Our Blessed Mother" Mary. The most radical thing about her was also the most easily overlooked: Mary, through no fault of her own, stood out from the crowd of all other women specifically because of her identity as mother. She was, as the liturgy proclaimed, "blessed . . . among women," but her prestige came by association: "Blessed is the fruit of thy womb, Jesus." Despite—or maybe because of—her preeminence, there was something unseemly about Mary, a mother singled out for devotion, her life-size statue displayed in a cozy blue niche at the side of the main altar. As if to set her apart from us, our Mary was always pictured with absurdly blond hair. Like our teachers, the sisterhood of Marys who moved hugely among us, she commanded respect, but she represented an impossible ideal: at once mother and virgin, exceptional and humble, a prototype recommended but inimitable. In these contradictions, Mary complicated our self-expectations in ways both inspiring and disturbing. She was clearly adjunct, even "among women."

The rest of the women in our religious stories were easier to take. Mostly silent, they drifted in and out of the Gospels like specters, occasionally brought forward to swell a scene: ask for a miracle, minister to the dead, wash dusty feet with their hair. Most of them were also named Mary. These girls fit neatly into a cultural model we recognized. They were handmaidens, ancillae, the wise or foolish bridesmaids dealing with the practical needs of everyday life. At Jesus' first healing, we discover the familiar pattern in Peter's mother-in-law, who lies sick with a deadly fever. When Jesus went to her, the Gospel reports, "the fever left her and she began to wait upon them" (Mark 1:29–31). In other words, after the miracle, things returned to normal. Even Mary Magdalene, who initially stood out—and in the worst way—was neatly folded back into the humble crowd as soon as Jesus cast out her devils. The next we heard of Magdalene, she was wiping Jesus' feet with her hair.

On those few occasions when a woman moved to the center of a story, Catholic girls paid attention. In the story of Mary and Martha, for example, we noticed that Mary, the intellectual sister, challenged the handmaiden tradition in interesting ways. In Luke's account, Martha is the good servant, mightily "distracted by waiting on many needs." Her dreamy sister, meanwhile, "took her place at the Lord's feet, and listened to his words"—in biblical terms, she "studied with" Jesus (Luke 10:38–42). Although Jesus approves the studious sister's choice, the Gospel frames Mary's interest as a betrayal of her sister. Long before AAUW research confirmed that girls face disadvantages in the classroom, my friends and I discovered that aspiring to academic achievement marked you as, in De Salvo's image, an odd sort of *puttana*, a "bad girl" with glasses. And, of course, to stand out as ambitious only reinforced the norm for other girls as complacent. Mary and Martha seemed hopelessly irreconcilable.

In this construction of the female as handmaiden, the Virgin Mother reigns supreme. But in those few narratives that center on the Virgin, we discover suggestions of a subversive complexity, a double vision of motherhood sustaining both selflessness and authority. One of the first things we noticed was that Mary was quiet. In fact, she speaks only four times in all the Gospels. Typically, Mary listens. Indeed, one of the most common images of the Virgin shows her kneeling and staring into the light as a huge, swanlike angel hovers over her, delivering the good news of her motherhood. In this, the Annunciation story, Mary professes by listening. By straining to hear and understand, she comes to power. Her question to the angel—"How shall this be?"—is genuinely inquisitive, even stunned. But it is also—and already—accepting, implying a radical openness to the mysterious message: "And Mary said, Behold the handmaid of the Lord; let it be unto me according to thy word" (Luke 1:24–38).

Mary's "let it be" can easily be read as reinscribing a restrictive ideal of female submissiveness, and such a reading has been reinforced by centuries of encoded moral teaching. This interpretation, however, violates the narrative impulse of the story, with its framing of Mary's answer as active consent. In the 1960s we would have said that at that moment she makes an existential leap.

The mode of joyful acceptance carries over to the Visitation story, in which Mary's cousin Elizabeth knows without being told that Mary is carrying the Messiah. Mary responds with the Magnificat, praising God for lifting up his handmaid in the only way possible for that time and place: the bearing of a son. It is here, in her longest speech, that Mary employs a richly evocative and tellingly active verb with powerful implications for a feminist pedagogy: "My soul doth *magnify* the Lord." With this word, she begins to define a womanly way of being active in the world. In addition to the traditional functions of ministering and witnessing, Mary represents the mother as *magnifying*—of making visible and tangible what had otherwise been only an idea, an abstract promise unfulfilled.

WHAT DO THESE MARY TALES tell us about the women academics who grew up hearing them? To begin with, I would suggest that, although Mary was not the best model for our careers, she turns out to be not so bad a model for our classrooms. If our Mary stories encouraged us to take on a tradition of service that makes us oddly comfortable in the role of adjuncts, they also presented us with a variant model of authority, one that has less to do with disseminating expertise than with shaping a community of learners, even in the very classrooms where we serve as undervalued "instructors."

Comparisons of teaching and parenting are inevitable, and occasionally problematic. What is unique about the teaching model of *mothering*, especially as embodied in the Virgin Mother, is its recognition that our students always come to us as *other* people, already half-formed, whom we help to become what they were meant to be rather than to become versions of us. Mary does not represent an ideal of self-reproduction, but a choice to accept and creatively transform the intrinsically other. Like the Socratic method, the Marian method enacts the slow and sure progress of dialectic, based on the capacity to "mind" someone without dominating. It is a pedagogy that comes naturally—if usually by necessity—to adjunct faculty.

Despite my mother's warnings, I went to the MLA convention that December to compete for the tenure-track job. The next fall, I returned to the same university where I had been teaching as an adjunct for 12 years, but now as an assistant professor teaching writing courses at all levels. My "new" field of specialization was one I had acquired through years of re-searching and teaching composition as an adjunct. Having now occupied both sides of the tenure divide, I can attest that in terms of what ideally goes on in the college classroom—rigorous, effective pedagogy grounded in scholarly inquiry—the distinction between "regular" faculty and "adjunct" faculty is not as clear as institutional structures suggest. And yet, for those of us struggling to define a place for ourselves within these thickly textured institutions, the shorthand markers of rank and title continue to matter.

Linguists tell us that the language of an institution changes more slowly than its culture. It has been almost 15 years since Carolyn Heilbrun (1990), in "The Politics of Mind," observed that women working "at the margin" of the university were no longer content to focus their energies on a feminist critique of those confines: "Rather," she claimed, "they profoundly desire to alter the nature of discourse that defines margins and centers" (p. 35). It may be time to reexamine the scarlet A-word, not necessarily to argue for a change in title but to recognize the centrality of what "adjunct" faculty actually do. Just as other marginalized groups have taken up the names and roles that their cultures defined for them and worked within those traditions to transform them, so adjunct faculty might well discover in the title of adjunct instructor a trope of abjection that proves both restrictive and empowering. Etymologically, a *professor* speaks forth, which suggests that his or her primary bond is with the topic professed. An *instructor*, by contrast, builds in; with its root *struere*, that title suggests an effort to build a structure out of interdependent parts. Because the instructor's primary bond is with the student, the ultimate instructor may well be the adjunct, whose locus of activity is situated at the periphery of the faculty, within a nexus of participants who study together.

In a recent book on women's life writing, Sarah Wider (1997) describes what she calls the "great man's model" of biography as governed by the as-sumption "that a center demands a periphery." In writing a woman's life,

Wider experiments with an alternative model of composition, describing "multiple, nonconcentric circles" in which "overlapping circles of numerous centers intersect" (p. 8). Wider's geometric model is useful for describing a decentered pedagogy with particular relevance for adjunct instructors. For too long now, those of us regularly assigned to teach introductory courses have been viewed as engaged in academic child care, nurturing young scholars in the skills that will prepare them for more rigorous intellectual work in the disciplines. In constructing an adjunct pedagogy, we might begin by challenging the notion that preparatory work is trivial; in fact, it is foundational. In an age in which information is easily accessible, the model of higher education as a provider of information is increasingly outmoded. Composition faculty have led the way in generating community-based, collaborative models of pedagogy. The interactive methodologies to which students are introduced in these basic courses have profoundly altered students' expectations for academic discourse at all levels.

Recent studies on gender and pedagogy, most notably those by Gesa E. Kirsch (1993) and Eileen E. Schell (1998), have alerted academic women to the challenges to professional authority posed by cultural definitions associating women with child rearing. Adjunct teaching poses similar challenges and for many of the same reasons. Adjunct faculty, both women and men, work without the warrant that comes with institutional investment, and we feel this critical exclusion in our classrooms. Clever consumers that they are, our students worry about our competence, sometimes asking us difficult questions in what they hope are tactful ways: "What is an adjunct? Is that one of those European degrees?" "Do you have a regular PhD?" "Should we call you 'Professor' or what?" Lacking the undergirding of institutional support, the adjunct instructor must continually renegotiate authority behind the classroom door.

Out of these pressures a teaching style emerges based on "overlapping circles of numerous centers." In such a classroom, knowledge is generated collaboratively, with all of us focused squarely on the material of our discipline. This approach effectively challenges the assumption that professorial authority is a warrant conferred from on high. As Kirsch (1993) argues, by teaching our students *how* scholars establish authority, we "demystify the making of knowledge" (p. 134). The adjunct's first teaching task, then, is to demonstrate to students that intellectual authority is something generated by immersion in the object of study. Together, students and teacher "in-struct," building a knowledge community one step at a time. To have been mistaken for a passive vessel makes adjuncts wary of mistaking our students for such. Consequently, early and deliberately, we talk about pedagogy and method: why we are doing what we are doing. As a writing teacher, I have become accustomed to working in the shadows, straining to perceive the half-spoken possibilities implicit in my students' halting efforts to make sense. Like Mary, I try to "magnify" the amorphous "message" taking shape around me, fostering a dialogue that integrates abstract knowledge with my own and my students' experience.

In such a classroom, teaching is largely a receptive act, a matter of watching and waiting, and it is radically situational. I absorb and return information in a complicated process of listening, followed by patient questions and slow reshaping. I look for patterns, slow things down, ask for clarification, and repeat what I hear in order to provide a resonating base for the many voices gathered in this noisy place. To teach in the Marian way is to find your fullest realization in relation to other people—your students—and in this sense, all teaching professionals can be seen as adjunct to the central work of education.

Once again, the personal proves political—and also pedagogical. A few years ago, I was invited by the journal *Thought and Action* to address the question of adjunct labor in higher education. By what seemed an ironic coincidence, I was that same month nominated for a college-wide teaching award, which required that I compose a statement of teaching philosophy. Not surprisingly, when I began to write, the two assignments overlapped, and I found myself reflecting on the many ways that my years of adjunct labor had shaped my performance in the classroom. The resulting article (Tilden, 1999) made tentative steps toward articulating the adjunct philosophy of teaching that I have been developing here, one that I am still proud to bring to my classes.

None of this speaks very directly to the economic and political dilemmas of adjunct faculty and the administrators who struggle to define an institutional place for them. We all recognize that adjuncts don't "fit" at any tenure-granting institution; that is precisely the meaning of "adjunct": extra, or—more to the point—ancillary. Did I find myself constrained by my adjunct status? In almost every dealing that I had outside the classroom—in the department, the college, my disciplinary community—the answer is *yes*. In the classroom, however, I continue to find the adjunct model enabling and expansive. In the deepest sense, "adjunct" is what all educators, tenured or not, should strive to be.

If adjunct faculty can no longer be content to complain about their marginalized situation, neither can they realistically expect to move to the tenured center: There is no room at the inn (and precious little office space, either). What all of us, faculty and administrators, *can* do is to recognize that the undergraduate classroom, itself too-long marginalized, is struggling to reclaim its place at the center of higher education. With their greater involvement in foundational skills and core discipline requirements, adjuncts can claim a new and rightful centrality for the courses they teach.

Those of us who have shaped our professional identities outside the tenure track are actively seeking ways to realign ourselves with the rest of the profession. As we continue to push for equity, we must resist the pressure to reduce ourselves to political cartoons, whether of militancy or abjection. We are both Mary and Martha, and for teaching professionals, the paradox is ultimately enabling. From within our classrooms, we are quietly changing the terms that define margins and centers. My mother was right: We are dangerous people. But we try not to stand out.

REFERENCES

De Salvo, L. (1985). Portrait of the *Puttana* as a middle-aged Woolf scholar. In H. Barolini (Ed.), *The dream book* (pp. 93–99). New York: Schocken Books.

Heilbrun, C. G. (1990). The politics of mind. In S. L. Gabriel & I. Smithson (Eds.), *Gender in the classroom: Power and pedagogy* (pp. 28–40). Urbana: University of Illinois Press.

Kirsch, G. E. (1993). *Women writing the academy: Audience, authority, and transformation.* Carbondale and Edwardsville: Southern Illinois University Press.

Schell, E. E. (1998). *Gypsy academics and mother-teachers: Gender, contingent labor, and writing instruction.* Portsmouth, NH: Boynton/Cook.

Tilden, N. (1999). Learning to read and write: Still a miracle. *Thought and Action: The NEA Higher Education Journal, 15*(2), 43–46.

Torgovnick, M. (1994). *Crossing Ocean Parkway.* Chicago: University of Chicago Press.

Wider, S. (1997). *Anna Tilden, Unitarian culture and the problem of self-representation.* Athens: University of Georgia Press.

12

Pregnant with Meaning: A Mother's Sojourn in the Academy

Nancy Gerber

In *Of Woman Born,* Adrienne Rich (1976) refers to the phenomenon of "matrophobia," which is not fear of motherhood but rather fear of turning into one's mother (p. 236). The dread of reproducing our mothers' oppression is related to ambivalence about possibilities for an authentic, empowered maternal identity. For women seeking fictional models of questing mothers, Western imaginative literature provides few examples of women who can nurture themselves and their aspirations while mothering their children.

What do we think of when we think of the literature of mothers and motherhood? The mad Medea, who, following Jason's duplicity and desertion, devours her own children? The manipulative Rebekah, who advises her son Jacob to dress as his brother Esau in order to trick their father into giving Jacob the coveted paternal blessing? The self-less Marmee of *Little Women,* who advises her daughters that nothing is as satisfying for a woman as sacrificing her own needs and desires in order to be useful to others?

Shortly after I gave birth to my first son, I found myself yearning for a vocation I could call my own. I knew that my son was not "mine" in the same way that my clothing was mine or my name was mine; I also knew that one day the urge to protect and envelop would be replaced by the necessity to let go and set free. And on long walks around the neighborhood or silent afternoons while my son dozed, my mind would drift along a quiet but insistent current that always led to the same question: Who am I? Who am I now that I'm a mother?

Motherhood causes a seismic shift in a woman's identity. Any imagined sense of wholeness, of belonging fully to one's self, explodes into myriad bits and pieces. Jane Lazarre, in her memoir of new motherhood, *The Mother Knot* (1976), worries that she might have a heart attack from the emotional intensity of being a mother (p. 75). Fortunately, the scattered fragments of a new mother's identity eventually return to their center and coalesce into something larger and grander than what existed before. But until that process begins to take shape, we live in terror that what was a "self" is irretrievably lost.

At a certain point, I knew that I could no longer ignore my soul's longing for something substantive and meaningful. Weighty, and also durable. Something that would simultaneously hold me to earth and allow my imagination to soar. And so, with trepidation and exhilaration, I entered a master's program in literature at the Rutgers University campus in Newark, reclaiming a course of study I had abandoned nine years earlier when I graduated from college.

Motherhood shaped my experience of graduate study and academic life. The evening of my very first class, I discovered that my two-year-old son had been playing with an open bottle of Advil while at a neighbor's house. Panic-stricken, I phoned the pediatrician, who told me to give him ipecac. I've always believed that it's important to be prepared in case of emergencies, so I had six unopened bottles of ipecac in my medicine cabinet. When my mother, our temporary babysitter, arrived, I motioned toward her grandson, who was clutching his stomach and vomiting on the stairs. "He'll be OK," I said. "Sorry, but I have to run, or I'll be late for class." I drove down the Garden State Parkway squinting my tears and sobbing aloud, "This is too hard. I'll never be able to do this." My dream of self-fulfillment had become a nightmare of full-catastrophe mothering, tinctured with a heavy dose of guilt and self-doubt.

Fortunately, life settled into a more predictable pattern. I found a sitter, a lovely, responsible high school student who was able to stay from 5 P.M. until my husband came home from work or I came home from school. Josh started nursery school, leaving my mornings free for reading and writing. I was energized by the changes that had taken place in the academy since my graduation. In 1978, when I received my bachelor's degree, there were no courses in women's studies or feminist thought at my alma mater, the University of Pennsylvania. My professors insisted that most literature was written by men and that it was not important that George Eliot was really a woman. In Newark, I encountered, for the first time, feminist literary criticism, as well as courses informed by critical theories of race and class. I finished the master's program in four years—three years of part-time study and one year of leave after I gave birth to my second son—and was proud of my achievement.

But I still wasn't satisfied. The sense of solidity I had been seeking eluded me; ahead loomed a large, barren plain. After the elation of finishing my master's wore off, I was left with the nagging question: What next?

As Julia Kristeva (1987) notes, "The only thing Freud tells us concerning motherhood is that the desire for a child is a transformation of penis envy" (p. 255). Motherhood is still uncharted territory; the psychoanalytic literature provides no road map for the questing mother. As Jessica Benjamin (1988) observes in *The Bonds of Love,* no psychological theory has adequately articulated the complexities of maternal subjectivity (p. 23). After muddling about for a while wondering if I should teach high school English or study for a more practical degree, such as a master's in library science, I finally understood that what I really wanted was to finish what I had begun and continue for my doctorate. I applied to the doctoral program in literature at Rutgers in New Brunswick (because the Newark campus does not offer this degree) and was thrilled to be accepted.

Now there was a new Pandora's box of complications. There were two children, in two different schools with two different schedules—and no babysitter. Because my classes were held in the daytime rather than in the evenings, I could no longer rely on high school students. The search for a babysitter had always filled me with dread, but I was able to hire the friend of a woman who watched one of my neighbor's children. The commute to school jumped from 40 minutes round trip to nearly two hours. There was also a heavier workload, more pressure, and competition from other students. In Newark, most of my fellow students had been high school teachers seeking additional qualifications; in New Brunswick, most were seeking tenure-track positions in the academy. Because the stakes were higher, we were a less congenial group. I entered the program in 1991 as an unfunded, part-time student, an option that has been discontinued in the English department because of the competitiveness of the job market. Although my part-time status contributed to my sense of marginality, it was the path I had chosen, and I was fortunate to have such a choice. What truly marginalized me, I felt, was the fact that I was a mother.

Not that I was the only student who was a mother. Indeed, many of the faculty were mothers. However, conversations on motherhood and mothering were relegated to hallways and classroom breaks. It was difficult to put the topic on the table for serious discussion, although it did emerge from time to time, in deliberations on the outraged mother of 19th-century slave narratives and in analyses of gender, modernism, and the fiction of Virginia Woolf. Nonetheless, what had once been tangential to my academic interests suddenly moved to the center. I became obsessed with mothers in literature and motherhood in general. At Rutgers, I felt an overwhelming urge to talk about my kids. At home, I was burning to talk about mothers I encountered in fiction. This split continued for several years as I wore myself out trying to fuse the experience of motherhood with my intellectual interests. Along the way, I devoured the critical and theoretical literature, searching for a model or paradigm that spoke to my concerns.

I have often wondered what caused such a change in consciousness—why motherhood became a kind of obsession. I think it had to do, in part, with my sense of alienation and isolation. I was closer in age and experience to the faculty, yet clearly I was not their equal in terms of status. The knowledge shared by mothers—our sense of connection to the human community—could not be voiced in the classroom, and there weren't any support networks at that time for women with children. I felt that I could be heard as a mother in the academy only if I studied motherhood.

Plenty had been written on the subject, particularly during the genesis of feminist criticism. Adrienne Rich's *Of Woman Born* (1976) was an important early text that contextualized motherhood within the patriarchy, differentiating between mothering as a set of psychosocial experiences named by women and motherhood as an institution defined and controlled by men (Abbey & O'Reilly, 1998, p. 74). Nancy Chodorow's *The Reproduction of Mothering* (1978), another landmark text, attempted to fill in the gaps of the androcentric Freudian narrative of psychosexual development. Although Chodorow's argument tended to pathologize mother-daughter attachment and framed women's growth in the context of a male-dominated nuclear family, her work paved the way for feminist analyses of mother-daughter relationships and the significance of the pre-Oedipal period. Ten years later, Sara Ruddick's *Maternal Thinking* (1989) argued that the duality of maternal subjectivity—a position that simultaneously recognized self and other—could form the basis for a global politics of tolerance. Marianne Hirsch's *The Mother/Daughter Plot* (1989) extended the work of Chodorow by reading women's writings in which mother-daughter relationships shaped both theme and narrative structure. In spite of these rich, important works, I still did not find what I was looking for—a set of matricentric narratives that located the mother at the center of her own story.

I was aided in my search by several women faculty members, feminist mentors who nurtured my scholarly interest in mothers and mothering.

Cheryl Wall, whom I met in the fall of 1992 when I took her class on black women writers, had introduced me to Gwendolyn Brooks and her only published novel, *Maud Martha* (1953/1987). The novel touched me at a very deep level; I identified with the eponymous heroine's search for meaning and order, with her quiet humor, and, perhaps most of all, with her motherhood. In *Maud Martha,* motherhood is represented as an expansive, empowering subjectivity; after giving birth to a daughter, the heroine finds her voice, denouncing a racist Santa Claus who has insulted the child. This was my first encounter with a fictional heroine who was both artist *and* mother. Alicia Ostriker, another professor at Rutgers, inspired me to think seriously about motherhood through her class lectures and in her poetry, where pregnancy and birth figured as themes as significant and universal as war and battle.

I spent three lonely years in course work, during which time I made few friends. At home I continued to struggle with feelings of isolation and fragmentation—of not quite belonging to the world of at-home mothers and not really belonging to the academy either. Between mornings spent on reading and writing and afternoons with my kids, I could go days without talking to another adult. By the time my husband returned from work, I was tired and irritable, envious of my husband's sense of accomplishment and his integration into the world of adults. I felt invisible as a mother and as a scholar; I yearned to belong to a community of mother-scholars with whom I could identify.

Shortly after I finished my course work, my father suffered a massive stroke. As he was shuttled between hospitals, nursing homes, and rehabilitation centers, I considered postponing my qualifying exam. My days were spent visiting him, making phone calls to doctors and family members, and taking care of my kids. I was exhausted and grief-stricken. Three months after the stroke, he returned home, and the outline of my life resumed a more familiar shape. I shelved my phone calls and my grief and began to study for the exam.

At this point in my studies I seriously began to wonder whether the doctorate was worth all the agony. My father was paralyzed, and it was evident that he would not recover. Part of me ached to chuck the exams and to have my life back, to be able to make plans without feeling guilty, to be out in the world without feeling split in two, to spend time with my family without worrying about books and notes and exam questions. By now I had spent seven years in graduate school, and I was tired. But I also knew that if I quit now, I would never return. It was an agonizing period.

Cheryl Wall, who had agreed to chair my orals committee, came to my rescue and encouraged me to continue. She also suggested that I study with another student, a mother who happened to live nearby but with whom I had had little contact because we had never been in class together. And, to my surprise, I enjoyed preparing for the exam. I made note cards for each text on my list and took pleasure as the connections among books and authors grew. The note cards and preparation helped take my mind off my worries about my father, and coffee with my study partner helped me feel connected to the world and the academy.

After six months of intensive studying, I passed the exam. Ahead loomed the biggest hurdle: the dissertation. At Rutgers, the qualifying exam is divided into four overlapping categories in order to facilitate the process of finding a dissertation topic. Miraculously, or so it seemed at the time, the four categories I had chosen—bildungsroman for genre, Edith Wharton for literary figure, feminist criticism with a concentration on the maternal for methodology, and the years 1880 to 1990 for literary period—led me to my subject, the mother as artist. Although Edith Wharton's overbearing and needy mothers did not lend themselves to such a study, I had already found my first text for discussion: Brooks's *Maud Martha*.

I finally felt at home. The subject of the mother-artist had been born out of my own search for narratives of questing mothers. Cheryl Wall and the members of my dissertation committee—Abena Busia, Carol Smith, and Fran Bartkowski—all of whom were mothers—encouraged me to work on "I Stand Here Ironing" and "Tell Me a Riddle" by Tillie Olsen and *The Shawl* by Cynthia Ozick. The committee felt strongly that I should add another contemporary text. We spoke about the stories of Grace Paley as a possibility, but I felt that those fictions, much as I admired them, were not consistent in tone with the others I had chosen. I also considered Paule Marshall's *Praisesong for the Widow* but discarded it because Avey Johnson's motherhood is tangential to her development. I had begun to despair of finding my final text until I read Edwidge Danticat's *Breath, Eyes, Memory* for a book group. My list of texts was now complete.

Writing the dissertation was the high point of my graduate career. I no longer had to commute regularly to New Brunswick. I no longer needed sitters, who had been difficult to find because of my erratic schedule. I could determine my writing time and deadlines. But most of all, I was finally able to fuse the split between mothering and scholarship by working on a scholarly study of fictional mothers whose yearnings and struggles I knew and recognized because they were my own.

It would be tempting to say that the writing just flowed out of me like mother's milk. It would be tempting . . . but it would be a lie. The dissertation process is fraught with its own particular set of difficulties: the challenge of producing a work of original scholarship, the challenge of keeping to a schedule in order to stay connected to the work, the challenge of believing that one day the project will actually be completed. As anyone knows who has been involved in this process, the last few months feel as though one is trying to finish the New York Marathon. Several things kept me going during this stretch: the encouragement of my dissertation committee, with whom I met twice a year; my desire to complete the program; and the passion I felt about my subject.

It was evident to me that the mother-artists in the texts I was studying shared certain traits in common: a gift for figurative language, an ability to work with domestic materials, and a desire to be heard. The roles of race, ethnicity, and social class in these texts also emerged as important categories of analysis. In fact, the texts were linked not only by motherhood and artistry but also by the class position of the protagonists, who, in spite of differences in race and ethnicity, were all working-class women.

The analysis of social class opened up my discussion of the mother as artist in ways I had not anticipated. I began to see that the experience of working-class mothers and their relationship to domesticity was very different than that of middle-class mothers. As bell hooks (1984) has noted, sexism operates in the domestic sphere for women regardless of race or class; nonetheless, the boundaries between home and work are more fluid for working-class women and women of color than they are for white, middle-class women (pp. 133–135). I also discovered that the narrative of the mother as self-sacrificing and self-less is rooted in Western middle-class discourse; for instance, as hooks (1984) observes, mothers are seen as figures of strength and resilience in African diasporic communities.

In developing my argument, I was also influenced by the writings of Alice Walker (1983) and Virginia Woolf (1929/1989, 1942). Walker's essay "In Search of Our Mothers' Gardens" introduced me to the concept of the "motherline," a feminist genealogy of wisdom handed down from mothers to daughters across generations. Walker insists that the mother is the artist; she locates her own mother, whose stories had inspired Walker to write her own, in a motherline that includes not only slave mothers but celebrated artists such as Bessie Smith and Aretha Franklin. Walker's refusal to privilege writing over orality, or writing over art forms such as music, inspired me to conceptualize art in a less rigid way. For example, the unnamed mother of "I Stand Here Ironing" is clearly a storyteller, but she is also an artist who is writing her story with the iron. The movement of the iron over dress mimics the motion of pen over paper; the act of ironing creates the narrative frame of the story.

Virginia Woolf's (1929/1989) notion that the body of the written text, like the bodies of women, is marked by difference was also helpful to my discussion. In *A Room of One's Own,* she observes that women's texts will have a different form, one shaped by interruption and disruption (p. 78). Indeed, this poetics of rupture seemed to resonate in the texts I was studying: *Maud Martha* is written as a series of short vignettes; "Tell Me a Riddle" is structured by Eva's memories, which move back and forth between the present and the past; *The Shawl* is a narrative of loss and absence following the death of the protagonist's infant daughter in a Nazi concentration camp. I took a certain delight in using Woolf against herself, because she was very ambivalent about the idea of mothers as artists (she watched her sister, the painter Vanessa Bell, exhaust herself trying to care for both her children and the painter Duncan Grant, with whom Bell lived). In "Professions for Women," Woolf (1942) writes about the Angel in the House, who is described in maternal terms, as a figure who prevents women from writing.

It took me four years to complete the dissertation. Twelve years after I left Josh vomiting on the stairs, I had my doctorate. My children had inspired me to take this journey, but it was a voyage I had taken for myself. It has taken several years for the realization that I finished to sink in.

But it is almost a cliché to note that finishing one set of problems begets a new set. I felt like a soufflé that had collapsed: The energy from writing my dissertation was still running in me but had nowhere to go. Fortunately, a colleague mentioned that she had seen a call for papers from a group operating out of York University in Toronto called the Association for Research on Mothering (www.yorku.ca.crm). Here, at last, was what I was looking for, a community of scholars interested in mothers and mothering. My connections to this organization have been professionally and personally rewarding. A visit to the publishers' exhibit at the MLA convention held in Washington, DC, in 2000 resulted in a book contract for my dissertation, *Portrait of the Mother-Artist: Class and Creativity in Contemporary American Fiction* (Gerber, 2003).

There are "nourishing mothers" (the translation for *alma mater*) in the academy, and I count myself lucky to have worked with some of them. I would not describe the academy as a community of nurturing mothers, because it has traditionally institutionalized and rewarded masculinity. Yet mothers and mothers' concerns have been marginalized not only in the academy but also within feminist thought. But there is hope; there is a small but growing group of scholars working on mothers' stories, and their work, along with projects such as this collection of essays, will help shift mothering from the margins of theory and engagement toward the center.

REFERENCES

Abbey, S., & O'Reilly, A. (Eds.). (1998). *Redefining motherhood: Changing identities and patterns.* Toronto: Second Story Press.

Benjamin, J. (1988). *The bonds of love: Psychoanalysis, feminism, and the problem of domination.* New York: Pantheon.

Brooks, G. (1987). *Maud Martha.* In G. Brooks, *Blacks.* Chicago: Third World Press. (Original work published 1953)

Chodorow, N. (1978). *The reproduction of mothering: Psychoanalysis and the sociology of gender.* Berkeley: University of California Press.

Gerber, N. (2003). *Portrait of the mother-artist: Class and creativity in contemporary American fiction.* Lanham, MD: Lexington Books.

Hirsch, M. (1989). *The mother/daughter plot: Narrative, psychoanalysis, feminism.* Bloomington: Indiana University Press.

hooks, b. (1984). *Feminist theory: From margin to center.* Boston: Beacon Press.

Kristeva, J. (1987). *Tales of love.* New York: Columbia University Press.

Lazarre, J. (1976) *The mother knot.* Boston: Beacon Press.

Rich, A. (1976). *Of woman born: Motherhood as experience and institution.* New York: Norton.

Ruddick, S. (1989). *Maternal thinking: Toward a politics of peace.* Boston: Beacon Press.

Walker, A. (1983). *In search of our mothers' gardens: Womanist prose.* New York: Harcourt.

Woolf, V. (1942). Professions for women. In V. Woolf, *The death of the moth and other essays* (pp. 284–289). New York: Harcourt.

Woolf, V. (1989). *A room of one's own.* New York: Harvest/HBJ. (Original work published 1929)

13

Elemental MoThEr

Michelle M. Francl-Donnay

"You're not the same person today," puzzles the parent at commencement weekend, seeing me in my academic robes. (I was last seen in tennis shoes and shorts chasing two small boys up a tree on the campus green.) "Which of you is the real one?" she wants to know. "Neither one, they are both figments of my imagination," I respond flippantly, and we laugh, but internally I am shrieking "Good question . . . what *am* I doing?" It is a question I have asked myself countless times, in innumerable places, and with varying degrees of panic in my internal voice. It comes unbidden late at night, it seeps into the tiny cracks formed in the structure of my life, it's the undercurrent that threatens to tip my lifeboat. Mother? Scholar? Which of me is the real one? What *am* I doing?

The pressed flower card taped to the wall next to my desk at home is carefully inscribed to "MoThEr" in a scrawl poised somewhere between kindergarten and first grade. I smile as my mind's eye produces an image of the often sticky ball of ebullience that is my youngest son. The next time I spy the pink construction paper talisman, Christopher has vanished and in his place is a litany of chemical elements: "Molybdenum, Thorium, Erbium." I have the same sensation as when I look at the women in the classic optical illusion of the young woman and the old. Who do you see in the picture? At any given moment you see only one woman or the other, yet both are always there. The images cannot be separated—no line exists that divides the image of the beautiful woman from the crone. The whole of each is present within the other. You have only to switch your focal point, and the image changes. There is no blurring of the two images, you see one—or the other. This is my life. I am a mother and a professor, my life flicks back and forth between the two personae. Change the focus, and *mother* becomes Mo, Th, Er.

How do I combine my roles to create the ambiguous illusion of scholar and mother in my life? Can, and does, parenting shape my scholarship?

Should it? What does it mean to my children to have a mother who is a scientist and professor? What *am* I doing?

Path Integrals

Integration is a vital tool for physical chemists—it enables you to sum up tiny, seemingly inconsequential pieces and construct a meaningful whole. Path integrals are familiar to both the thermodynamicist and the quantum mechanic. You can integrate the same quantity, the same formula, over two different paths, and the final values can differ wildly. Put another way, if you don't know the path, the answer is meaningless. Similarly, I cannot separate the path that's led me to be both mother and scholar from the final result. If I had come to it in another way, it would have a completely different meaning, be an utterly different result.

Years ago I happened across a yellowed, crumbling piece of paper my mother had kept from my kindergarten days. I had drawn a picture of myself in a lab coat in front of a bench covered with chemical apparatuses, captioned "When I grow up I want to get a PhD in chemistry and teach." Although in the decades that followed kindergarten I certainly tried on many different hats—from marine biologist to nun—in the end, I did exactly what I told my kindergarten teacher I would do. I majored in chemistry, went on to graduate school, got my PhD in quantum chemistry, took a postdoctoral fellowship, and got a job teaching at a small liberal arts college. A straight path, seemingly trivial to integrate. Tracing my path via my curriculum vitae, though, is a bit like tracking a whale on the surface of the sea. There are subtle signs of its passage, a certain sheen on the water, an eddy here and there, a plume of vapor, but its frequent changes in depth are entirely hidden. My CV obscures a personal history, full of unseen depths and heights—one that is far from linear and consequently more difficult to integrate into the final illusion.

I grew up in a house rich in books and learning. My parents are both chemists who met and married in graduate school. My father completed his PhD, and my mother stayed home and raised us all. My mother put life into my childhood imaginings, scattering books about like so many secret doors into other worlds. More than a muse, she was a willing accomplice in my scholarly excavations, searching with me through her library for the answers to my questions, as excited by our discoveries as I was. Her half-dozen children notwithstanding, my mother's intellectual curiosity never faded, and I never saw my mother as less of a scholar or scientist than my

father, despite her lack of an elaborate laboratory. My childhood hero-
ines—Marie Curie, Dorothy Hodgkins, and Eugenie Clark—each seemed
to have carefully woven a life-text that included both spectacular science
and motherhood. From my child's vantage point there seemed to be no
conflict between motherhood and science; indeed, scholarship seemed to
be an integral part of motherhood.

In fine family tradition, I, too, married another chemist midway
through my graduate career. The Princeton postdoc that appears on my
CV was the result of a (successful) national search for two jobs within 50
miles of each other. Despite my graduate adviser's admonitions "not to put
all your eggs in one basket" in looking for an academic job, I did, seeking
a position near Tom's industrial job. Miraculously, the basket didn't drop,
and I landed a job at a liberal arts college for women less than an hour from
home. Miracles seem to have their price, or perhaps one is entitled only to a
limited number of them. In the midst of the spring of my first year at Bryn
Mawr College, the college president called me out of an evening faculty
meeting to tell me that my husband had been pulled out of the college pool
with an apparent heart attack. Tom died less than eight hours later during
unsuccessful surgery to repair an aneurysm. I was a widow at 29.

A bit more than three years after Tom died, the college hired a new
mathematician with interests in dynamical systems and—as it turned
out—me. Now tenured, secure in my career as well as in a rebuilt life, I
married Victor. We are close colleagues in both teaching and research,
but our most substantial collaboration involves raising Michael, eight, and
Christopher, six, who, as fourth-generation academics, are fully conversant
with academic rank, the rigors of publishing, and the rancor of academic
politics.

Both my family and my scholarly life are crucial—one does not trump
the other. When I was widowed, it was as if half of me had been cut off, and
the contents of what remained had simply spilled out on the floor, leaving a
shapeless mass behind. My academic existence became the scaffolding on
which I could rebuild my life. It enabled a connection to carefree childhood
days, where I could escape the pains of the present by diving into the secret
worlds contained in my books and my work. I could not have done without
it. I still cannot; it represents a safe haven, a door into a place apart. Yet I
also value my relationship with my husband and children beyond price.
Knowing well that today might be the last day I can spend with them, I am
reluctant to relegate them to the margins of my life, even momentarily. So,
for me, the question can never be how do I "balance" a career and family.

Mother and scholar must mysteriously be one. Can the academy and the larger world embrace this ambiguous figure, one who is entirely a mother and simultaneously wholly a scholar?

A Grim Life

Last spring I gave a paper at an international conference. There had been an open bar and a sumptuous dinner, complete with an after-dinner talk—the first given by a woman at this meeting in its 30-year history. A prestigious electron diffraction spectroscopist, the speaker had spent the bulk of her career in her husband's lab in Germany, finally "retiring" in the United States to a position of her own. Afterward, a clump of chemists lingered by the elevators, dissecting the talk, when suddenly an older colleague blurted out that science was, he thought, "a grim life for a young woman." He went on to say that you could neither do enough science to be taken seriously nor take adequate care of your children, so it is rather a lot of drudge work, without any chance of reward. Fortified by a glass of wine and surrounded by a group of graduate students and young women faculty, I rose to the bait. I certainly had not found my life to be "grim" at all. I enjoyed what I did as a chemist and as a parent. I am a successful scientist—tenured, promoted, on a list of highly cited scientists—and had managed much of this while raising two young sons. Let's just say that my adversary's response, "Well, la-di-da for you!" did not exactly encourage further serious discourse on the issue.

One is tempted to dismiss my elder colleague's cantankerous comments as the product of too many years and too much alcohol. Unfortunately, both anecdote and analysis suggest otherwise. The National Survey of Faculty, conducted by the Mapping Project at Penn State (Drago & Colbeck, 2002), attempts to address these issues quantitatively. The survey, which looks at the ways in which faculty do, or do not, balance work and family, grew out of recent work suggesting that an image of the "ideal worker" is emerging not only in the corporate world but within academia as well. Ideal workers do not have substantial commitments outside of work. Because women, even professional women, carry the bulk of the burden of child and household care, they are less likely to meet that ideal. For the average man, who contributes 10 hours a week to the care of the household and whose contribution does not significantly change when children arrive on the scene, the ideal may be achievable. If it is not, it won't be because of domestic duties.

Women faculty seem well aware of the unwritten rule that you must not create additional distractions in your life. The National Survey of Faculty compares men and women in the fields of chemistry and English, noting that in both fields at any rank, at any type of institution, women faculty are less likely then men to be married or in committed relationships. The average number of children per woman faculty member is also substantially lower—again regardless of discipline, rank, or type of institution. The survey's authors attribute this directly to "bias avoidance behaviors" in women. Women know that having a family will cost them. They will pay the price, first in hours of domestic work that their male peers will likely not spend, and ultimately in their reputation for academic seriousness. It is a Faustian bargain that women must strike—sacrifice your immortality for scholarly heft.[1]

Common wisdom has it that women choose jobs off the tenure track to make more time for family, particularly child rearing. The Mapping Project challenges this supposition. Women not on the tenure track are actually less likely to engage in family formation than women who are. Supervisory and institutional support to women for balancing work and family appear no more evident at community colleges than at Level I research institutions. Women are not choosing to avoid research institutions in order to better manage the dueling demands of career and family. The academy as a whole emerges as an uninviting space in which to bring a family—if you are a woman.

The Sore Task

Are women simply imagining the bias, or is academe really so unwelcoming? In a recent *New York Times* article (Cohen, 2002), a senior administrator at a large state university complained that parents' "maternity leaves, restricted scheduling and all sorts of 'emergencies'" unfairly shift work onto those who have no children. Is there is a reality behind her remarks? Data from the Bureau of Labor Statistics indicate that highly paid professional women in the general work force do not have a higher absentee rate than men, even factoring in maternity leaves. Despite the movement toward family-friendly policies such as maternity leave and slowing of the tenure clock, most faculty—men and women—do not take advantage of them. Finally, at least on my campus, restricted scheduling does not appear to be the sole prerogative of women—or parents, for that matter. Many an attempt to schedule a meeting has been scuttled by a childless male colleague's flatly stated, "I do not come to campus on Mondays."

Why then the bias? The curmudgeonly chemist implies it is because they do less work. So does the senior administrator who worries that this burdens colleagues. This surprises me, for much of what I consider the work of the academy cannot be readily shifted onto coworkers. Scholarly work that for any reason is not done remains undone and is not taken up by my colleagues. I strongly suspect that few institutions have so much committee and advising work that a lack of participation by a particular faculty member at a particular moment creates an overload for her colleagues. I have yet to see academic parents trolling the halls looking for colleagues to grade their papers or prepare their lectures for them. I find it hard to believe that mothers are shirking truly *necessary* work and thus forcing colleagues to pick up the slack, and I instead wonder whether we are merely counting hours.

How much necessary work is there to do in academe? Shakespeare's Marcellus might have been referring to faculty when he observed

> Why such impress of shipwrights, whose sore task
> Does not divide the Sunday from the week;
> What might be toward, that this sweaty haste
> Doth make the night joint-labourer with the day:
> Who is 't that can inform me?
> —*Hamlet* I.i.75–79

The labor of the faculty is unceasing, and more is always better. Part of this appears to stem from current cultural perceptions that "ideal workers" are those who are wholly committed to their jobs, but it seems particularly ingrained in the academy. Does the tight academic job market drive us to it? If we don't work endless hours, there are a dozen others who will gladly take our places and work to keep them. Or is it that the vestiges of the old clerical and monastic model of the university make it peculiarly unaccommodating to families and women?

I learned in graduate school that not all time is created equal. The calculus of hours compels the conclusion that the more time you spend in the lab, regardless of whether you are working or trying to sink baskets in the lab trash can, the more dedicated you are. Hours after midnight count more than hours before noon, so graduate students who work from 7 A.M.

to 9 P.M. obviously are not as hardworking as those who work from noon to midnight. The resulting patterns do not conduce to caring for small children, either in the late hours or in the assimilation of what, in fact, is leisure time into the working day (or night). Once leisure becomes subsumed into what counts for working hours, the "sore task does not divide the Sunday from the week," and the job appears to require more hours than it actually does. These are the patterns of those who are liminal in the family structure and who therefore have few constraints placed on their time—or of those whose family structure is completely congruent with work, as it is for a monastic. Mothers are neither liminal nor monastic. This insidious conflation of leisure with work makes it very difficult for an academic to judge the necessary hours for the tasks at hand.

Linear Combinations

My research area is quantum mechanics or, as one bumper sticker quipped, "the dreams stuff is made of." A theorem says that you can take a set of solutions to a quantum mechanical problem, as long as they are of the same energy, add them up any way you like, and the new state function is still a solution to your original problem—and it has the same energy. The only caveat is that you can't create something from nothing—if you start with a function that describes one particle, that is what you will get in the end. Quantum mechanics generate such linear combinations often, always to craft a solution that is in some way more convenient for the task at hand. Can I construct a solution to my life that has the same energy, i.e., reputation, as the purely scholarly solution? Can I take a linear combination of two 24/7 jobs and get something that doesn't require more hours in a week than exist? All the theorem demands is that motherhood and quantum mechanics have the same academic heft. Right.

At first go, it's hard to argue ab initio that motherhood brings the same scholarly challenges as quantum chemistry, though I would begin by pointing out that a stubborn eight-year-old can be more demanding of my cognitive skills than any differential equation I've encountered to date—and the equations never talk back. I will settle for an inductive proof: If the resulting linear combination of parenthood and scholarship retains the reputation of my childless days, then motherhood must be of the appropriate energy to include in the mix. The academic culture should not view motherhood as a competitor to scholarly work but as a cognate activity, even when the research does not explicitly treat of parenting. I will argue that even quantum chemistry research can be changed—without compromising the results—by my role as mother.

My children see the rainbow in a puddle, wonder about it, touch it, and explore it, while I see only diffraction and an oily mess to step around. It is hard for adults to realize that our organized view of the world keeps us from thinking about it in new ways, but with children around to remind me, I suspect I have an easier time of it. I recently spent many hours of supercomputer time trying without much success to unravel the mystery of why a particular molecule has an unusual and strained structure. The answer finally came not from my painstakingly acquired solutions to complex differential equations, but from playing with a paper cutout of the molecule made weeks before while teaching the neighborhood cohort of five-year-olds how to make paper dolls. In order to find the solution, I had to stop seeing the sophisticated differential equations, with which I had always solved these types of problems in the past, and start seeing again the molecule itself. Beyond unraveling the mystery at hand, the process ultimately led to a new research area, in which the techniques of differential geometry are applied to molecular structure.

Louis Pasteur, whose careful observation of the small differences in crystals eventually led to the discovery of chirality in chemistry, noted that "chance favors the prepared mind." I would add that the mind is prepared by chance, and the young children I live with take the chances offered to notice the minutiae, to create their own patterns from it, rather than to see what they are "supposed" to see. The inverse olefin effect had been seen more than three decades ago but never satisfactorily explained. The counterintuitive behavior of the molecules was long attributed to the larger metal atom in a catalyst, which much like a spider in a web is the center of chemists' attention—it is what we are "supposed" to see. It was not until I was contemplating a graph of one of the orbitals of the transition state, which I had pinned to my office wall in conscious imitation of the art galleries my kids create on our home walls, that I realized that the metal is not the critical component controlling the reactivity—it is the other end of the molecule that contains the clue. As my children know, sometimes the most interesting thing in a web is not the spider but the detritus entangled in it.

Parenting thus feeds my scholarly life in much the same way as a colleague's artistic work feeds his scholarship in aesthetics. Neither of us reflects directly on our other commitments in our academic work, but these experiences provide perspectives that influence our methods as well as our results. My scholarship has certainly been challenged, and changed, by the addition of children to my life. Although I won't argue that I would never have solved these problems if I were not a mother, the solutions would have been different, and certainly the course of my research would have been altered. The linear combination of motherhood and quantum mechanics provides a solution—although a different (and perhaps, contrary to the usual practice of quantum mechanics, less convenient) one than I might have constructed without children—that is no less productive.

All About My Mum

> I like to make-up stories with my mum.
> I like to race with my mum.
> I like to read to my mum.
> I like to hug my mum.
> —Michael, 7

If you want information about a quantum mechanical function, linear combination or not, you must look to the observables. Mathematically, operators are used to extract from the state functions the values of the observables. I cannot so easily write down the rules to extract my reality from the state I have crafted. My son Michael had no such inhibitions and on the petals of a paper (chrysanthe)mum make clear the values he observes in me.

If you asked my children (I did) what they think about having a mother who is a professor and a scientist, they would tell you that no one else in their class has a mother who knows how to make ice cream from liquid air. They will also say that I can explain *anything*. My sons accept the ambiguous image of me as mother and scholar. Their relationship to me is not circumscribed by one image or the other. Teaching and discovery are the essence of both motherhood and scholarship, lessons imparted to me long ago by my mother. In many ways my children and students easily recognize that both images—scholar and mother—are drawn with the same lines. If only the academy could be as accepting.

Illusions

I would contend that it is time to shift the conversation from the competition between motherhood and scholarship toward the recognition that motherhood can be an integral part of a productive scholarly life. The two roles are not mutually exclusive. Each builds on the other to create a single image that functions as the moment demands. Mothers need not learn to juggle here, but to draw. When we purge from the academy the traces of the monastic tradition that views work outside the cloister as profane, we will have a more welcoming and, ultimately, a more diverse and exciting place not only for mothers, but for anyone who works outside its doors.

"Which of you is the real one?" I had the answer almost right. The two personae, mother and scholar, are not so much figments of *my* imagination, but fragments only in *your* imagination. Without the ability to see mother and scholar simultaneously or to see a single image in which both subsist, the world shifts its focus and the images flick past. It is only an illusion, for the lines I've drawn for myself render a single figure, at all times mother *and* scholar.

ACKNOWLEDGMENTS

My path to motherhood is not mine alone. I could not move between the worlds of mother and scholar as easily as I do without the encouragement, love, and support of Victor Donnay. We long ago agreed that we each do 75% of the child care, and his imitation of the "mother hovercraft" is a powerful weapon in my battle against the cultural forces that push mothers toward being the ones who bear the brunt of organizing the family life. I am grateful to share parenting with someone who more than holds his own—and who has a sense of humor about it!

REFERENCES

Cohen, H. (2002, August 4). The baby bias. *New York Times,* Education Life supplement, p. 25.

Drago, R., & Colbeck, C., for the Mapping Project at Pennsylvania State University. (2002). *Preliminary results from the National Survey of Faculty.* Retrieved February 8, 2003, from http://lsir.la.psu.edu/workfam/prelimresults.htm

Hagan, J., & Kay, F. (1995). *Gender in practice: A study of lawyers' lives.* New York: Oxford University Press.

NOTES

1. This sense of falling short of the ideal is not limited to academia. Hagan and Kay (1995) note that a substantially larger percentage of male lawyers in Toronto and Ottawa were partners. Among the strongest predictors of success in attaining partnership were law school grades, specialization, and children. The predictors are gender sensitive. Women must have higher grades than men (are we surprised?). Men who have children are more likely to become partner than men who do not. Having children is not an asset for women, however: Motherhood is negatively associated with promotion success. One sees not only bias avoidance here but the potential for actual bias.

14

Chuck E. Cheese at Noon: Adventures in Parenting and Higher Education

Susan Jacobowitz

My life in academe has almost always been entwined with my life as a mother. I started my MFA when I was 29 and my daughter was three; we lived on campus in student housing with other graduate students and their children at Mills College in Oakland. We were probably the only student group on campus agitating for a sandbox. Our children played in the parking lot alongside our apartments, so speed bumps were a big priority for us as well. The others mothers and I called ourselves MUCK (the Mothers' Underwood Collective, named for the street we lived on) and coordinated our schedules to allow for group child care with all of us taking turns. We used to have co-op dinners, sharing many a pot of macaroni and cheese.

We were all sad when the group broke up—we all scattered in different directions. My daughter Harper thought that people moved only when a parent received a degree. "Where did your mother graduate to?" I overheard her asking a friend who was moving. We moved from Mills to the University of California at Davis, where I started studying for my doctorate and where I became a single mother when my husband and I divorced. After a year there in student housing (two bedrooms, 600 square feet), my daughter and I moved on to Brandeis University, where I transferred so that I could work with faculty in my areas of specialization: the Holocaust and Jewish studies. We went into student housing once again. The apartment was full of derelict furniture, and there was a big burn mark in the shape of an iron in the middle of the carpet in the room we used as a living room. Every time anyone in the building would cook, the fire alarm would go off and we'd all have to wait outside on the curb for the fire department.

Once I tried to disable the alarm, only to set it off, finding out too late that I had tampered with the sprinkler system—an offense punishable by arrest—instead of the smoke alarm. Lights went off and sirens wailed—I had to grab my daughter out of the bathtub and run. Then I had to shamefacedly explain to a police officer that I had only been trying to make dinner.

Sometimes I feel as if my daughter grew up in my pocket. She occasionally came with me to classes; I'm pretty sure she was the only child in her first-grade class to attend a dissertation defense. She's always been poised and good in groups and able to establish friendships with people of all ages. My life was about combining my first priority—Harper—with my second and third priorities, which involved supporting us and managing to complete my education. In addition to working as a teaching assistant, I worked as a temp in legal offices, did transcription work for a real estate assessor late at night, and worked at every on-campus job I could find. Once I even answered telephones at a massage parlor when we needed to build up enough money to move out of student housing. There were challenges. I used to set my alarm for 4:00 in the morning so that I could study Hebrew in the predawn quiet. I had to change departments when promised funding failed to come through. Once I missed a class because my daughter was ill and had to endure a lecture from a professor who warned me "never to let it happen again." But there are other memories I cherish: the wonderful friends we made, the close-knit communities of which we were a part, that sense that I was always working toward a goal, getting somewhere. To our close friends, Harper was almost like a communal child. Several times she was taken on special outings, or friends met her school bus for me. We would have Friday night dinners where I felt as if, because we could not go out into the world, the world came in to us. Even though all of my cousins in California owned homes and drove Acuras while I was unrelentingly poor, I usually still felt myself fortunate. I remember that feeling of my young daughter trailing after me . . . handing out candy to secretaries and students for Halloween, snapping a picture of the chair of my department for a book she wrote entitled "My Mother Goes to Brandeis University."

I didn't have a certain kind of freedom within the academy that I think those without children are better able to experience or derive benefit from. Lectures and events scheduled in the evening were almost impossible for me to attend; meetings and social events were very difficult as well, even if they were scheduled in the afternoon. I always felt a little tentative bringing the only child to the opening party for the department early in each new semester, although the memory of my daughter comfortably mingling with my professors still amazes me. Celebrations for passing orals or finishing dissertations took place in bars, at places you couldn't take children and at times that were inconvenient for those of us who had responsibilities at home or for whom babysitting was a luxury. Nobody ever seemed to want to meet up at Chuck E. Cheese at noon. It was hard to pursue publishing to build my CV and even harder to present material at conferences—I once had a paper accepted at a conference but had to cancel as the conference date drew closer, realizing that I couldn't really afford to get there and had no one to take care of my daughter.

My life was defined by having a school bus to meet, by having someone else's life to consider. Yet I never felt that Harper was a hindrance or an inconvenience. When people used to say to me, "I don't know how you do it," I used to wonder how people without children did it. I couldn't imagine life without that source of joy and satisfaction. Harper was both my motivation and my inspiration. I wanted to be able to take care of her by having a profession and earning a good living, and I wanted to set a good example and make her proud. She was always pulling for me. Years before, when I had been anxiously awaiting a letter to see if I had gotten into any PhD programs, she just knew that I was anxious for a letter. She had her preschool teacher address and mail an envelope to me with a beautiful drawing that she had made inside, so that I wouldn't be disappointed about not receiving a letter.

It's a challenge to reflect upon the meaning or significance of motherhood without feeling as if you are falling into Hallmark card territory or kitsch. Some of what we feel must be biological, the result of thousands of years of evolution. My father's past strongly influenced my feelings about family. He was a child survivor of the Holocaust, deported in the spring of 1944 at the age of 15 and liberated almost exactly a year later, on April 29, 1945. His mother and four youngest siblings died at Auschwitz. I went to Ukraine in 1993, to see the house where my father and his family had lived. Then I followed the trail of their deportation to a ghetto in a brickyard in Munkács and on to Auschwitz. I said Kaddish for my father's family and tried to find a record of what had happened to my grandmother and the two little boys and two little girls who would have been my aunts and uncles. Because they were liquidated upon arrival, there are no records. The children may have been thrown alive into burning pits. My mother was born in Chicago, but her parents were immigrants from Poland and Austria. While they were raising five children in America, every member of their extended families in Europe perished.

This, then, has always seemed to me one of the greatest gifts one can experience in life: to get to bear children you can nourish and protect, that you get to see grow and thrive. Once when I was taking a graduate seminar in American poetry, I became exasperated at all of the tortured angst expressed by many of the poets we were reading. How was it possible, I asked, that some of these people didn't feel fortunate—blessed—just to be able to wake up in the morning with all of their children asleep in their beds, safe and sound? This is the thing that so many people have been and will be denied. This is one of the things that I've never been able to take for granted. It's a gift not to be born into a tragic time.

As fate would have it, my life as a professor has been marked by my commitment to motherhood as well. I remarried when I was working on my dissertation, moved to Long Island, and began teaching as an adjunct at Queensborough Community College in Bayside, New York, when I was five months pregnant. I became more and more nervous as finals approached, wondering which would come first: labor or the end of the semester. As it happened, I gave my finals on May 22 and spent the next day grading. I woke up on the 24th to find that my water had broken. I went to the hospital with my husband and older daughter, but I made them wait while I dropped off my grades at the registrar's office at QCC on the way. That's where I found out that when you're in labor, people let you go right to the head of any line.

And so it continues. The first semester after my second daughter, Adi, was born, I was offered a full-time substitute line. It was an unprecedented opportunity for me to develop professionally, so I accepted, even though I had a three-month-old infant at home. I taught four classes in what remains an almost incomprehensible blur of preparation, grading, sleepless nights, and breastfeeding. I taught in a block so that I never had to be away from my daughter for more than four or five hours at a time. I somehow managed to garner wonderful evaluations from my students, and in the spring, teaching as an adjunct again, I applied and was hired for a full-time, tenure-track position in the department where I had been teaching.

What do you do when every part of your life is active and yet every part is precious, when there's nothing you are willing to leave behind? I have an adolescent and a toddler and am completing a dissertation while working full time. There have been wild ups and downs—days when I despair, days when I just don't think it would be possible for me to ever have perhaps one more child, that that part of my life might have to come to an end. There are days when I feel stretched to the limit physically, psychologically, and financially. I hate to say goodbye to my daughter at the door, to feel that I can't afford the luxury of making her my only priority. Then there are days when I feel elated to have so many good things in my life—rewarding and challenging work, a wonderful family. I take comfort when I see my friends dealing with the same challenges, when I don't feel so isolated in the struggle: One friend who is trying to complete a dissertation has an infant and two-year-old twins; another has two children under the age of 18 months. I wonder how—or even if—the academy will adapt once the normative graduate student or young instructor is pumping breast milk and running around with stuffed animals dropping out of her briefcase. One woman I met who was teaching at an institution in Boston had her tenure clock run out—she just couldn't generate the support material she needed with the added demands of two small children. She told me that, behind a closed door, working, she kept feeling the pull of her family. She had waited a long time to have children and found it hard to separate herself. And this was a woman who almost always had a live-in nanny available to help her.

If we are committed to our children and to our families, perhaps it shapes some of the choices we make in the job market. I don't want a job that would require me to log 80 billable hours a week, or one in which I would be expected to leave the fact of my parenthood behind when I enter the workplace. After the events of September 11, 2001, the *New York Times Magazine* ran a picture of men who worked in the financial industry under the heading "What Were They Thinking?" The men were survivors from the 60th floor of 2 World Trade Center who worked in the municipal bonds department of Morgan Stanley. One man was quoted saying, "Before all this, I'd be afraid to ask for a day off—or a morning off—to take my kid to the first day of school. It's true. We spent more time there than with most of our family members." Howard Lutnick, of Cantor Fitzgerald, would have died alongside his brother and other employees if he hadn't been heading in late after dropping his son off at his first day of "big boy" school. Another man in the photograph offered, "I'm going to walk out Friday at 12:30 and drive down and see my daughter for parents' weekend. Ordinarily, I wouldn't leave that early. People always got a hard time about it. But now

I couldn't care less. If you have something to do with your family, go do it, because you might not get another chance." I wonder how much the culture of the workplace might change and adapt.

Combining parenthood with the academy definitely takes support. The understanding of my family has been key—I have an involved partner and a supportive older daughter, and my mother even came to live nearby to help me once my second daughter was born. In addition, I've had the support of my students, colleagues, and supervisors. I was nervous about interviewing for an adjunct job while pregnant. I was wearing a maternity suit, but it was hard to know whether someone who had never met me before would be able to tell that I was pregnant. I don't think anyone did notice. Once I started to show even more and was waddling around in stretch pants and maternity jumpers, I received only encouraging and enthusiastic comments. I even received a key to the elevator so that I didn't have to huff and puff my way up four flights of stairs.

Even with all of the support, I've had my bad days. The combined stress of handling my daughter so much and grading so many papers the first semester after she was born gave me tendonitis in both thumbs and arms. I've had my days of rage and frustration where I despair of ever being able to do it all up to the standards I want to hold—where I wish that I could be my husband, comforted by the thought that the baby is being left behind with me. My husband has gone away on a few business trips, which is something I can't even imagine. I still try to get home in time to meet the bus. I've been away overnight only once, to celebrate my wedding anniversary, and Adi is nearly two. She still doesn't sleep through the night. The last time I had an official departmental observation of my teaching, I had been up four times the night before with a screaming baby.

Many of the women who were role models for me in academe had no children. Many were single, and one, a lesbian, told me that she always felt put into a strange position when she was asked to represent the needs of female faculty members who were mothers and wives. When she was getting her degree, she wasn't allowed to teach as a teaching assistant because she was a woman—they just gave her the fellowship money. Two other women who inspired me were mothers. One had two young sons and such tremendous vitality that she had finished her dissertation during her older son's first year of life. She could frost cupcakes for a Boy Scout meeting, stuff a turkey, and discuss ideas for a master's thesis all at the same time. She made it look easy. She was the first professor I saw welcoming students into her home and reaching out to students in more personal and meaningful ways. I sometimes felt that she had "discovered" me as a student—her mentoring gave me tremendous confidence, and we became fast friends.

Another woman who shared part of her story with me had had two children, very far apart in age. One child was in college studying for a PhD in English while the other was still in elementary school. There must have been about 15 years between the two children. I used to see my professor walking around campus with her younger daughter in tow, having picked her up from soccer practice. She was a little bit older to have such a young child and told me that when she became pregnant with her second daughter, all of her friends and colleagues just assumed that it was a mistake and inconvenient, and that she would schedule an abortion. When she told people she was going to have her second child, they were incredulous. She told me that she had been thrilled to have both of her daughters, that she had anticipated the birth of her younger girl just as eagerly as she had awaited the birth of her older daughter.

Motherhood has had a tremendous impact on every part of my life, from the metaphysical to the mundane. Like many women, I have my professional and creative ambitions. I worry that I won't be taken as seriously as a professional or as an artist—or that I won't be as rewarded or as successful—as some who have fewer demands put upon them. Katharine Hepburn described not having had children because she didn't feel that she could successfully combine a career with motherhood. I can respect her decision as honorable—and I certainly don't feel that having children is or should be for everyone—but for most of us, men and women, it's an unrealistic and even inhuman sacrifice to demand.

My parents, who raised children in a comfortable suburb while my father worked and my mother stayed home, sometimes express pity for me. I'm so busy, pulled in different directions, and I have to do so much. But I feel fortunate. I truly believe that in some alchemical, synergistic way, one feeds the other—that my love for my work enhances what I bring to my children as a parent and that the love I bear for my children brings something extra to my work. I wouldn't want to check my identity at the door, and the fact that I am a mother is as integral a part of my identity as my ethnicity, religion, or heritage. I have received a tremendous gift that my paternal grandmother was destined never to know—my children grow and thrive, and we are together. I know that I have special feelings for my students who are combining parenthood with education. I encourage them because I believe in what they are doing, and I hope that I can bring greater sensitivity to their struggles and the challenges they face than the professor who chastised me for being absent to take care of an ailing child. I hope that I can provide some inspiration for them as well. Commitment to both education and parenting—to parenthood and the academy—isn't always easy. This is what I might tell them: You may have to get up at 4:00 in the morning, and you may never drive an Acura. There will be days when you feel a little crazy. But it can—and will—be done.

15

Great Expectations: An Academic's Crash Course in Parenthood

Heather Bouwman

Late in the semester several months after I had given birth to my son, I stayed a few minutes after a faculty meeting at the large state university where I taught to chat with a young female colleague. We lamented about how tired we were after grading exams; I added that I was about to go home and try to take a nap with the baby. Joining in our discussion, a senior female colleague reported that she hadn't taken a nap since she was both pregnant and sick with the flu—18 years ago. She just didn't have time to schedule naps into her day.

This woman, whom I admire deeply, has raised children, begun and headed a strong program within the English department, and published widely in her field; she is a true, bona fide superwoman. I am not. I consider myself on track if I can get dressed in the morning without inadvertently choosing a skirt covered in cat hair or a shirt layered with baby vomit. As I have experienced them, administrative policies regarding parental leave and tenure, although extremely important, are only part of the picture; just as important are the informal practices and deeply entrenched attitudes (many of them unconsciously held or unarticulated) of members of one's own department—and one's own attitudes and goals (many of them also unconsciously held or unarticulated). At the time of this conversation with my two colleagues, I knew of my university's parental leave policy (basically nonexistent); I had been allowed by my dean to stop my tenure clock for the year; I had been given a cushy mentoring assignment (in lieu of one third of my teaching course load) by a sympathetic department head. But comments like this colleague's scared me. Was I supposed to be a superwoman, capable of soothing a crying infant with one hand and efficiently typing clever scholarship with the other? I knew I couldn't do it—I, the woman who regularly forgot to fasten her nursing bra before she stumbled out of the house on the way to class. Was there room in the academy for someone like me?

I didn't hang around at that research-intensive institution long enough to find out. At the end of my first semester of trying to teach and parent, I sat down and took stock of my situation. And I knew it was time to leave. This essay is the map of the journey to that decision, the tracing of the trail to the very different teaching job I now hold at a very different kind of university, and the lay of the terrain between here and there. It is a record of how one not-very-super woman has thus far made it, with equal parts grace and disaster, at balancing the baby and the books. And it is, in a sense, a manifesto for the average parent, the one who messes up and forgets her meeting, the one who can't get out the door in a clean outfit; there is room for us at the university, too.

I had dreams of being a superparent—as, I suspect, many academics do—but mine were made particularly unrealistic by the fact that neither my husband nor I had any experience with children other than what we had read in books. And our research led us to believe—as, I should add, we still do, though less inflexibly—in the value of what is called "attachment parenting." As part of this model we decided (all before the baby's birth) that I should nurse exclusively and on demand for the first six months and continue nursing for at least a year; that our baby should sleep with us rather than in a crib in his own room; and that we should try, as much as possible, to coordinate our schedules so that the baby would be with one of us rather than an outside child-care provider. For two academics (me in the second year of a tenure-track job, and my husband a graduate student), these plans were perhaps unrealistic—if we also planned to keep our sanity. When, after our son's birth, we threw an exceptionally high-need infant into the mix, facing each daily challenge became akin to wading naked into a hurricane.

During the pregnancy, when I was still planning on supermom status, there were already clues—had I chosen to heed them—that I was not cut out for such an assignment. Early in my pregnancy I bought a maternity suit, imagining myself as a chic pregnant woman, attending conferences in said suit while people whispered in awe, "How does she do it all?" The reality is that at the first conference I attended as a pregnant woman, then four months along, I was not showing enough to justify wearing the stylish suit. Instead, I looked dumpy in my loose-waist nonmaternity skirt, and I spent most of my talk trying not to throw up. Later that evening, at a Mexican restaurant with the rest of my panel, I lay on the floor of the women's restroom (whose tile pattern is still fixed in my memory), heaving and wondering what had gone wrong and what I was doing 300 miles away from my own clean bathroom. By the time I was about six months pregnant, I could wear the chic suit, and briefly I looked and felt the image I had imagined—breezy, confident, successful, productive. By the third trimester, however, when my cats had taken to sitting on my belly as if it were their private warming table, I was huge and uncomfortable, and the last place I wanted to be was anywhere that demanded heels and maternity hose. The suit disappeared into the deep recesses of the closet, never again to reemerge until garage-sale time. I simply wanted to wear a pair of huge sweats and sit home, near the bathroom, with the cats.

I titter now to think about it, but I actually said, sometime in the late, tired, and uncomfortable days of my pregnancy, "When the baby's born, I'll finally be able to get some work done again." Our son's early days were very intense, as he was what is kindly called a "high-need baby," but I imagine that, although my and my husband's crash into parenthood was a big, flaming one, almost every parent can relate to the bucolic Gerber-ad expectations not always meeting up with the squalling late-night reality. This disjunction is probably especially true when the mother, on whom early infancy traditionally lays its head the heaviest, works full time in a position in which taking time off is detrimental to one's career and in which being at less than full productivity is frowned upon—exactly the type of job most academics have. And even when official models may be in place to allow for the academic to take parental leave or to gear down for a period, the unofficial attitude at some (many?) schools is that only a real wuss would actually take advantage of such models.

At the school where I taught when my son was born, the only leave policy in place was the federally mandated 12 weeks without pay—not an option for my family, since my husband was a graduate student and my paycheck was our primary source of income. I was allowed—after obtaining a note from my doctor stating that parenthood was time-consuming (no, this is not a joke)—to stop my tenure clock for a year. But I was, to my knowledge, the only person in my department *ever* to have stopped the clock for a baby. Suddenly, then, I was the woman who couldn't cut it. When my two-year evaluations came back from my tenured colleagues (technically, because I had stopped the clock, I was treated as if I were repeating my second year, so I had my second-year evaluations all over again), they were substantially lower than my two-year evaluations had been the previous year, a phenomenon both I and the head of my department found troubling (though I for much more personal reasons than she). Clearly, there was a message here from my colleagues, however unintended: I was really not in my second year, but my third year, and trying to take time off the clock to have a baby was cheating.

There were many and weighty reasons for my decision, during my son's first year of life, to look for another position at another university—I wanted to teach in a liberal arts college, we wanted to move back to the Midwest, I wanted more freedom in my research and publishing life, and so on—but none had the same felt urgency as the realization that, as an academic who is also a mother, I could never cut it at the large research-intensive institution where I was working at that time. I am sure there are people who can—I have even met and stood in awe of such people—but I am not one of them. So that winter, I sat down one morning in my office and wrote a list of my accomplishments during the previous six months. I had given birth to our son in May; now, in December, I reflected on my decision to stop the clock for the year. What, I considered, would I have to show for myself if I were to go through the weighty third-year review now? The list I constructed was both utterly depressing and instructive. Here is what I had accomplished in my professional life that fall:

1. Number of courses taught: one (usual load is three).
2. Course releases granted for an internal research leave: two. Research completed as part of the research leave: none.
3. Number of workshops organized: one, for graduate students on teaching.
4. Number of papers presented: one (at a small, unimportant conference whose key attraction was that it was held near my parents' home, and thus they could babysit while I gave my paper).
5. Number of articles written: none. Revised: none. Published: none. Completed no real scholarly work of any kind (save the conference paper, above).
6. Committees served on: two (but missed one meeting and several deadlines).

I tried to be generous with myself (I didn't list the fact, for example, that my teaching evaluations were, by a slight margin, the lowest they'd ever been), but I also felt compelled to list teaching and publishing accomplishments as I thought my colleagues would perceive them. The list was short, perhaps mercifully so. I concluded with a separate tally of personal "accomplishments," many of them constituting the most memorable moments of the semester, which would never, ever make the third-year review folder or be formally evaluated by my colleagues:

1. Number of times, this semester, that I've worn a pooped-on shirt (without realizing it) to the office: one.
2. Number of times I've met with colleagues while wearing said pooped-on shirt: one.
3. Number of times I've walked to campus (just over a mile) with the flaps down on my nursing bra: two.
4. Number of times I've taught class that way: one.
5. Number of times I've noticeably leaked milk while in conference with a senior colleague: one (note: different senior colleague than pooped-shirt colleagues).
6. Number of times I've slept through a committee meeting because I fell asleep while nursing the baby: one.
7. Number of times I've felt as if I've gotten a full night's sleep: zero.
8. Number of committee deadlines I've missed because something with the baby has taken precedence over committee work: three.
9. Number of times I've worn a one-piece dress to the office only to have my husband drop by later with an inconsolable baby, at which point I have to take the entire dress off, in my locked office, in order to nurse him: two.
10. Number of times I don't remember, afterward, what happened in class that day because I've been so sleep deprived that I can't maintain my concentration: about 15 (can't remember exact number; too tired).
11. Number of times I've mentioned the baby in class: almost daily.
12. Number of times, premotherhood, I used to find it annoying when people constantly talked about their kids: countless.

The happy ending to this story, of course, is that I have found a teaching position I'm very happy with in a university where I feel much more comfortable and supported as both a mother and an academic. In the process of moving, we reorganized our lives and schedules, and as a result I've been much more successful at my new job. The following, then is what it took to make me succeed: (1) a more supportive work environment; (2) a stay-at-home spouse and reorganized schedule; and (3) a commitment to juggling and negotiation.

In my move, I've found both a university and a department with more supportive policies and attitudes toward family life. In an informal poll (conducted by me and based on my knowledge of departmental members), in my first university, in an English department of about 35 full-time faculty, 3 members (besides me) had children under age 10. In my new university, with a faculty of about 28 full-time faculty, 8 members (again, besides me) have children under age 10. In the old university, there was only one other woman in the department with young children (and she was a superwoman who applied for and received tenure in a record three years, among other things). In my new department, seven of the eight are women, and most of these women freely talk about child-care issues, nursing concerns, sleep problems, and childhood illnesses with me and among themselves, in the hallways, at meetings, and at parties. They bring their children into the office, where they have space set aside for toys. The official parental leave policies at my new university are really good. But what really makes this university work for me, as a parent who can't always separate family life and academic life, are the myriad ways in which my college and my own department are, for lack of a better term, *child-friendly.*

By child-friendly I do not simply mean that the women (and men) in my new department seem much more interested in me as a parent than were the members of my last department—though that's certainly some of what I mean. But child-friendliness also evidences itself in some measurable ways: for example, office layout, campus layout, and policies regarding such things as gym or pool use. In my old university, my office was not a safe environment for a small child: The floor tiles were loose and raised, mysterious wires dangled from the walls, paint was peeling, and random pieces of pipe and ceiling tile on occasion fell from the ceiling (I should note that, since my time, this building has since been torn down and replaced with a gorgeous new building); in my new university, my office is clean, safe, spacious, carpeted, and with enough shelving to house my books and Gabriel's toys. My old university bragged of one of the largest campuses in the country; in practical terms this meant it was about a five-minute walk from the English building to the closest food court or coffee shop and about a 10-minute walk to one that was open late in the day. In my new university, I don't actually have to go outside to get to the coffee shop, so if Gabriel visits me in the winter, we can simply walk out of my office and through the tunnel to get a muffin or a drink. At my old university, the gym was student owned and frowned on children in the building; at my new university, the gym is college owned, faculty are welcome there, and the student workers usually greet Gabriel when we bring him in. These are small considerations, perhaps, but they add up. And they add up not just for me, but for other faculty members, too, I think: I often see other kids on campus (it helps that the campus day-care facility—sadly, *way* out of my price range and with no drop-off care—is across the street from the English department), and I see kids in my department, even attending meetings or at office hours on occasion.

As important as the new work environment is the new home environment. For the first time, I have a "wife": Steffen elected to stay home with Gabriel for the year and provide primary child care. So although I still relieve him often, I can generally count on from three to six hours of absolutely uninterrupted time each day to work. This semester, as I teach three courses and have office hours on Mondays, Wednesdays, and Fridays, Steffen stays with Gabriel; as Steffen teaches a martial arts class part time in late afternoons and early evenings, I stay with Gabriel (we often attend the class). On the two weekdays I don't teach, I work in the office for about three hours in the morning, and we spend the early afternoon together as a family. On weekends I work a few hours each day, and I generally work a couple of hours each evening after Gabriel is in bed. Most late evenings—grading or thesis binges excepted—are personal time for Steffen and me. Is this a complicated schedule? Not really, though I'd like more time to read mystery novels, and we both would like to go on an actual date again before Gabriel moves out of the house. But I suspect most parents feel this way. It is an eminently workable schedule, and though my work time is more compressed than it was before Gabriel, I (usually) am able to use it more effectively than I did before Gabriel. There's just no time off.

Our plan of keeping Gabriel at home and spending lots of time together as a family would not work if Steffen worked full time at a traditional job. It's only his decision to stay home with Gabriel that has enabled this schedule to work. But there are also constant negotiations—semester by semester and even week by week ("I'll cover for you this weekend if I can get more grading time today and tomorrow")—as we both, on some level, argue for optimal work-times and Gabriel-times (Steffen prefers late-night work, I like late mornings, and Gabriel is most cranky in late afternoons).

My husband and I have made a lot of changes in our lives: We tag-team our child care for at least part of every day; we live within a half-mile of campus so that we can meet up with each other or do a child handoff at a moment's notice; my office has three bookshelves devoted entirely to toys (though my son currently prefers the stapler to anything on the toy shelf). More important, we've cut some things we used to think were essential or at least important; in fact, as I've become better at juggling motherhood and academia, I've become, in a weird way, worse at some aspects of both. I don't keep up on foreign films, attend many readings, or even consider going to more than about one academic conference a year—and I still base my conference choices on location and child-care options available. At home we cook less and pay less attention to our cats than we used to. We don't keep Gabriel to nearly as strict a bedtime as we ought. We have utterly given up on such "unnecessary" items as mopping floors and making sure our son has clean, matching socks (I write this hoping my mom won't read it and be appalled). Sometimes, when we switch child care at odd times of day, we don't keep track of how much juice he's had or when he needs his diaper changed next (always a bad combination). Yet we survive.

What constantly surprises me (happily, I might admit) is that choices that I made as a parent in my old university that were regarded as weird or even suicidal (tag-teaming our child care, for example) are here regarded as normal or at least acceptable, and the fact that I attempt these things has suddenly altered my status from potentially failing academic to great parent. Partly this change is because research expectations are here both broader and shallower than they were at the large state university: I am no longer expected to publish a book-length work in my field and am allowed to count many publications that are technically outside my field toward tenure. But to a large extent this change in status stems from a palpably different attitude that my new university has toward family—an attitude that probably stems in part from the fact that it's a Catholic university—in which, as far as I can tell from my year here, it sees family as central to one's life, rather than as peripheral to one's academic life. When I received a research grant last summer, child-care costs for Gabriel were included in the grant monies; when I go to conferences, he attends with me, and no one seems to think that's abnormal; when I visit my office at odd times of day or evening, he generally accompanies me. A month or so ago, when Gabriel was visiting me during the day, one of my colleagues saw us in the hallway as we walked to my office carrying my mail. "Baby and books. You're a supermom," he said to me. And I think he was only half joking.

That moment with my colleague, actually, brought about an epiphany (such as I experience them; please don't expect Joyce) in which I suddenly realized that *supermom* here has a different meaning than the traditional image I had in mind of the woman who doesn't nap for 18 years to head a successful academic program and publish prolifically while raising her children. Here, instead, supermom means not someone who can separate family as much as possible from work, but rather someone who can successfully integrate her family into her work—even if that means taking naps occasionally. It means someone who works, publishes, teaches, shows up for committees—of course it means these things—but it also leaves room for someone who is still struggling to pull herself all together. It simply means someone who's trying, not to do everything, but to achieve some sort of balance in her life. Oh, I thought (yes, here's the epiphany): that's me.

As I complete this essay, now several days late for its deadline, I am pregnant with our second child and dog-tired, this morning, from waking up with a two-year-old who *still* (!!!) doesn't sleep through the night. I didn't get as much work done as I had intended this weekend because we were attending a Raffi concert for a big chunk of Saturday, so instead I finished grading my first big round of papers for the semester by staying up exceptionally late for several nights straight. Upon finishing this essay, I plan to get a long-overdue haircut (it's been about six months) and take Gabriel to play in the bookstore across the street from the hair place (weird, I know, but he really likes the ramps there). Tonight I'll spend my evening prepping for class.

After two years of combined motherhood and academia, I firmly believe that to be a bona fide supermom-slash-superacademic you really need full-time child care and/or actual superpowers. Others may be capable of parenting with grace and full attention while at the same time composing cutting-edge scholarship suitable for *PMLA,* but I am not. Ratcheting down—and broadening—the scholarship expectations in my career has possibly taken me out of competition for those darned Newberry Fellowships (but was I really in the running anyway?) but has made me a much happier and saner person. Moving to a teaching-centered university that seems to really value family life has lowered my risk of ulcers and allowed me to spend time with Gabriel without feeling guilty about research time lost. And I have rediscovered in the past year that achieving my goals—to be both a good teacher and a good parent—takes not only a supportive work environment but also, for me, several other key ingredients: commitment, the total backing of your significant other, and skills in compromise and juggling. These are, admittedly, hard to find all in one place. I am deeply happy that, in the past couple of years, I've not only found the work environment but also found, in myself, a commitment to both teaching and parenting; in my husband, support and love; and in our relationship together, the ability to give and take successfully.

Well, so far. With the next child, I'm sure we'll start the process all over again.

16

The Two-Thousand-Mile Commute

Lynn Z. Bloom

"I hate to wash floors," I announced. "If you love me," said my fiancé du jour, "you'll wash the floors after we're married." "I might do it," I said, "but I'll always hate it"—grounds sufficient in what they implied to break off our engagement. Martin responded to this litmus test, "I'm stronger than you are. Either I'll wash the floors or we'll get someone else to do it, but you'll never have to wash a floor." Thus when Martin and I married in 1958, just before we began doctoral work—his in social psychology, mine in English—at the University of Michigan, we adopted a single principle to govern our lives together: We would do whatever we could to enhance each other's personal and professional lives. From that, all else has followed, for the next 46 years and counting. . . .

This principle, our version of the Golden Rule, made de facto feminists of us both, before the term was common. It meant, at the outset, that we would both work on our doctorates full time, that we would share the responsibilities for earning money and running the household (the proportions of each have varied over the years, with each of us assuming responsibility for what we could do—or liked to do—best), and that if one or the other of us needed extra help to accomplish something important, they'd get it. It also meant that when some male students in my doctoral program would say to me, "I'm glad *my* wife isn't in graduate school"—at a time when women were resented for "taking a man's seat"—I could cheerfully reply, "I'm glad I'm not your wife."

We moved to Cleveland from Ann Arbor when Bard was 10 days old, and nine months later I finished my dissertation. I wrote the last hundred pages with a squirming baby on my lap by day and rewrote them again at night and on weekends when Martin was home to handle Bard's round-the-clock energy. Laird was born two years and one textbook later. Although I was teaching part time, by design I was away from the children no more than 18 hours a week until the boys were in school full time, because Martin and I felt very strongly that if we wanted our children to grow up the way we thought they should, we'd better spend lots of time with them. As a social psychologist, Martin could earn a great deal more money than I could in English, so we agreed that I'd postpone full-time teaching until the boys were in school. Thus, during our sons' preschool years, I was never away from them overnight, with the exception of a single week's research trip to Boston and a few single-night research trips during the five years I spent writing the biography of America's most widely read author, pediatrician Benjamin Spock. Little did I know that six years later I'd be commuting a thousand miles each way to work every week.

Martin's research job kept him out of the house, alas, during most of the children's waking hours, except on weekends, when the boys followed him like Lorenz's ducklings and I hit the electric typewriter full speed ahead. But on weekdays I could hardly say to Bard and Laird, "Go away, don't bother me, I'm writing about Doctor Spock." So I learned to work in short batches of time snatched from car pools, nursery school schedules, housework, and entertaining friends and international visitors. By the time *Doctor Spock: Biography of a Conservative Radical* was published, we had moved to Indianapolis for Martin's first academic job and its more accommodating schedule.

In—and Out—of a Real Job

A year after our move to Indianapolis, our children started school, and I got my first real job, at 36, a tenure-track assistant professorship at Butler University, a convenient five minutes from home, teaching four courses a semester. Martin saw the boys off to school so I could teach in the mornings and be home by the time they arrived for lunch (no school lunches at this 1970s neighborhood school), and he did bedtime duty on the nights I taught. I loved the job—my colleagues, the students, and the variety of courses—and I received early tenure and promotion.

During this time our phone was tapped because Spock, my biographical subject, now notorious for leading protests against the Vietnam War, was under FBI surveillance. When I'd pick up the receiver to dial out, I'd hear mysterious clicks, breathing, but never a voice. Sometimes the line would go dead. Here's what the eavesdroppers would have heard: conversations with colleagues about books and with students about assignments; arrangements with neighbors about car pools, play groups, peace marches, integration efforts, and the elementary school's annual geranium and pansy sale (run, of course, by the Blooms); negotiations with babysitters; discussions with editors of my other books-in-process, but with Spock only to make appointments for interviews. Whether the FBI ever provided a context for the fragments of lives they overheard, I do not know, but they evidently didn't carry a grudge, for every member of my family—Martin, Bard, Laird, and myself—has over the years received a number of federal fellowships and research grants, which would presumably have been denied if I'd been blacklisted.

After five happy years in Indianapolis, the FBI notwithstanding, Martin was offered his dream job at Washington University in St. Louis, and I cheerfully resigned from Butler for the move. Our overarching operative principle was intact, and I was confident—with the arrogance of a Michigan PhD who came of age when deans were lamenting, "It's going to be hell on wheels faculty-wise around here," coupled with the ease of finding the job at Butler—that I could again get a good job at the best place in town.

Wrong! In 1974's dismal job market—prognostic of today's—I could find no job except part-time work as an adjunct at three universities, where I came and went, invisible, under cover of lightness and darkness. I had no faculty contacts, fringe benefits; no stationery, telephone—not even an ID or a library card. I was treated as an illegal alien. Nowhere did I have an office, until at the plushest school I was finally allowed to share space with a TA—and, as it turned out, her cat, confined to quarters. This office symbolized my status on all three jobs. As I've explained in "Teaching College English as a Woman": "It was in a building across campus from the English Department, where no one could see us. It was under a stairwell, so we couldn't stand up. It had no windows, so we couldn't see out, but it did have a Satanic poster on the wall—shades of the underworld. The TA had the desk, so I got to sit on the floor next to the kitty litter. I stayed there, in the redolent dark, for a full thirty seconds" (Bloom, 1992, p. 82). In those 30 seconds I decided in a flash of insight that if I were ever to do this again, I would deserve what I get. I did finish the semester. But I never went back to that office, and I made two resolutions: never again to take another job that supported such an exploitative system and—when and if I ever got another tenure-track job—to do what I could to help to change that very system. (The latter is another story.)

The Critical Job Search

That year of miserable marginality impelled me to look in desperation for a full-time, tenure-track job. I would soon be 41 and feared my career would end before it had scarcely begun. While our sons, now in junior high, were doing their homework, Martin and I took long evening walks around the neighborhood, exercising the dog and entertaining options. Should I stay home and write full time? I enjoyed that; I was publishing apace; and I'd gotten two new book contracts during our first four months in St. Louis. I could be home when the boys came home from school, which I insisted on, and cook ad lib, a favorite pastime. Nevertheless, I hadn't spent all that time earning a PhD not to use it—and to get paid appropriately. But the real reason was that I loved to teach; real students in actual classrooms were adrenaline to my teacher's blood. And, as a faculty child myself, I loved the rationale and rhythm of the academic life (in which Labor Day is inevitably New Year's Day), even committee meetings. I loved being identified as a college professor, as much as I loved being identified—in other contexts—as Martin's wife or Bard's and Laird's mother. With that identity gone, too soon, too soon, I felt bereft, in anticipatory mourning for an unlived life.

For a while it was hard for Martin to understand the intensity of this desire, especially given the appeal—though not the financial assurance—of a writer's career. I really wanted both; actually, I wanted it all, however immodest those aspirations might have been. "I'm your best friend," he said, and I hurt his feelings when I told—as usual—the truth: "Yes, but you can't be my *only* friend." As we renegotiated our Golden Rule, it became clear that "to enhance each others' personal and professional lives" meant arranging our family life so we could each have equivalent careers. Since we had comparable academic training and I had been, by design, off the career track when our children were little, I needed to scramble to get back on the train. I thought I would have to settle for a local—although the possibilities in St. Louis ranged from dim to nil, if my experiences as an adjunct were predictive. But what I really wanted was a fast express.

In his new understanding, Martin encouraged me to apply for jobs the length and breadth of the MLA *Job List*. With no institutional affiliation to provide an entrée, I was surprised to receive invitations for a dozen interviews at the MLA meeting from schools around the country. Two I remember very well, even three decades later. In the worst, the yawns of the three interviewers, eager to escape to the convention bar, reaffirmed the in-house favorite daughter's hammerlock on the job. And I remember the best, because it was so much fun, with the University of New Mexico. Fourteen faculty crowded the department chair's small hotel room, sitting on the bed, the floor, or standing; as candidate, I got one of the two chairs. Although the job had been advertised as Renaissance lit, which I had taught at Butler, the interviewers had picked up on my work in biography and autobiography and composition—all my favorite subjects—and geared the interview to these. The discussion was verbal volleyball, with myself the only player on one side of the net. Someone would lob a title over the net and I'd hit it back; I'd read every book and article they mentioned, and more. We talked about big ideas and invented whole programs in that interview, which though scheduled for 45 minutes lasted two hours. These people could be friends, I thought, and I could hardly wait to meet the students—a mixture of Hispanic, Native American, and Anglos—from an exotic culture far beyond the Mississippi.

As the results of the interviews came in, with invitations to visit campuses far beyond driving distance, the reality of what I might be getting into began to dawn. To accept a tenure-track job with all its attendant rights, responsibilities, and privileges, I would have to commute overnight or longer. Could I really do this? To even contemplate a long-distance commute violated my whole understanding of what marriage and motherhood meant. Despite the fact that Martin and I considered ourselves feminists, given our operative principle that translated into a marriage much more collaborative than many we knew of at the time,[2] I believed that a mother who loved her family and wanted them to thrive was always available to her husband and children.

A call from New Mexico in February wonderfully focused our minds, as Samuel Johnson said of an impending hanging. "Come for an interview," invited the cordial chairman, himself the father of seven. "I must tell you," he said, "that state law says that if we pay your expenses for an interview, you have to be willing to take the job if we offer it to you." "I'll call you back," I said. This was the perfect job, a chance to teach autobiography, women's lit, and graduate courses in composition research—three new fields that were just beginning—in the flagship school of the most exotic stateside location I could imagine, with research support and the chance to direct the writing program. "What if they offer me the job?" I wailed to Martin. "I can't take it. Albuquerque is a thousand miles away; I'd have to be there three or four nights a week. I can't be away from home so long." "Oh yes you can," he said without hesitation. "I'll come," I told the chair.

I loved New Mexico but was convinced I'd blown the interview. My interview talk was on point of view in Gertrude Stein's autobiographies. In my innocent heterosexism, I didn't realize that to talk about Stein was to signal UNM's large lesbian community that I was ready to join them. So from all venues of the campus they arrived for the lecture, their blue jeans and cowboy boots a frontier contrast to the sedate suits I was used to in the effete East. Although the English faculty seemed happy with my interpretation, the lesbian contingent was growing restless; their unending questions pushed for a lesbian reading, and I resisted—gently, at first, as I tried to escape a confrontation. "How can you *not* read Stein as a work of lesbianism?" someone asserted, and I got mad. (A decade later, I'd have agreed. One learns.) Into my mind came my favorite scene from *Huck Finn,* when Huck refuses to turn Jim in to the slave hunters, in defiance of the law and the locals. "You can't pray a lie," I thought. "OK, I'll go to hell, and lose this job"—which by then I desperately wanted—"but I have to say what I think." So I took a deep breath, clung to the podium, and said, "Any set of readings that allows only a single -ism, whether it's Freudianism, Marxism, feminism"—I paused—"or lesbianism, is too narrow." Whereupon the hecklers rose and strode out as a white-maned English professor shouted, "Gertrude Stein was a beautiful woman." I returned home, convinced that the beautiful job had fled the room along with my antagonists.

Even if I were to get an out-of-town job (other possibilities were emerging; I had even had one interview in an airport phone booth as I left for New Mexico), we never entertained the possibility of moving the children, then in seventh and eighth grades. We had a big old house in St. Louis in a superb school system. The boys were well ensconced in school. Martin's office was two blocks away from their school and four blocks from our house, so he could easily bike home to be there when they got home from school. Besides, he said, on any new job I'd need to concentrate on learning all of the complicated things I'd need to know to do the work well; I shouldn't be bothering about housework or child care. "But what if something goes wrong at home while I'm away?" "I'll handle it," he said. My protests were getting weaker. Then the New Mexico department chair called to offer me the job. "We were impressed with the way you stood up to the hecklers. We didn't care what you said, just the fact that you didn't back down under all that pressure was important. Come ahead." And he offered me an associate professorship at double my previous salary and a teaching schedule tailored to my commuter flights. Yet I hesitated. "My commuting expenses will cost half my salary," I said to Martin. "Yes," he replied; there went the raise. "Go for it." And so I did.

The Exhilaration of the Long-Distance Commuter

Every couple invents their own marriage and has to reinvent it as life circumstances change—geographic and career moves; the arrival (and departure) of children, aging parents, and other relatives; the waxing and waning of income, health, and affairs of the world. For many of these changes we have models—we can talk it over with those who have preceded us, we can read up on it (and nowadays, check it out on the Web). But in the mid-1970s if there were precedents, especially for the wife and mother as the commuter, we didn't know about them. Marital lore says that extreme commuting works if the couple has a very strong marriage, which can literally "go the distance," or a very weak one, which benefits from separation, but that uncertain marriages can't take the instability and are likely to dissolve. With no model for long-distance commuting—we came from traditional families and lived in a neighborhood where the mothers who worked were within easy reach of home—we had to invent and reinvent the dimensions as we imagined the possibilities. We didn't ask our sons' opinion, but they seemed unfazed by the prospect of my absence. I was afraid my neighbors would shun me, but they seemed as intrigued as I was by the prospect of my new job and said they wished they'd had comparable opportunities. The women's writing group I'd been leading decided to adapt their meeting times to my commuting schedule.

We soon settled on the model that worked well during my three-year affiliation with UNM. Three weeks out of four I flew from St. Louis to Albuquerque—a straight route, no change of planes—on a Monday or Tuesday morning and returned home on Thursday night. The fourth weekend I stayed in Albuquerque—to cut down on costs, catch up on work, cook meals to freeze and thaw during my shorter stays, and explore the state. And I worked hard, in my office with a balcony and huge windows facing the ever-changing Sandia Mountains; 14-hour days and evenings meant I could get most of the class preparation and administrative work done in situ. I was so busy I scarcely had time to get lonesome—except during the occasional solitary dinner and at bedtime. I graded papers on the plane—the two-plus-hour flight was just long enough to finish a set. That left the three-day weekends in St. Louis free to write—a great deal, as it turned out—to spend lots of time with my family, and to cook a lot for them to eat during my absence, thus assuaging my initial guilt at leaving the children during the week. The Friday trips Martin and I took to the grocery store had the frisson of a honeymoon. The boys, busy with school and after-school activities, accepted my departures—and arrivals—with aplomb. After all, they could count on their dad to be home when they were, and—especially after he switched from full-time research to a professorial job—Martin always spent lots of time with them, even for a time becoming Cub Scout Den Mother (the Scouts had no alternative language at the time for den fathers).

Indeed, when I asked Bard and Laird as I began this essay how they had felt about my commuting, each shrugged. "No big deal. That was just what you did." "We were busy all the time you were away." "We expected it, just as we expected a scramble of housecleaning on Thursday nights before we went to pick you up at the airport." This experience also set a pattern that our sons' wives have benefited from, as they freely travel on business while their husbands tend the household. So I soon got over the guilt, though I kept on cooking and acting as communication central, in charge of scheduling everyone's appointments and serving as a concierge for the family's social life and recreation. By this time, however, Martin was baking bread regularly, which he does to this day; as his culinary repertoire expanded, the boys too were developing a lifelong love of cooking. When we were interviewed about our "alternative lifestyle," Martin and I always maintained that it wasn't alternative, it just occurred in two different places.

Not only was the New Mexico job the right job, it came at the right time in my life and that of our family. I wanted to get in on the ground floor of research in the areas I was hired to work in; as it has turned out, all three—autobiography, women writers, and composition studies—have moved since then from far left field to the mainstream. I wanted to direct a big undergraduate writing program, do research on it, and help train TAs to teach it. UNM not only provided research funding, but a crack typist, a program secretary—herself a fine creative writer—and an administrative assistant who handled with aplomb all queries, including the usual grammar mavens and threateners of lawsuits over grades, and took me to the airport, a fast mile from campus. I learned a lot about multiculturalism in this state where Anglos were in a minority; I taught a much wider range of students—in income and age, as well as ethnicity—than I'd ever taught before. I learned about high- and low-stakes testing of writing; I learned, often the hard way, about academic politics, for good and for ill. Thanks to the mentorship of many, particularly my last and best landlady, who had been the first woman commissioner of Bernalillo County and knew everyone in the state, I learned from the inside what it was like to live in the still fairly wild West, with mountains and canyons and mesas and Indian reservations that our family explored during spring breaks. What I learned would have been utterly impossible had I never left home and instead settled for the alternative—part-time adjunct jobs in St. Louis.

I learned, too, that it was possible to take huge risks, with my family and my career, because the foundation was in place. All the things that might have derailed either the commuting, our marriage, or our children didn't happen. Although I was three weeks late to school at the outset of the job because of recuperation from unexpected gallbladder surgery, all of us stayed healthy, and happy. Martin and I had neither the time nor the inclination to develop dangerous liaisons. Our sons' grades remained stellar, their behavior (to our knowledge) wholesome, as might be expected of the children of nerds. The airline crews never struck, the flights were never canceled or rerouted, and in those innocent times I could rush from class through the Albuquerque airport's adobe corridors and onto the plane in 10 minutes flat. By chance, trouble struck only when we were together: our dog was mangled to death by a mastiff; Laird broke a tooth in a sports accident; on a camping trip in Sweden I was attacked by a rapist on drugs within 200 feet of my sleeping family.

On the Road Again

The attempted rape, coupled with the unavailability of jobs for Martin in Albuquerque (UNM had no social work school), made us decide after three years that it was time to stop commuting. Because English jobs were still scarce, we agreed that I would find the job first. Fortunately, the range of my new experiences, particularly as writing director, provided a plethora of possibilities in cities and towns where Martin could also find work. For this move, the boys had a vote; Williamsburg, Virginia, beat San Diego four to nothing. As an enticement for Martin to stay at Washington University, his Social Work dean offered me the best part-time job I'd ever encountered: to teach a course in social science writing and edit a social work journal the school published. If that had been an option four years earlier, I'd have accepted it, no question. "I'll take it if you want me to," I told Martin, for his job was both agreeable and prestigious. "Nope," he said cheerfully, "you deserve the best job you can get in your field, not mine. Here, you'd be just as isolated professionally as you were when we first came." And so we moved, where I encountered nonstop professional harassment, beginning the day I arrived; Laird was nearly killed in a car crash; and Martin was diagnosed with a brain tumor. We all survived.[3]

Except for the traumas just identified, this story sounds too good to be true. Although readers make great allowances for misery and maelstroms, they distrust happy stories, and they often can't stand the tellers. To ensure reader sympathy, I or my family should have experienced a major crisis, trauma, breakdown, or horrendous problem that we overcame only after great storm and stress. Preferably more than one, to make the narrative of the 2,000-mile commute compelling. But those bad things didn't happen as the consequences of commuting; they are not inevitable. The many morals of this story of personal and professional risk taking are evident. Like many other adventures in life, the big risks that could have culminated in catastrophe had even greater potential for change, growth, and a great deal of fun—not only for myself but for our entire family. We chose the long, adventuresome open road over a dead-end street. That 2,000-mile journey, back and forth, back and forth a dozen times a semester, led not only to the Land of Enchantment, but to the wide world of the possible, from that day to this.

REFERENCES

Bloom, L. Z. (1992). Teaching college English as a woman. *College English, 54,* 818–825.

NOTES

1. This essay is dedicated, with gratitude and love, to Martin, Bard, and Laird Bloom, and to the memory of Joseph Zavadil, mentor and friend.
2. To celebrate finishing *Doctor Spock,* Martin and I took the boys camping throughout Europe for a summer, renting out our house in Indianapolis to an older law student and his family, whom we had never met. The wife met us at the airport on our return, with a defiant welcome: "I've seen how you live, I know there's a different way to do it than the one I have, and I'm divorcing my husband." And so she did.
3. I elaborate on the first two phenomena in "Teaching College English as a Woman" (Bloom, 1992).

17

Science Mom

Rachel Fink

There are moments—wondrous, spine-tingling, feel-it-in-your-gut kind of moments—when everything in your life comes together. On a cold, dreary June day my kids yelled "Look, Mom!" and I turned to see each of them holding a large, dripping horseshoe crab. As I snapped a photo of their beaming faces, it hit me: *This is perfection.* Here we were, in the marine resources building at the Marine Biological Laboratory in Woods Hole, where much of my academic scholarship has been centered. Bringing my children to dig among the sea creatures symbolized how intertwined my professional and personal lives have become.

The kids came to us via paperwork and heart-stopping fear, endless bureaucracy and the faith that somehow, somehow, after years of fruitless medical procedures, international adoption would let us build a family. In contrast, the professional side of my life seemed to come quite easily. From my earliest days I wanted to end up teaching biology at a small New England college, and that is exactly what I am doing today as a 46-year-old professor at Mount Holyoke. When I look back, it all seems so *linear.* My parents are teachers and scientists, I loved school all the way through, and I headed off to college at Cornell because its catalog had the largest number of biology courses. A summer at their Shoals marine lab convinced me that ocean life was my passion, and I can pinpoint exactly when I decided to become an embryologist. The summer after my junior year of college I took a course at the University of Washington's marine laboratory in Friday Harbor. As bald eagles flew overhead and orcas breached offshore, I became nursemaid to every kind of marine invertebrate larva that could be coaxed to grow in our custard dishes. In a room sloshing with seawater tables, I watched starfish larvae and baby sea cucumbers, and my notebook grew fat with diagrams of comb jelly eggs and barnacle sperm. The hours looking through the microscope, as a single fertilized egg transformed into a scallop or anemone, so thoroughly captivated me that I have never stopped learning about development.

I went from Cornell to Duke, landing in the laboratory of an energetic developmental biologist who taught me to work with sea urchin embryos and who instilled in me an understanding of how to design an experiment. My adviser often said that I went into embryology because I was so maternal—a comment that at the time drove me nuts, because it sounded so sexist, but that I now see has a lot of truth to it. He also introduced me to the politics of being a scientist, and allowing me to watch him succeed in the hard, hard world of academic science was his greatest gift.

After finishing my thesis, I traded North Carolina barbecue for the incredible pizza of New Haven and became the last postdoctoral fellow of a craggy embryologist from Yale. It was Trink who took me to Woods Hole for the first time, thus escorting me into the scientific mecca that is created each summer as tides and water currents bring an extraordinary array of marine creatures to the nearshore waters. After decades at the Marine Biological Laboratory, Trink's lab on the second floor of Whitman looked out over the Sound, and on a clear day I could see Martha's Vineyard behind the first of the Elizabeth Islands. My postdoc brought me two of the great passions of my life: the Marine Biological Laboratory and the embryos of the killifish.

Although the waters around Woods Hole are teeming with life, *my* summer field guide would have but one entry: the killifish *Fundulus heteroclitus*. From May to July, the estuaries on the Cape are full of these little fish, no bigger than sardines, that dart between the eelgrass and swim through waters both salty and fresh. The locals call them mummichaug, and when they are ripe they produce embryos so large and transparent they could make commercial caviar blush. Each summer season I scoop up a handful of fish and sort them into males and females by dropping them into two buckets. Back in the lab, I eye them from above as they wiggle through the water. The outline of a gravid female has a curve I can see in my sleep, and I know just how to hold a fish so she relaxes in my hand, her eyes covered by the curve of my pinky and ring finger. A gentle rub on her belly, and her tail starts to twitch as the eggs pour forth. A single fish can produce dozens of eggs, and I collect them in a finger bowl with a tiny bit of seawater on the bottom. The size of a BB, each egg is covered by a protective shell, so hard it can be picked up without being squished. After collecting eggs, I throw the female back in the tank and go for a male. His vent is tiny and delicate, and I barely touch it with the tip of a fingernail. At this time of year, the lightest pressure can cause sperm release, and when his anal fins are dripping with milt, I touch him to the bottom of the dish containing the eggs. I can see the milky cloud, and quickly swirl the dish. Eggs meet sperm, and a new generation is created. Wiping my hands on my pants, I grab a lab marker, write the time of fertilization on the dish, and get ready for an experiment. I have spent years filming the movements of individual cells as they crawl, squirm, divide, and specialize in these wondrous embryos.

When it was time to apply for jobs, I was quite choosy and hit the jackpot when Mount Holyoke called to invite me for an interview. Clothed in my favorite embroidered vest, black pleated skirt, and lucky boots, I drove to the Pioneer Valley and was charmed by the wide hallways, friendly faculty, and enthusiastic students. It took no time at all for me to accept their offer, and I decorated my new office with colored photomicrographs of sea urchin larvae and cleaving cells. Those early years at Mount Holyoke were, I assume, fairly typical for a new faculty member. Writing lectures all night, frenzied summer months of research, trying to learn how to grade a zillion student papers—along with life in a new location and the realization that "this is it," the place I could spend the rest of my life as an academic. I was very successful as a scientist and was proud of publishing papers, being elected to national society committees, and winning prestigious grants. I was running with the big boys, and it was quite heady stuff. I was somehow doing it all, and it felt very, very good.

After a few years at Mount Holyoke, I fell in love, and I can remember the exact place we were standing the first time I visited his house when he told me he had always wanted to have kids. I looked at him and thought, "This is the man for me." I was 33 years old and had never understood why I had been able to make my professional life scoot forward on a nice track without finding a lifemate along the way. Tom was the college astronomy professor, and his gentle Southern charm, passion for eclectic music, enthusiasm for village life, and strong family ties won me over—we were married six months to the day from our first date.

We built our life in a small ranch house three blocks from the Mount Holyoke campus and bumped and clunked our way through the "learning to know each other" part of making a relationship work. As we negotiated which brand of detergent to buy, how to deal with window treatments, and just what constituted a *short* woods walk, one fiercely strong thread that wove a love pattern between us was the knowledge that we wanted to become parents. Together. Soon. Even with all of the biological background in reproductive physiology I had spent my professional life gathering, I found myself superstitious, romantic, and (in retrospect) unfathomably naive about our chances of becoming pregnant the first time we had unprotected sex. As month after month went by, I realized that medical intervention was to be a part of our lives, and we began what was to become five years of torture in the world of assisted reproductive technology. For me, it overshadowed everything and colored my world in ways that will be with me for the rest of my life.

One day, after my husband had injected my thigh with the daily dose of Lupron, I sat in my office trying to listen to a research report from one of my best-ever students. I looked at her—brilliant, eager, enthused—and instead of reveling in her success, I was entombed in feelings of drug-induced paranoia, sad down to my toes, skin crawling with discomfort, doubting whether I could ever again successfully teach a student anything. I remember making my husband lie to anyone who called on the telephone—"She's in the bathtub," "She ran out to the store," "She's taking a nap"—so that I wouldn't have to tell another soul that I had, once again, failed to conceive. I remember hating the doctors who talked to me as if I had no scientific knowledge whatsoever, who wouldn't tell me the details of pH or cell counts or micrograms/ml or true odds for success. And I remember the embryos—our embryos—created after weeks of injections and surgery and micromanipulation. How could I not focus on those embryos? So much like the urchin and fish embryos I worked with by the thousands in my academic life, and yet so monumentally different. The handful of times embryos were transferred to my body was the most pregnant I had ever been. Lying on the gurney I was full of hope despite all of the statistics. But I was soon to be zapped, once again, by the brutality of failure.

It was Tom—my warrior gentle man who wanted to be a father as much as I wanted to be a mother—who finally convinced me that although my dreams of being pregnant seemed to be unreachable, the world was full of children who could bring love and laughter and sticky fingers into our lives. Almost one year from when we applied, we found ourselves on an airplane heading to Guangzhou, China, to meet our daughter, Li Xiao Qin. Nothing in my life had prepared me for the reality of sitting in an institutionally ugly room in an orphanage in Southern China. Tom and I sat there for what seemed like forever, until finally a broad-faced caretaker carried in the tiniest nine-month-old I had ever seen and put her in my arms. I was instantly, completely, irretrievably transformed, and I have been, ever since, first and foremost, Rose's mother.

I was able to take parental/adoption leave and had almost eight months as a new mother, without any professional demands. And when I did go back to teaching, we had a day-care center on campus where Rose was safe and loved and social. I found the juggling act of new parenthood and professorhood much easier than the previous double life of infertility treatments. Now I could laughingly (proudly) shout about new-mother fatigue, the need to rush out of a meeting to pick up my child, or how distracting it was to switch from being "Dr. Fink" to "Mommy." After those endless years of wanting to parent, I dove in completely, and it all felt so *right*. I was more or less at peace with being on the "Mommy Track." I let my microscopes sit idle, and I didn't go to national meetings—I sort of tuned out to the sense that if you don't stay in the game, the world of cell biology will pass you by. I was too enchanted with buying corduroy overalls in size 2T, reading *Good Night, Gorilla* for the umpteenth time, and watching Rose ride on her daddy's shoulders. I was happy in the classroom and taught up a storm. I justified the lack of scientific research as the reality of family life and reveled in the wonders of parenting.

I hate old wives' tales. But I will say after five years of high-tech reproductive failures, I was knocked off my feet by the reality of "As soon as you adopt that baby from China, you'll get pregnant." It had always felt particularly ironic that year after year I would lecture about reproduction as my body exhibited a stubborn refusal to be fruitful. But the February after Rose came home was different, and sure enough, one day I found myself looking at a beating heart on an ultrasound screen as the technician moved the wand over my body. The next day in class, colored chalk in hand, I turned to the blackboard and drew a huge, luminous egg. My happiness was so intense I almost laughed out loud as I drew a zesty sperm and wove a tale of cells and fates and specialization—deaf to the sounds of microscopic unzippings as the chemical Velcro that embedded my baby in my womb, molecule by molecule, let go.

Two years after traveling to China, my sister accompanied me to Vietnam to bring home another child. Sweating in the thick August air, I was nauseated with terror when it came time to enter the orphanage. Looking through a window, I caught a glimpse of Hieu, wearing a faded yellow basketball jersey—tiny, lethargic, unsuspecting. I was told later that I cried out and elbowed my way into the building, and suddenly, at long last, he was in my arms. Our lives fused as I fed him fresh lychees, and, promising him a new world, we boarded a plane for home. Tom met his son in the middle of the night at Kennedy airport, and a few hours later, I lay next to Rose and watched her wake up. As she blinked open her eyes, her first words were "Where is my brother?" and I realized my motherheart would soon learn lessons never before imagined.

While I am enjoying this time of small children, I know I will not be able to manage a research program anywhere near the intensity of what I once had. But as Rose and Hieu have grown and I find myself waving them off on the school bus, I realize that their worlds have enlarged in ways that allow me the freedom to focus on the questions that first won my research heart: How do cells within an embryo crawl? How does a fish embryo make skin? What signals an embryonic cell to change direction? I joined forces with a colleague at a nearby institution and in the last two years have learned how to create fish embryos whose cells synthesize brightly labeled proteins. Amazingly, I am now once again spending hours at a microscope, sitting in a darkened room, watching fluorescent cells reveal things about early embryos that no one else has ever seen. It has been thrilling to realize that my research self was not lost by becoming a mother and that the excitement of discovery is still as sweet. My children know I am a scientist, and both love to come to my fish tanks—especially at breeding season. They can sort the killifish into males and females as easily as I can, and my son is in heaven if I allow him to hold a ripe female and, by gentle rubbing, release her eggs. I once overheard a classmate tell him, "My mommy is at work," and Hieu asked, "Oh, is she at Woods Hole collecting fish?"

Our desire to be parents led us to create a multicultural family, and the academic community has embraced our children with love and happiness and much collective wisdom. Colleagues and friends join us in celebrating Chinese New Year and Tet. I now see my students not only as eager minds ready to learn developmental biology, but also as ambassadors from family lives that might inform how I parent. Our children have babysitters from Bulgaria, Honduras, Korea, and New York City. They participate in the yearly Asian festival on campus as well as the basketball clinics and departmental picnics. We now feel "routine," in all the lovely meanings of that word. The morning routine of making sure our long-haired, graceful, radiant Rose has her notebooks and biteplate and eyeglasses and extra pair of sneakers, ready for another busy day as a third grader. The routine of waking up my snugglepuss little boy, who will cling to me warm and soft and full of love, before demanding French toast and extra lunch money (for chips) and the black swishy pants he wants to wear, again. The routine of saying goodbye to my husband, cramming in the details of who-will-pick-up-the-kids-today and don't-forget-to-give-the-dog-breakfast. The routine of heading to a job that is familiar and ever-changing, rewarding and frustrating, and always worth doing.

But it is only at certain moments that it all seems easy—moments when it *is* doable, to be a mom and an academic scientist. Much of the time I live with a sense of compromise brought on by conflict and fatigue. I really, truly do not think you can "have it all," if the definition of "all" comes from magazines and talk shows and outlandish expectations of perfection. My institution has been mostly supportive of my choices, and the academic life is overwhelmingly privileged. I don't have to worry about feeding or housing my family; I don't have to worry about losing my job; and I have a tolerant and intellectual community in which to raise my kids. But I am definitely a second-class scientist in the eyes of the administration, failing to bring in the big bucks, failing to publish the big articles. I was looked over for promotion, and the pain of being leapfrogged by a younger, more aggressive male colleague surprised me with its sharpness. My passion for sitting at the microscope, for the dizzying buzz of a day well spent with a colleague, the thrill of just finishing a grant proposal—none of these seemed to count when the senior faculty looked at my vita.

And in thinking about my vita I wondered why it had to be so impersonal. Why is it impossible to portray a *real life* on a professional summary? It is a format that has evolved from a culture that believes it possible to separate work world from home life. When I print out a résumé, I am always frustrated by what is *not* on it. Where do you write "Those were the two and a half years when my son suffered from night terrors so profound I staggered in to class on a few hours of interrupted sleep"? How could I shout "Can you believe I managed to start a new research program at this stage of my life? It will take me a few more years to put out some papers—but look at me!" The fact is, I can't often meld my personal and professional lives in ways that maximize both. So instead I careen from one world to the other. In the morning I might deal with a troubled advisee, lecture on fruit fly genes, and try to fix an overflowing seawater tank at work—then glance at the clock and zoom off to make Guatemalan trouble dolls with my daughter's third-grade class. At times I am dizzy from the seesawing, but then again, there are moments—oh, those wonderful moments—when it all clicks. My kids at home, and my students in the classroom, get the best and the worst of me as I manage to change "scientist mom" from an oxymoron to a life choice full of wonder and pure, pure joy.

III

Change

Change can occur on many fronts, and the essays in this section provide a number of different perspectives on how change is occurring or can occur for parents in academia. Individual, interpersonal, policy, and systemic changes can all contribute to warming the climate of academia for parents, as the essayists included in this section demonstrate.

It sounds easy to make change at the personal level, but in reality, individual-level change, without institutional or cultural support, requires a considerable degree of determination. Suzanne M. Cox, whose field is developmental psychology, receives support for her commitment to attachment parenting from her scholarly work on attachment theory and support in coparenting from her self-employed husband. These sources of support have enabled her to combine a full-time academic career with extensive involvement with her four children. Whereas Cox describes the intellectual traditions that support her chosen life, Rachel Hile Bassett relates how her lived experiences as a mother and scholar helped her to move beyond the ideologies of "intensive mothering" (Hays, 1996) and "ideal workers" (Williams, 2000) that had limited her sense of how she could create her life, discovering in the process the benefits that coparenting could provide for her whole family.

At the interface between individual and institutional change, Christina Brantner describes the interpersonal work academic parents can do to ensure that family-friendly policies work in practice. Based on her own experiences, Brantner emphasizes the importance of cooperative work with department and students to cover work during leave time. Brantner's experiences exemplify how well-functioning departments can support an on-leave parent without any one person becoming overburdened from the extra work, and she offers advice for receiving equitable treatment even from less well-functioning departments.

Change for parents in the academy is necessary not only for professors, but for students as well, and students actually have a longer history of activism on behalf of parents. Kathleen B. Jones describes the collective student action she was part of in the early 1970s to get child care on her campus and how their success in getting the center and keeping it going resulted from cooperation and continual negotiation among the parents involved. But student concerns must become visible to those with power for lasting change to occur: Jones notes that the same questions she and her peers asked 30 years ago about caregiving and academia are still salient yet still largely unanswered. In her essay, Alison M. Thomas explains how recognizing her students' needs for family-friendly policies made her realize that the "honorary man" pattern she had followed up to that point—never allowing family life to interfere with work responsibilities, in order not to be kicked out of the club—was detrimental not only to her students, but to her own family life as well.

Thomas's realization leads us to the crux: Family-friendly policies make academia "friendlier" only to the privileged and only to visible caregivers. Only radical change can make caregiving easier for both students and professors, for both biological mothers and all the other academics with other, less obvious caregiving responsibilities. Both Anna Wilson and co-authors Gayle Letherby, Jen Marchbank, Karen Ramsay, and John Shiels argue for more radical changes within the university than policy changes that allow "accommodations" for parents with academic careers. Letherby and colleagues build their argument on the point that academia (following broader cultural workplace norms) dichotomizes workers into mothers and "others," basing both on biological understandings. Caring responsibilities of those who aren't biological mothers—fathers, children of aging parents, caregivers for ill partners and friends, stepparents or foster parents—are generally not visible. Letherby and colleagues propose a revision of the culture of academic work to make academic institutions less "greedy" of workers' time, making it possible even for academics with "invisible" caring responsibilities to achieve work-family balance.

Anna Wilson bases her argument for radical change within the academy on an analogy between queer parenting and mothering in the academy. Queer theorists have noted that heteronormative discourses of femininity and motherhood create a sense of motherhood as a unitary and monolithic thing. Liberal discourses on queer parenting have acceded to this view, such that liberals, though supportive of gays' and lesbians' right to parent, see the goal of queer parenting as replicating what nice liberal straight couples do as parents. Liberalism thus embraces pluralism at the expense of glossing over very real differences, such as the possibility that different *outcomes* between queer and straight parents might be part of a richer and more real pluralism. Turning to the academy, Wilson notes that, just as conservatives and liberals have more in common with each other on the question of queer parenting than either shares with a more radical view, academics—both the conservatives who want to deny tenure to everyone not exactly like them and the liberals who want to extend the tenure clock, provide maternity leave, and so forth—assume that the current system is "natural" and can be tinkered with but not fundamentally changed. Thus the binary of "dyke/mother" can be seen as parallel to academia's binary of "professor/mother": Liberal policies will allow the mother to "pass" as a real professor, but they don't even aim at systemic change. True systemic change to encourage participation of currently marginalized groups will make academia not only more welcoming for caregivers of all sorts, it will also enrich academia's areas of inquiry, influencing the questions asked and the answers found, making the world of academia fuller in its knowledge.

REFERENCES

Hays, S. (1996). *The cultural contradictions of motherhood.* New Haven, CT: Yale University Press.

Williams, J. (2000). *Unbending gender: Why family and work conflict and what to do about it.* New York: Oxford University Press.

18

Boomerangst

Kathleen B. Jones

I'm a boomer, part of the generation that tried to combine mothering with politics, begging the question of whether such a balancing act was possible or even desirable. It was never an abstract question to me. I wasn't debating theory; I was living the contradictions.

One cold January day in 1969, a month shy of my 20th birthday, I gave birth to a 7-pound 12-ounce baby boy. At the time, I was a college student majoring in dance. I felt both totally unprepared and unequivocally eager to be a mother. As an only child reared by a mostly single "working mom," herself the only child of otherwise Irish Catholic parents, I'd never plumbed the mysteries of child care, never had dutiful responsibilities to siblings. And as for tending the neighbors' kids, I preferred minding world events. In adolescence I was an avid debater on a competitive and highly successful high school team and spent my evenings designing ways to catch opponents using faulty logic or entrap them during cross-examination. Tending toddlers wasn't my thing; I was a champion at argumentation, the queen of Catholic forensics. I even married my debate coach. Ah, the battles we waged besting each other!

For the first six months after my son Jed was born I was a full-time mother and homemaker. In our six-story apartment building populated with assorted, mostly white lower-middle-class families, husbands worked; wives scoured and cleaned, cuddled and clothed children—and shopped. Pushing caravans of baby-filled strollers, the brigade of women who would be soccer moms ambled up and down the long avenue, stopping at the A&P, congregating in the small concrete patches of playgrounds to share stories of Johnny's first words or Janie's first steps or to trade news about discounts on baby clothes or the wisdom of using Pampers instead of a diaper service.

I was an oddball mother. With my books and papers in a backpack and friends from college visiting me with news of the latest demonstrations and artsy events, I didn't fit.

But I was an oddball student, too. Most of my friends weren't serious about relationships. They were serious about art or politics. I was the only one among them who had to balance care of an infant with dance rehearsals that ended at midnight or political meetings that overlapped the dinner hour.

In those days, there was no university child care. And my husband lacked the inclination to help at home. So I hired an infant-care specialist to stay with Jed while I went to class and stayed up late at night writing manifestos about the importance of cultural revolution in the new society.

I crammed my remaining year of courses into a single semester, completed my senior choreography project and honors thesis in political science while taking Jed with me to political meetings and rehearsals—I had decided to continue in dance but major in political science—and graduated in August 1970, the year of Kent State and Jackson State, of secret bombing campaigns in Cambodia. That fall I entered graduate school and was awarded a research fellowship. To stretch my fellowship far enough to cover the cost of babysitting and minimize the time I spent away from my son meant calculating the time I permitted myself for classes and research down to the minutest fraction. Including transportation by bus and subway from Brooklyn to Manhattan and back, I crammed a full-time schedule of courses, some library time, and the occasional coffee break with fellow students into less than 15 hours a week. The professor I worked for didn't mind my carting truckloads of documents home so I could finish researching strategic arms control in the security of my own living room.

Whenever Jed was napping or late in the evenings when everyone was asleep, I'd spend hours combing through the UN General Assembly debates on arms control and disarmament, looking for nuance and pattern among the millions of hollow phrases tossed into the murky policy mix. MIRVs and ABMs, the NPT and TBT—this strange alphabet soup filled my head. To the tunes from *Mr. Roger's Neighborhood* or *Sesame Street,* I wrote some plausible defense of nuclear arms reduction.

The immediacy of my need for balance, the fact that my child was an infant, and my need to downplay the difficulty of taking care of everything conspired to keep me isolated. Yet, I'd glimpsed the possibility of a collective solution when I'd marched with thousands of other women in New York City during the national "strike" on August 26, 1970, demanding pay equity, free abortion on demand, and even 24-hour child care.

By the fall of 1971 I had a graduate teaching fellowship at Brooklyn College. One crisp day I happened past a demonstration outside a Quonset hut the university had set up for temporary classrooms. A petite woman with a close-cropped Afro talked animatedly into a megaphone, trying to drum up support for some political action. Other women passed out leaflets; a few toddlers tried to find ways to amuse themselves with makeshift games played on the grassy area in front of the building.

"Brooklyn College must provide child care. In the interests of justice, we demand the university fulfill its promise for educational equity and provide us with a clean, lighted place for our children's program."

"What's this about?" I asked another woman standing nearby.

"We're occupying the building until the college gives us a better facility for our kids. They gave us the basement under the theater building. It's dark and rat infested. We're taking over *this* building until the college owns up to its obligations. Wanna help?"

Help? A classroom of comparative politics students waited for me to lead them in a discussion, ironically enough, about the Cultural Revolution in China. And I had to be home right after class to relieve the babysitter. I took the leaflet about upcoming meetings. "I'll be back," I said, racing to class. But when I returned, the building had been emptied out.

"Everyone got arrested that day," Gracie, the woman with the Afro, told me at the meeting of the child-care coalition the following week. "But we were released almost immediately. And we got our point across. We can sure use your help, though, especially since you're a graduate student. And you're faculty, you're a teaching assistant."

And so began an organizing effort that I co-chaired with Gracie at Brooklyn College. Our victories included acquiring a beautiful space for our child-care cooperative. The college gave us wide, high-ceilinged rooms above the library. They were light and airy, with windows overlooking the quad. Afternoons, you could hear announcements of upcoming demonstrations mix with the faint chords of sitar music, the cacophony of song and spirit that marked that decade of disrupted dreams.

The cooperative required parents to donate time to run the center, fathers as well as mothers. We hired a fully licensed preschool teacher and several professional staff, including a cook, to help plan the program. News of our success spread to other campuses.

I don't even remember who told me about the dozen or so women and men who already had been meeting informally to discuss the possibility of the Graduate Program's providing child care on site. But when I found them, I found the road to sanity. If there was a child-care program at Brooklyn and one at the Graduate Center, then I could take Jed with me to school, whether I was in class teaching or being a student myself.

In the same year that we were given the new space for the center at Brooklyn, graduate students who were parents, myself among them, successfully lobbied the program to create a child-care center. On the third floor of the Graduate Center's 42nd Street facility, an old office building that had been renovated into classrooms and faculty offices, we created a day-care program.

When we inherited the space, it was anything but child-friendly. Clever engineers retrofitted a bathroom to accommodate the needs of small people with dirty hands. And when we couldn't find any safe park within reasonable walking distance to take the kids to—these were the days before Bryant Park's rejuvenation—our urban planning and architecture colleagues helped us create an indoor play area, complete with jungle gym, tricycles, and cushioned floor. We formed a board of directors, of which I became chair, and hired our first full-time teacher. A journalist colleague helped us create a nifty pamphlet to get the word out about our affordable, high-quality program, available to children of faculty, staff, and students. In it we bragged that you could bring your kids to campus, go to class, and have lunch with them on break! The brochure featured Jed playing Superman, while Jed's best friend, Greg, graced the cover, festooned in a giant cowboy hat, riding a wooden scooter and pretending to be John Wayne.

On graduate seminar days, Jed and I took the subway from uptown to Times Square. Walking past the late-night movie theaters and peep shows and the electronics stores perpetually going out of business, we'd reach the oasis at 33 West 42nd Street, across from Bryant Park. We'd take the elevator up to the third floor, where Jed went to "school," and then I'd continue to the ninth floor, where the political science department had its offices. Most days I'd take the elevator down to lunch with Jed. Some early evenings, before the center closed, I'd ride up to the cafeteria and hang out with friends, talking about books or the peace movement or women's issues.

The child-care center gave us parents peace of mind. Our kids were near while we studied; we were near them if an emergency arose. And, surrounded as we all were by the cultural cornucopia of New York City, our kids got an education beyond the classroom walls. If I needed esoteric texts for my research, Jed and I wandered across the street and walked up the concrete steps between the graceful lions and into that blissful space—the great reading room of the main branch of the New York City Public Library.

Under the light of green glass lamps, with my books and note cards litter-
ing the worn wooden tables where thousands had written before me, I'd
pore over rare texts on 18th-century political theory and history while Jed
scribbled in his notebook, pretending to record his "research."

After our success at Brooklyn and at the Graduate Center, we expanded
our single-campus organization into the City University-Wide Day Care
Coalition, garnering support from Eleanor Holmes Norton, then commissioner of human rights of the City of New York. Norton helped us craft a
press release, and with cameras popping and tape recorders whirring, we
announced our demands: We wanted to secure the support of the chancellor's office for space and financing to create subsidized child care as part
of the university's commitment to educational equity. I think we amazed
ourselves when the strategy worked. The chancellor's office announced that
priority be given to the issue in all master plans. After that, the remaining
senior colleges in the City University system received support for child
care.

Our group pushed the connection between educational equity and
social change a few steps further with the idea for a multidisciplinary research and teacher-training program, a kind of lab school that could serve
the needs of our kids, provide a field school for those in early childhood
education, and enable us to balance our lives better. We wanted a place
for a new curriculum—one that stressed antiracism and antisexism—to
be implemented at an early age. It was a bold idea, which has since been
enacted on a number of campuses, including the one where I currently
teach. We felt as if we were part of the larger educational reform movement
that was burgeoning then, one that linked the importance of child care not
only to efforts to meet the needs of college students with preschool-age
children, but also to the vision that collective social responsibility for the
future hinged on democracy in the private as well as public realm.

I became interested in the connection between child-care reform
and social reform for both intellectual and personal reasons. As someone
connected to the women's movement, but not one of its leaders, I came to
the movement's questions through the door of Firestone's *Dialectics of Sex*
(1970). In it I read that "women have been found exceedingly useful and
cheap as a transient, often highly skilled labor supply, not to mention the
economic value of their traditional function, the reproduction and rearing
of the next generation of children, a job for which they are now patronized
. . . rather than paid." That analysis of the exploitation of love resonated not
only because its argument was strong, though disturbing, but also because,

by the spring of 1971, my personal life had begun to unravel. My mother had died the year before. Now my marriage was ending.

The summer of 1971 I had separated from my husband and moved into a tiny apartment in Brooklyn Heights with my toddler son. Because the day-care program at the Graduate Center looked promising, I knew, or thought I knew, that I'd be able to balance school and motherhood. I soon swapped the Brooklyn sublet for a Soho apartment. It had a tub-in kitchen, sleeping loft in a tiny bedroom for Jed, and room for my sofa sleeper in the living room, my books in crates along the wall. Everything fit. Or so it seemed.

I'd fallen into a bohemian, leftist routine, replete with starving artists and suffering Kerouac-ian souls. There were the all-night conversations about Hemingway and Marcuse, followed sometimes by midnight movies in Times Square or a late-night meal at Ratners' in the East Village. I taught 8 A.M. classes at Brooklyn College, attended grad seminars two nights a week, and chaired the day-care center's board of directors. I didn't sleep much. It wasn't exactly superwoman syndrome. But close.

It only worked because D and C and I, three single women with young children, had created our own little extended family. Each of us had a male partner who disdained sharing domestic chores, each of us had professional aspirations, and each of us had a young boy-child who happened to thrive with the addition of two brothers and two mothers into the equation. We rotated sleepovers twice a week so that one night we each had all three kids in exchange for two kidless nights a week.

On those nights alone I caught up with lecture notes or seminar papers or organizing or dance classes. Or maybe even a bit of private romance. It didn't elude any of us that we were a network of women who cared for one another enough to help each other stay sane.

In the early 1970s it was the rare male among the radical men I knew who bothered himself with domesticity. Even when a group of friends and colleagues tried to carry principles of equity and genderless roles and responsibilities into alternative educational organizations, old patterns proved resolutely difficult to alter.

I remember one short-lived group that sprouted in New York City in the early 1970s. An eclectic group of lawyers, artists, writers, and academics, myself among them, created the Free Association, a sort of storefront "open university" that operated in a not-too-pricey midtown walkup. We offered noncredit courses in politics taught by the likes of Stanley Aronowitz and other Democratic Socialists, as well as writing and art workshops—and general leftist camaraderie. A few of us had young children, so the group decided child care was essential. But staffing was another matter. Mostly, it was the mothers who took turns caring for one another's children so that the other mothers could rotate in and out of lectures by the mostly male, mostly childless "faculty."

When the mothers brought the matter of the sex and motherhood status of the caretakers to the general board for discussion, we were greeted with the predictable blank stare and not overly enthused assent to alternate child minding between the men and the women, the mothers and the non-mothers. Yet, without constant reminding, old habits persisted.

By the time I left New York for Kentucky in 1975, public higher education funding for services and programs, such as child care, was at an all-time low. Nationally, we had lost the debate in 1972, the year Nixon vetoed legislation that would have provided a federal child-care policy. Despite its having passed both houses of Congress, child care had been condemned as something bordering on a communist plot. By then, my son had entered elementary school, and my immediate attention shifted to after-school care. A few Kentucky schools and community centers provided activities for young children. Between those programs and the ability to juggle my schedule, I managed to make things work, teaching part time and trying to write a dissertation. I hadn't quite finished my dissertation when I was offered a tenure-track job in North Carolina. It was 1977, and jobs were scarce. I took the offer and moved my family to Wilmington, where I became the only woman in a five-person political science department. But within a month my new husband had gotten a job in Jacksonville, 50 miles northeast of Wilmington, and the job required him to live within shouting distance of his patients. So we moved to Jacksonville, North Carolina, famous for Camp LeJeune Marines, porno strip joints, and little else in the way of entertainment or culture beyond the blue-light specials at Kmart. And I drove 50 miles to Wilmington and 50 miles back every day to teach.

The university had given me until May to complete my dissertation or lose my job. The threat motivated me to write. But reality made timely completion a challenge. I taught four different courses on a schedule covering five days a week. Travel time to and from work was an hour or more each way on North Carolina 17, a rural highway landscape interrupted only by the occasional pine tree and Holly Ridge, a town halfway along the route through which one could drive no more than 25 miles per hour or almost certainly be stopped by the highway patrol. I had an eight-year-old with a keen interest in Little League and a husband resistant to taking on his share of household responsibilities. And I needed to finish a dissertation on Marx as quickly as possible in a place where the *Werke* were a couple hundred miles away in Chapel Hill's library, at a time before computers, when typing meant a lot of labor and when multiple revisions were costly.

Then I got pregnant.

It wasn't a mistake. We'd been trying to have a child and had almost given up. But the timing was less than ideal. A few weeks after I'd returned from my dissertation defense, I met with the department chair to discuss the implications.

"Oh, I see." He seemed nervous. "How will you manage?"

"I'll be fine. The pregnancy isn't disabling."

"I mean, uh, uh, uh, how will . . . will you continue teaching?"

"Just like I have before."

"And what about, what about after the baby is born?"

"What about it?"

"Well, you, you, you . . ."

"Did you ask Lee that question, too?" Lee was another junior faculty member who'd been hired the year before me and whose wife, I knew, was pregnant.

"Well, no, but . . ."

"Then you don't need to ask me."

Still, the chair was a considerate man, in the tradition of white Southern gentlemen, and agreed, under the circumstances, to give me a teaching schedule of Monday/Wednesday/Friday the following fall, during my last trimester of pregnancy.

"And make sure we have your doctor's phone number." I had a doctor in both towns. "Just in case."

One late November night somewhere along Highway 17 I felt contractions start. False labor. Still, largely because of the drive, I decided to stop teaching the last week of the semester. My son, Ari, was born December 1, 1978. I graded my term papers while nursing him into the late hours of the night. Six weeks later, I was back teaching, driving 100 miles a day again. Within a year, I was one among a circle of women faculty who were designing the first courses for a women's studies program on the campus.

The second marriage ended, but not before I'd moved to California. I had resigned my position at North Carolina when the dean there denied me a leave that my department had supported. I'd always thought it had something to do with the student branch of the National Organization for

Women that I'd organized, which had sponsored the visit of Sonia Johnson right after her excommunication and just before her publication of *From Housewife to Heretic*. Her visit wasn't warmly welcomed by the Mormon church across the street from the campus, a point the Mormons made clear to the dean. But it might have been because of the Democratic Socialist Club I'd helped launch. Or maybe I just didn't belong.

But "mothering" and academia still don't belong together. And by mothering I don't mean only the work that women do with children. I mean any kind of caretaking, whether for children, for elderly or incapacitated loved ones, or for partners, whether gay or straight. Or for each other.

Unions have not made the work of care a priority benefit. But faculty and staff have sometimes found clever ways to accommodate the needs of personal life. Because paid leave is uncommon and often inadequate, they've pooled sick leave to allow a parent time off after a birth. Yet the principle has not been extended to adoptions or to elder care. Nor has it been made gender or sexual orientation neutral.

After 30 years of teaching, 23 of which I've spent in the oldest women's studies department in the country, I find myself asking the same questions we asked in the movement long ago: Can we combine intimacy with social action; can we integrate emotions and politics? Will we recognize that the demands of care still don't fit the clockworks of careers in the academy? And if these questions remain salient, then why don't we talk more publicly about the peculiar ways that caretaking engages us deeply and intimately in the business of what it means to be limited, to be human, to have a life and not just a career? I wonder what we are afraid to discover.

One thing I learned from my days near Camp LeJeune: The academy, especially as embodied by large research institutions, is like the Marines—if they wanted you to have a family and a personal life, they'd have issued you one.

REFERENCES

Firestone, S. (1970). *The dialectic of sex: The case for feminist revolution*. New York: Bantam Books.

Johnson, S. (1981). *From housewife to heretic*. New York: Doubleday.

19

Terms of Inclusion?
Rejecting the Role of "Honorary Man" in the Ivory Tower

Alison M. Thomas

In spite of all the fine rhetoric of equal opportunities, the opening up of higher education to women—who are today a highly visible presence on university campuses—has nevertheless occurred at minimal cost to the previously established patriarchal structures of the university system. The numbers of women entering higher education as undergraduates may have increased dramatically, but relatively few proceed to careers in academia, and of those who do, only a tiny proportion succeed in reaching the highest levels of the professoriat (Hague, 1999; Herbold, 1995; "Report," 2002). Men thus remain dominant in academia, even more than they do in most other professions (Stalker & Prentice, 1998). The most obvious reason why this is so is that universities have so far done little to accommodate to women: Rather, it has been for us to accommodate to the existing "ivory tower" culture.

Even today, universities continue to operate on the basis of a set of expectations about the role of the Scholar (generically male) that have hardly altered over several centuries and are thus clearly out of step with the massive social changes that have occurred over the past 40 years or more in the world beyond the portals of academia. The particular problem this presents for women is that the Scholar, traditionally remote from the everyday world in his ivory tower and thereby removed from its trivial distractions, is *still* expected to be free to commit himself totally to his field of study—irrespective of any other commitments he might have.

As I will argue in this essay, although the iconic figure of the Scholar may be perceived as a worthy role model for those male and female academics who have no children or other family responsibilities (or for those

who have partners willing to shoulder these for them), this kind of dedication to work is simply not compatible with maintaining other commitments—such as active involvement in "hands-on" parenting—and as such
is especially problematic for women academics who wish to have children.
The persistence of the "ivory tower scholar" as the one and only legitimate
role model available to us thus preserves a culture that makes universities
an inherently discriminatory environment for women.

Historically, at least, the Scholar's ability to prioritize his work in this
way was made possible by the domestic support work done by others, such
as female university staff and his wife or mother. Although many men may
still benefit from such support, far fewer aspiring female scholars have the
luxury of an equivalent level of behind-the-scenes assistance, and so this
model of academic scholarship is already less easily attainable for women
than for men. However, it is the decision to have children that has the
greatest impact in terms of differentiating the academic careers of women
and men. For although the career impact of having children has generally
been minimal for male academics (because child care either has been the
responsibility of their partner or has been bought from a nanny or other
child-care provider), women seldom shed their family responsibilities so
lightly—even when they can afford to delegate daytime child care to others.
We thus continue to bear more of the burden of raising a family than our
male counterparts (Vasil, 1993), and so it is not surprising to learn that although having children is generally associated with career success for men,
the same is not true for women (Miree & Frieze, 1999). In other words, the
career costs of having children fall disproportionately on women, not men,
in academia as elsewhere.

How, then, in the context of our contemporary awareness of the need
for equal opportunities, has this ivory tower culture been able to persist
unchallenged for so long? One reason, I suspect, is that its very dominance
means that those who publicly question it thereby risk exposing themselves
as less committed to making their scholarship the first priority in their lives.
As a consequence, academic women who struggle with the conflicts they
experience between work and family are more likely to leave academia than
to speak out for change (Herbold, 1995). This in itself helps explain how
universities have succeeded in reproducing this particular set of academic
values, generation by generation. Those women who succeed in academia
are generally those who have learned to accommodate to the system—in
many cases, by avoiding such conflicts altogether through choosing not to
have children at all. (Is it merely coincidence that women who succeed in

academia are much less likely to have children than their male counterparts [Hague, 1999]? I think not.)

Thus, both the men and the women who persist and succeed within the system and rise to its upper echelons have typically been socialized to respect and perpetuate the same values themselves. Indeed, in reflecting upon some of my own experiences within the ivory tower, both before and after having children, I will show how easily we can be drawn into reproducing this system of values ourselves.

MY INITIATION INTO THE PATRIARCHAL WORLD of academia in the mid-1970s was accompanied by an act of blatant discrimination when, as a politically naive 19-year-old, I was offered a place at one of the first co-educational colleges at Cambridge. A congratulatory letter from the (male) admissions tutor informed me that, had I been a man, I would have been awarded an entrance scholarship; however, college ordinances (established centuries before it was even conceivable that women should be educated alongside men, and therefore exempt from the terms of the Sex Discrimination Act) meant that as a woman I could not become a Scholar.

At the time I accepted this without question. Thrilled and a little overwhelmed to be given a place at Cambridge at all, I was too dazzled by this new environment to find fault with it: My feelings of pride at meriting such an award overcame any sense of injustice at being denied it merely on account of my gender. I had already in effect been socialized to feel gratitude for what privileges I had been granted, rather than resentment over what I was being denied. Indeed, as women in academia we experience many and frequent reminders that we are granted inclusion only on the condition that we display due loyalty—and that we do not draw attention to ourselves as women. We are expected to blend in with our surroundings and become "honorary men." We are not to make an issue of our difference.

This unwritten expectation was for me entirely compatible with my understanding of the goals of the "women's liberation" movement of the time—that is, demonstrating that we could do everything that men did. Being more a tomboy than a feminist at this stage in my life, I had not yet started to question the structural origins of gender inequalities but instead thrived on the challenge of being "one of the boys," both in intellect and in other domains, as a way of proving myself their equal. I took up rowing, training with weights at a time when it was still "unfeminine" to develop a muscled body, and I enjoyed the notoriety our rowing crew earned itself for daring to share the men's changing rooms and taking mixed showers—there being no facilities for women in the college boat-house in those days!

Although at that point in my life I had no problem seeing myself as an "honorary man," some years further on in my career I began to take a rather more critical view of my position as a woman in the patriarchal world of academia. Over a period of time in which the agenda of the women's movement was itself shifting (as we began to question the desirability of seeking equality by mimicking men), I slowly discovered for myself that the privileges of membership in this elite club might ultimately fail to compensate for the attendant liabilities—especially the career workaholism that accompanies the frenzied drive for academic productivity. However, this was something that crystallized for me only after several years of participating in the academic rat race myself, when one day I found myself involved in addressing the work-family conflicts of some of my students. It was this episode that led me—as a mother of two young children—to begin to question my own balancing of family and career and to ask myself whether the compromises I was making in my family life were justifiable.

BY THE TIME I BECAME A MOTHER, in my early 30s, I had a PhD and a tenured position at a London university, and I had in my own mind established a firm commitment to an academic career. Much to my mother's disappointment, it had never occurred to me to give this up to have children, and, insofar as I could envisage what was to come, I blithely assumed that becoming a mother would impinge only minimally on my professional role. In effect, I anticipated proceeding as before—in other words, continuing to follow the male career pattern of prioritizing my work. With hindsight, I realize that the almost complete invisibility of any kind of parenting activity at work, or even talk about family responsibilities—by male and female colleagues alike—probably contributed to my belief that combining motherhood and academic life would be unproblematic. At the time I did not question this: Insofar as I even registered the invisibility of family I interpreted it as confirmation of my expectations that work and family need not conflict with each other. (However, a rather different analysis makes more sense to me today—one that recognizes that there is simply no place for family in the academic world.)

For most of the first five years of my children's lives I strove hard to keep my work and my family life apart. Because my partner also had a time-consuming commitment to his job as a school teacher, we knew from the start that we would need help with child care. We were fortunate in finding a wonderful child-minder who looked after our twin children from breakfast time until 5 or 6 in the evening throughout their preschool years. Some days I didn't get home from London until after 7 P.M., and so on those days the amount of active parenting I did was negligible. As my husband taught in a boarding school that involved him in school activities all day on Saturdays, on those days it was he who saw very little of the children. We had both grown up in families in which our fathers' roles as family breadwinners made them largely absent from our day-to-day lives. This was something we both regretted, yet, during the school term at least, we were ourselves fast turning into a family with not one but two absentee breadwinner parents. In my case, the perceived urgency of the need to continue participating in the academic rat race was preventing me from even seeing, let alone questioning, what I was doing.

What opened my eyes to this was an incident involving some of the mature students I taught, who were themselves mothers of young school-age children. When my own children were still toddlers (at a time when I could have benefited from a reduction, rather than an increase, in my workload!), I had been given responsibility for organizing examinations for students within the sociology department. Intent primarily on avoiding timetable clashes, I ended up scheduling several exams for a week when the local elementary schools were due to have a mid-term break—without it even occurring to me that this might pose problems for students with school-age children. Some of my female students explained that they were unable to arrange child care for that period in order to free themselves to study for and attend their exams, and they asked me if it would be possible to alter the exam dates for that reason. The basis of their appeal to me was that as a mother myself I must surely be able to sympathize with their situation.

I was both shocked and ashamed to admit to myself that this was probably the first time I had actually been required to think of myself as a mother in that context. I was accustomed to the daily routine of leaving my children with their child-minder and with that—I now realized—temporarily setting aside all the mental "baggage" that accompanies motherhood. In effect, I went to work leaving my identity as a mother at home, and I now realized that I had come to expect my students to do the same. I began to be more aware of the extent to which I had taken for granted being able to rely on an excellent and reliable caregiver myself, whereas so many of my students, it appeared, struggled constantly to make adequate arrangements for the care of their children, with the perpetual worry that these would break down, leaving them unable to attend class. I began to see the hypocrisy of the university's professed commitment to welcoming mature students such as these while making almost no effort to respond to their particular needs, as it could have done, for example, by expanding the small and heavily oversubscribed day care available on campus. I also began to feel increasingly uncomfortable with my own role in this: I, too, had been expecting students to accommodate to often arbitrary university schedules in ways that took no account of possible family commitments and thereby once again rendered these invisible.

It was, therefore, with a considerable sense of satisfaction that I sat down the day after my meeting with the students and rewrote the exam timetable to avoid the half-term holiday week—and then wrote a memo to my colleagues explaining my reasons for making these changes. It represented one small gesture toward recognizing the validity of these students' other identities as mothers—an identity that each retains long after ceasing to be a university student—and to making their family commitments visible. I also began to rethink my own priorities: Did I want to continue denying my identity as a mother in order to emulate the scholarly ideals of the ivory tower academic? It was slowly dawning on me that all this time I had been putting work first—trying to keep my career "on track"—at the expense of valuing precious time with my children, which was already evaporating fast as they were growing up. I came to the realization that after years of accommodating to the "masculine" world of academia without even noticing it, I could no longer do so.

This was not the result of some sudden reawakening of any dormant maternal instincts but was prompted rather by my rediscovery of the research literature on work-family conflict. I already knew that the male breadwinner pattern of parenting—for so long unquestioned—is now recognized to be one with considerable costs for both men and their children (cf. Coltrane, 1996; Lewis & O'Brien, 1987), and for the first time I made the connection between this and my own experience. I realized that I did not want to carry on following the male career pattern and thus remain a somewhat distanced breadwinner parent, as my father was to me: I wanted to be a full participant, rather than a spectator, in my children's lives. More and more I began to balk at the idea that it is necessary for any of us (women or men) to compromise our relationship with our children for the sake of career success—even if generations of men have done just that.

So when we moved from Britain to Vancouver a year or two later, we took advantage of the opportunity to make a fresh start and made a conscious decision not to seek after-school child care, instead juggling our schedules so that one or the other of us would be home by midafternoon when our children returned from school. This was something that had symbolic as well as practical implications for us both: It represented making more of a commitment to being actively involved in our children's daily lives.

There are, of course, costs to such decisions. On the days when I am the one at home, it means that my working day is generally somewhat shorter than it would otherwise have been—or else is suspended for a period of six or seven hours and resumed only after the children have gone to bed. That can work for some administrative tasks or grading papers, but for me it is not readily compatible with writing. Indeed, it is the thinking and writing time, when one needs to be uninterrupted for hours (if not days) at a time, that generally becomes elusive once one has children. (A period of time spent away from my children on a research trip a few years ago reminded me that the working day can be at least 50% longer and 100% more productive when one has nobody to worry about feeding, transporting, or shepherding into bed but oneself!) So although I have never felt that setting aside time for my family has resulted in my neglecting any aspect of my teaching responsibilities, I am keenly aware that I might be accused of having neglected my research, because at this stage in my life I have certainly published less than many of my (child-free) peers. Yet does this mean that I have failed to show sufficient commitment to my work?

In the current academic climate, it is still our research output that counts the most, and when it is assessed for hiring, tenure, and promotion decisions the assessment is done on the general assumption that all that limits our productivity is individual ability and effort. Implicit in this assumption is the belief that we are all equally able to dedicate our every waking hour to our research, just like the archetypal Scholar of times past, secluded from the mundane cares and unnecessary distractions of the world in his (sic) ivory tower. Yet this simply does not correspond to the realities of life for those of us actively involved in nurturing a family as well as our career. In this respect universities are, in effect, failing to provide equal opportunities to parents (of both sexes), although this—as I argued earlier—most often has the effect of discriminating against women.

To be fair, in recent years many universities have made some efforts toward formally recognizing that having children can hold women back, most notably by agreeing to stop the tenure clock for one year for women who take that time as maternity leave. Yet this is hardly more than a token gesture because it does nothing to address the reality that even after returning to work, most of these mothers will continue to put more time into raising their children over a further 17 or more years of their lives than will their male counterparts (Nakhaie, 2002). Few academics confine their research activity to the hours of the conventional working week, and it is the "after-hours" research time in evenings and at weekends that is largely lost by those who have children and choose to invest time in their relationship with them, rather than in their research output. This is something that needs to be recognized, because it will in most cases continue to contribute to productivity differences between men and women (and between women with and without children) over a far longer period of their academic careers than just a child's first year of life.

What, then, can be done to make universities more responsive to the needs of those with family commitments—and thus to make them more accommodating to women? Clearly, there are various practical steps that could be taken that would make things easier for both students and faculty members alike, such as improving the availability and affordability of on-campus child-care facilities for those with younger children. Just as important, however, would be a general reappraisal of the consequences of academic culture's tendency to render people's family commitments invisible; in particular, some acknowledgment that active parenting requires time and effort might help university managers to understand that those attempting to combine academic study with parenting (whether students or faculty) generally need more time to attain the same level than those who do not have such responsibilities. In the case of faculty seeking tenure or promotion, an editorial in the *Times Higher Education Supplement* ("Editorial," 1999) thus urged against penalizing people who take longer to reach "standard" publication thresholds at specific stages of their careers—and also recommended that more attention be paid to the quality rather than just the quantity of publications.

I would therefore suggest that it is time for a major reappraisal of the contemporary relevance of the role of the ivory tower Scholar. Few of us today (female or male) live in circumstances that permit us to withdraw from everyday life in pursuit of academic excellence. Recognizing and allowing for the importance of people's other commitments—whether these include responsibility for children, as I have explored here, or (increasingly) for aging parents—would bring universities in line with other more forward-thinking employers. Insofar as that might mean a lessening of pressure on faculty members to maintain a perpetual flow of research publications, that in itself could be an opportunity for us to reassess the balance between quality and quantity—and maybe to move toward placing greater emphasis on the former. Equally, it might provide a worthwhile opportunity to rethink the importance we should be attaching to teaching: For even if those of us who are putting time and energy into parenting do not top the productivity rankings during that period of our career, does that so irreparably diminish the contribution we make to academic life? Surely it does so only if one accepts "research output" as the sole yardstick of our academic worth, disregarding the equally important work of teaching that we do.

TO CONCLUDE, IN THIS ESSAY I have drawn upon my own experiences to show that as women we have generally been allowed into academia only on the condition that we act as "honorary men" and do not draw attention to our differences. For those women who do not have children this may be unproblematic, as it was once for me. However, anyone (woman or man) who chooses to have children and who seeks to be a participant, rather than a spectator, in their children's lives will soon discover that this is not easily compatible with the expectations of academic commitment that have been socialized into us. Universities make few real concessions to the importance of active parenting: If men are not expected to let parenthood get in the way of their productivity, neither are women, once their maternity leave is over and the tenure clock resumes its ticking. It is therefore apparent that changes of the kind needed to address this problem go well beyond what most equal-opportunity policies currently offer. If we want universities to start to accommodate to women—rather than vice versa— we need at this juncture to challenge the very foundations of the ivory tower culture and, in particular, its assumption that only those who dedicate themselves totally to their scholarship are capable of making a worthwhile contribution to academic life.

REFERENCES

Coltrane, S. (1996). *Family man: Fatherhood, housework, and gender equity.* New York: Oxford University Press.

Editorial. (1999, May 28). *Times Higher Education Supplement,* p. 16.

Hague, H. (1999, May 28). 9.2% of professors are women. *Times Higher Education Supplement,* pp. 20–21.

Herbold, H. (1995). Women who leave: Why women professors are cutting their ties to academia. *Monthly Forum on Women in Higher Education, 1*(2), 25–29.

Lewis, C., & O'Brien, M. (Eds.). (1987). *Reassessing fatherhood.* Buckingham: Open University Press.

Miree, C., & Frieze, I. (1999). Children and careers: A longitudinal study of the impact of young children on critical career outcomes of MBAs. *Sex Roles, 41,* 787–808.

Nakhaie, M. R. (2002). Gender differences in publication among university professors in Canada. *Canadian Review of Sociology and Anthropology, 39,* 151–179.

Report links family with career path. (2002, April). *CAUT Bulletin,* p. A12.

Stalker, J., & Prentice, S. (1998). *Illusion of inclusion: Women in post-secondary education.* Halifax, Nova Scotia: Fernwood.

Vasil, L. (1993). Gender differences in the academic career in New Zealand universities. *New Zealand Journal of Educational Studies, 28,* 143–153.

20

Through Foreign Eyes: Adoption Angles and Maternity-Leave Suggestions

Christina Brantner

I

First and foremost, I am a happily obsessed mother of two—not atypical among older and intellectual types. I am also single by choice, German by birth, part of a mixed-race family through life's interesting turns (my two adopted sons are African American), and, based on my university position, a resident alien (I could go on and on about being a quirky alien, but that's best left for another essay). And I'd like to stress one significant element in this puzzle right from the start: Without the flexibility of an academic schedule, it would have been nearly impossible for me to both continue a rewarding professional and international life (living months on end in Germany) and spend lots of formative baby time (plus now preschool time) with my sons. So I am *very grateful* to academia. Nonetheless, there are still countless ways to help the typical university environment grow into a more family-friendly one. And this is precisely what inspired me to contribute to this volume, because over my 20 years in academia I have observed far too many incidents of "antifamily" structures and acts. It is not enough to have a "family leave" policy at any given academic institution, although it is a necessary first step. For any reader contemplating a parental leave in the future, I hope to provide a model or two that go beyond the individual and anecdotal. My experiences with the "powers that be" were unique, frustrating, funny, and—in the end—supportive, which I hope will make this an interesting narrative. I mainly hope to show elements any new academic-parent-to-be could use to plan for a smoother transition from a more traditionally male academic role to a more inclusive one.

II

I am a literary scholar, not a sociologist, but one cannot help but notice that most American colleges and universities are run predominantly by men and are thus strictly hierarchical and based on the male life cycle[1] (this male life cycle means not only the supportive wife who cooks meals and cleans house for the professor husband, but it also means that the most vigorous research output is supposed to appear during what are a woman's best reproductive years). Thus, a nurturing climate for beings other than the traditional male[2] is by definition not part of the structures of this type of institution. And a propos male structures: They certainly are much worse in the German university system I came from—however, in their "benign paternity," German academics had to follow the federal directives allowing for a three-year unpaid maternity leave per child (which can be staggered with an additional child). If the husband's income alone is insufficient to feed the family, the German state extends a helping hand and supports the family for that time, and a woman's job is guaranteed by law once she comes back into the academic working world.

III

All of my thinking life, I have been a literary consumer and critic, devouring books, critiquing them, seducing other people to fall in love with them the way I did: a natural teacher of literature, I think. So it is no surprise that teaching German (women's) literature in German or translation and working on committees to foster the best environment to do that, I lived and breathed my dream "job" almost 24/7 (goodness, to be paid to do things you love!!). Work then was as much "work" for me as swimming around is for a fish in the water. Upon entering academia I found a home and a persona that felt natural and instinctively comfortable. The academic home stays the same after you become a mother, but the persona does not. And at first I did not even notice it. From the very beginning, colleagues' or superiors' views of you change. They suspect you are no longer the research or teaching machine you once were—that is, if you are a woman; I have not noticed this change of expectations for my male colleagues. But even within yourself, things change drastically: Maybe it was during the few moments of sleep I got in the first months with Benjamin that my subconscious rearranged my life's priorities. I confess I no longer make weekend or evening trips to campus to "finish up some work." I always had troubles with Thomas Mann and the like for their wordy (600-plus-page) novels and haven't finished a single such one in three years.

I was unprepared for the total makeover that my professional persona seems to have undergone without my consciously shaping it. And I am still in the process of finding out how much it has changed. This is *not* to say that things academic have become irrelevant. They just have lost the first and maybe even second ranking in my priorities. And the "motherly" new parts have not simply pushed the academic elements away. Somehow the new concerns and interests have grown into the old ones and helped them bloom in new ways: I do think that I look at my young college kids in the study abroad program in Berlin with different eyes. That might be more obvious. Less obvious maybe is my new strictness on sticking to my own classroom rules, when in earlier years I would have bent my rules all over the place: If my toddler gets a time-out for yanking the cat's tail (no discussion and no reneging), then the college student gets an F for a late paper (no discussion and no reneging). Do I think I am a better teacher since becoming a mother? As I always tell my students before going abroad, *better* is such a relative term. I have, for sure, become a different teacher. And whereas other teachers might arrive at a changed persona via a different route, motherhood is the one for me. I do think I am enforcing rules more strictly, but I also allow room for failure. I am available for help, but it takes two to tango. And lastly, the time a person spends learning in a college or university is not the be-all and end-all: It is terribly important as a choice to be offered, but opting for a different route can be all right, too.

IV

Adoption and the (academic) bureaucracy: When I started looking into the possible adoption of a domestic newborn in the late 1990s, adoption, if mentioned at all in what now would most likely be called a "family leave policy," was relegated to the same terms a biological father could get: a week or two off, if his wife had just given birth and was unable to care for the newborn right away. No awareness yet concerning the amount of time it takes for both newborns and older, foreign-born children to overcome the separation from their biological mothers or from different cultural and language surroundings. And no awareness of the adoptive parent's need for time to adjust—like any new parent. The federal regulations regarding adoptive leaves were in place years before most universities caught up. In my case, the University of Nebraska approved an "expanded adoption leave policy" in November 1999, in order to "bring university policy into compliance with state law" ("Regents approve"). This was 22 months after I had adopted my oldest son. Looking back at those months almost four years later, it is interesting to note how very excited members of my academic community were about my adoption and how unexciting the "system" actually made it for me, who like any new parent had not slept through a single night for many weeks.

When I had to make arrangements with staff and professorial colleagues, be it for insurance purposes, reassigning classes, or taking out a loan, many of them came out with adoption stories themselves, from siblings, from cousins, and often from themselves! I never knew just how many of the people I have regular dealings with are adopted and quite excited to share that story with an appreciative person. Without the flexibility of the professorial workload, a very supportive female chair of modern languages, equally supportive (female and male) colleagues in the German section, and of course the sisterhood of women's studies, I would not have been able to step out of my teaching and some administrative duties at all. Nevertheless, the unofficial and official "blessings" of my "adoptive leave" were months apart: Benjamin was born on January 2, 1999. I accepted him January 6 and flew to Mississippi to get him January 11, the exact day classes started and I was supposed to be in the classroom. My chair in modern languages and my colleagues in women's studies "reassigned" my duties as of that day—but official recognition through the dean's office (that particular dean has since left) did not come until May (!) 1999, about a week before the semester ended.

Three years later, almost to the day, my second son, Nikolas, came into my life in 2002. His birth mother, however, was able to do some longer-term planning, so I was able to get adoptive leave arrangements started a month before his arrival, fortunately again at the beginning of a spring semester. This time around, a decent enough policy (www.unl.edu/svcaa/hr/parentalleave.html) was in place, *and* I did not hold any administrative appointment. This helped, even with a new chair and dean who speedily figured out the "tail end" of the 12 weeks possible leave policy, giving me extra weeks of leave in order to avoid the ludicrous situation of me dancing into the classroom in week 13 and giving final grades in week 15 of the semester. In hindsight, the funniest moments were an exchange of e-mails between a higher administrator and me regarding this "adoptive leave" that I could take, he said, for eight weeks, unpaid of course. I shot back right away pointing out that I had only a single income, was not independently wealthy, and had not won the lottery lately, thus I needed, of course, a *paid* leave. Details, details—but boy, if you don't pay attention to them! This second time around, I again kept the nonteaching parts of my job, such as being the undergraduate adviser and overseeing the administration of the German study abroad program. But the main relief was the leave from teaching, especially since Nikolas was a very sick child in the first three months of his life.

V

White mother adopting two full African American (in adoption lingo that means both biological parents identified themselves as African American) sons: Interestingly, this is a "nonissue" in a lily-white town (Lincoln is 6.9% African American according to Census 2000) in the Midwest and at an institution reflecting this (Fall 2001: 2.3% African American faculty, 2.4% staff, 2.1% students). At first sight, my academic circles seem to be color blind, and whether that is "good" or "bad" could be another discussion. It is this liberal idea of "let everyone do his/her own thing." There were no white colleagues warning me about what it means to be a racially mixed family. And there were no questions from black colleagues about how I would (or even could!) try to preserve an African American heritage beyond taking the boys to the university's very inclusive Kwanzaa celebration.

As an academic, of course, I tried to tackle the mixed-race family issue first by reading up on it. As a German fully and especially aware of my country's Nazi past, I had to get used to, even physically, putting the word *race* in my mouth and uttering it. Neutrally. And then applying it in a regular, matter-of-fact way, to my new family. The psychological and sociological literature on how children—especially adopted children—of such families succeed in society seems not to show one clear path to be followed. Academics, lore has it, can't ever agree on anything, which is fine if one wants to be entertained in an abstract way. But if you look for clear instructions, good luck! Responsible adoption agencies do their best to screen parents and get them thinking about how this racial mix will affect the parent's and the child's future: to start thinking about how you as a mother will deal with an insulting racial remark in front of your child, or how you could preserve some of the child's heritage, such as by moving to a more diverse neighborhood. They might encourage you to weigh whether it would be better for the child to be in a financially better-funded "white" school or a poor "black" school, and whether you should change to or join a predominantly black church.

But even the best agency just gets you started thinking—they are in the business of placing children, not helping adoptive parents graduate with honors. So, you are on your own. And I have no answers of course, either. Not even a clear path in front of me. The path is still evolving, and once the baby is bigger and I have more time to read more articles it will no doubt shift further. But for right now I'm realizing the following plan: We will stay in this low-crime, predominantly white neighborhood because the school districts put the boys into academically excellent elementary and middle schools (very white) and then the city's most integrated high school, which is also academically very good. Thus in schooling I place the academic factor over the race factor. But I try to integrate the boys by attending a predominantly black church that is also politically active. However, because the older child speaks German as his main language and his English is a very distant second right now, I am waiting another year or so before integrating us regularly into that church so that Benjamin's English skills will be up to his full command. Our family will always be a curious one, I assume. We live long chunks of time abroad (sometimes summers, sometimes whole semesters). In addition, the boys will be bicultural and bilingual, will be academically nurtured, and will be raised by a single mother. We are creating our own path every day.

VI. First Action Model for Future Parent

Background: In the 1996 to 1997 academic year I became the one-year interim director of the University of Nebraska's Women's Studies Program. It was solely an undergraduate program with 30-some faculty teaching classes from a variety of disciplines: English literature, sociology, business, and beyond. The program had no tenured lines; all classes were taught either as overloads or as part of a departmental curriculum. Thus, I had done my apprenticeship when I got the job as program director for the five-year term in the fall of 1998, and my colleagues knew full well that I was in the waiting phase to adopt a child. "On the side," of course, I continued my regular load in the modern languages department and as director of the German study abroad program in Berlin, mainly recruiting students, training the new resident director of the upcoming year, and fighting the credit transfer battle at the end of each summer. I had my hands happily full that fall, putting in my usual 100-hour workweeks. Then, during the winter break when I was in Germany, I got *the* call: "Congratulations, you have a son in Mississippi to pick up ASAP."

A crazy-happy whirlwind came after that, and when most of the dust had settled, or so I thought, I was blessed with the cutest baby on earth, sleepless nights, and two and a half jobs. The department of modern languages relieved me of my teaching immediately, which was a great help, but they made it contingent on the women's studies department relieving me of all my duties there as well. I will spare you the months of administrative bean-counting quibbling from higher levels. The outcome was that I kept my student advising duties, taught a Business German class at home once a week, and continued to manage the study abroad in the German section. In women's studies, the advisory committee to the director and I had come up with a plan. At first we tried to get the dean of Arts and Sciences to realize that this was an emergency situation in a great program that needed immediate help and that he should hire an assistant director to keep the program going for one semester. This could have been done via a course buyout, costing at the most $1,500 for one of my colleagues to take on the directorship without working on an overload. My suggestions were met with outright laughter.

When members of the program talked to the senior vice chancellor in private, he promised he would help solve the situation equitably. For weeks, the dean and vice chancellor batted ideas back and forth. Later, we learned that the dean kept the problem "under consideration" and the vice chancellor could not initiate anything from his level (talk about useless male structures!). This official inattention to our problem forced us to solve it internally: We divided the work for the semester among Women's Studies Advisory Committee members. The main office, two graduate students, the secretary, and a work-study person handled the basic advising questions and sent the more detailed advising questions to me at home via e-mail. I met personally with students who needed more specific academic input. Furthermore, a colleague signed official business things that needed to be done "yesterday" and couldn't wait for me to come to campus a day or two later, and another colleague represented the Women's Studies Program on official university-wide committees. I continued to direct the weekly staff meetings, answer the frequent calls of the press, and meet with students at the university at least five to seven hours per week. My colleagues even bought a portable crib so I could have the baby with me in the office. And seeing me juggling all this, an undergraduate student in the program volunteered to entertain baby Benjamin for however many hours I needed per week to do women's studies business; Tina Gianbastiani even refused any pay! Although the official university structures proved largely incompatible with developing a modern family life, I was relieved and grateful that the individuals in my department and program turned out to be extremely supportive.

In the end, I think one can discern an outline of a model from this case that can work anywhere, providing that a couple of elements are in place. If colleagues are willing to help out for the good of the program, if the work to be distributed can be parceled out in small enough chunks so as not to overpower any single individual, and if students do their share, both the new family and the academic program can survive and even thrive. All of this, however, is unlikely to receive the explicit blessing of higher administration and has to be worked out, practically speaking, behind the scenes. Furthermore, if pregnant, one can work out a plan well ahead of time, get needed signatures and authorizations, and organize the smallest details so that one is comfortable with the arrangements. The trouble with adoption is, of course, that you cannot put any timetable on your plans. But go right ahead and spell them out in one of those "undated" planners, even if it involves five different scenarios. You will be happy you did it, because when the adoption happens, it still carries the element of surprise and a feeling of being unprepared. Thus, it is good to fall back on some thoroughly researched plans before you enter the sleepless night zone (besides, planning keeps you busy while you are waiting for the child).

Why do I recommend the above model when it didn't quite work out for me? Honestly, I do not think any person—even supermom or superdad—will be able to perform at the 100% job level they did before having a child, much less at the 250% level that I had tried to accomplish. So, if one is part of "only" one academic unit, that's where I can see the model being effective. It might even work for two units *if* you need less than (a combined) six hours sleep per night *and* don't mind handing your baby/child over to day care for 8 to 10 hours per (work)day. I was just not willing to sleep so little and hand my miraculous baby to anyone (except for Tina sometimes and close by) for any extended period of time.

VII. Second Model for Future Parent

Background: From January to July 2001 I led a study abroad group from the University of Nebraska–Lincoln on our Berlin program. Students took morning classes at a wonderful language institute, Deutsch-in-Deutschland-Berlin-Institute, while living with host families mainly in eastern Berlin. My role as resident director, besides being "mom away from home" to 15 more or less mature college students, was teaching two classes two afternoons per week plus countless opera and museum visits. All of this with a two-year-old in tow. And because Benjamin was attending a public day care for the first time, he was sick a lot, with high fevers and ear infections galore. So he needed to stay home a lot—when I had to be out teaching. Not having a family or any such support system in Berlin (and not being independently wealthy to pay for nanny services), I needed to enlist my students for help, and they very gladly cooperated. For museum visits we came up with a good pedagogical scheme: Teams of two (a language beginner and a more advanced student) would scout out an assigned museum and summarize (in writing to me) a tour to be given in German to the entire group. With my corrections, add-ons, and final blessings, the entire group then visited said museum, and the group wrote critiques of the given tour plus suggestions for improvement. It worked like magic! Thus the nearly 20 museum visits were covered in a pedagogically sound and effective way without my presence necessary most of the time.

And then there was the actual class time two afternoons a week. If Benjamin's illness started early enough in the week, I could call all students and move the class to a different afternoon. If, however, it was a sudden onset, I would call one student to take the tram to my apartment and stay with Benjamin that afternoon while I taught regular class, then come home and summarize it for the babysitting student over dinner. While it sounds like a hassle, it really was not.

So, how do you transfer this model onto a regular campus in the United States? Granted, on study abroad missions everyone is more flexible and creative because everyone is "on foreign turf" so to speak. However, in programs or departments small enough to have a close-knit community of teachers and students, I am convinced this can be done in the United States as well. Some topics could be addressed more effectively through group work or outings rather than during a physical class contact hour. And some smaller upper-level classes could well be held at a professor's home while a baby is in a crib or a toddler is playing around (this seems more practical than schlepping the kid[s] to a play-unfriendly classroom). Actually, I did this with a Business German class in the spring of 1999. I knew all but one of the eight students from previous semesters, so I felt comfortable asking them if they would be willing to meet off campus—and they trusted me that if they were unwilling, I would in no way "retaliate." We met once a week, and they submitted their homework via e-mail and carpooled to my house (some lived in campus dorms and did not have cars). I think it was one of the best Business German classes because they got to know the private side of their professor, they laughed about my monstrous cats' antics, and the baby enlivened an otherwise often rather stuffy class.

VIII. Action List for a Parent-To-Be (Adoptive and Biological)

Once you are certain that you are pregnant or have been accepted by an adoption agency via a completed home study, you start preparing for your maternity semester immediately, or at least next week. Here is a checklist for you to start with and amend:

- Read up on the Family Medical Leave Act of 1993 and get a copy.
- Check your university or college's policy on maternity/adoptive leave and make a copy for yourself and your chair.
- Invite your favorite colleagues for a cup of coffee and invite them to brainstorm with you about how your duties could be covered during your leave. If your unit is too small or tense, do the brainstorming with your chair. If that's not feasible, find a local AAUP member or a friendly women's studies colleague.
- Talk to other female colleagues with kids about how their department handled their leave: You'll be amazed how different those stories will be! If there is a Committee W of your local AAUP (a committee on the status of women), see whether they have done a report or study on that topic at your institution in the last 10 years; if so, get a copy.
- Depending on how experienced your chair is, try to make sure that your dean is in the know and supportive as well.
- If you are still on the tenure track, read up on the implications of having your tenure clock stopped and discuss this with a local AAUP person.
- If you have to or want to keep certain job duties during your leave, arrange for those that can be done with few meetings and via Internet.
- Once the arrangements for coverage of your duties are made (in

writing, please), talk to your majors at a regular meeting about why you will fade into the background for a while, and tell them you'd appreciate their support (not babysitting just yet, but fewer trips for you to the office once the child is there, dissertation chapters delivered to your house, etc.). If you need to do advising or even teach a class at your house or somewhere off campus, do check with your institution's legal department on the legality of this and how to protect yourself.

- Try to get just one more article sent out to be published than you had previously planned.
- If you often attend conferences, look at how many of those trips are necessary and how you would provide for baby next time.
- If you plan to bring baby to campus a lot while on leave or during the next semester (because of your lab research or such), rearrange your office or lab before the child's arrival so you have a safe corner for a portable crib.
- In the case of an adoption, talk to your health care provider *and* your local benefits office about when exactly coverage starts for baby—and get it in writing!
- Look around and find another mother/father fellow academic you admire and can emulate—and talk things over with her or him once the juggling of private and academic issues starts.
- Arrange for child care for the time after your leave.
- Once your maternity time starts, stick to the plan and don't let people renegotiate your duties.

IX

Current state of affairs in the fall of 2002 and outlook: Academia in general allows me the flexibility to be a relatively effective working mother under the circumstances. During a research semester such as this one, when the baby gets a virus for three days and needs to be "worn" by Mom, I can afford to do this and still catch up with my writing in the following week and not get behind schedule too much (what the kitchen looks like or the kids' rooms, that's really nobody's business). I am able to complete six solid hours of researching per day, and I am also on the road for two hours each day. This is a tad unusual for Lincoln, Nebraska, but the Montessori preschool/elementary school Benjamin attends is worth the extra effort, and Nikolas's nanny does not come to our house—instead, I take him to her nephew's house, which is not quite on the way to Benjamin's school. I have the usual juggling problems most working mothers do: Getting up at 6:30 A.M. and leaving the house by 8 A.M. gives me very little time with the boys in the morning. And their sleep needs are still such that when we get home around 5 P.M., the baby often wails for bed around 6 P.M., and Benjamin's bedtime starts around 7 P.M. (with books read, stories told, and songs sung it takes about 45 minutes). As an adoring mother I crave more time with them—but that does not seem possible right now. Still, I struggle with it. On a final note: In spite of some struggles, for me, single mother-hood within academia is very doable. I just wish I had had some sort of a list like the one I tried to put together in section VIII so I would have saved myself from some detours. Planning your work life for the time of "being with child" really pays off, especially if you stick to the conditions that free you up, keeping you home and with the new child.

NOTES

1. I am limiting myself to writing exclusively about the professorial side within academia; for (female) support staff none of the flexibility and few of the other "perks" are to be found. Female administrators seem to get into these positions later in life but would be in between the professors and the staff folks in the difficulties arranging their lives as mothers and professionals.
2. There are enough women in academia who internalized these male structures to such a degree that in order to become very successful they "out-maled" the males.

REFERENCE

Regents approve expanded adoption leave policy. (2000, November 2). *The Scarlet*, p. 3. Retrieved June 23, 2004, from www.unl.edu/scarlet/v10n29/v10n29nibs. html

21

Mothers and "Others" Providing Care Within and Outside of the Academy

Gayle Letherby, Jen Marchbank,
Karen Ramsay, and John Shiels

Introduction to the Authors

We are four British academics who are connected to each other in various ways. Gayle and John are partners; Jen, Gayle, and John are friends, as are Karen, Gayle, and John. Karen and Gayle once shared an office, as did Jen and Gayle in another institution. Although we have varied academic backgrounds (Gayle is a sociologist, Jen a political scientist, Karen a specialist in organizational studies, and John a sociologist specializing in criminology), we share a commitment to feminist politics. We also have varied connections as regards our research and writing interests: Gayle and Jen have written together about staff/student relationships and have conducted research on student experience; Gayle and Karen have performed research on managing nonmotherhood[1] and academic life; and Gayle and John have written an autobiographical piece on the gendered expectations of students. With respect to "mothering" outside of the academy our relationships are varied, too. John is a father of two who was given custody of his boys when his relationship with their mother ended 11 years ago; Karen is childless but recently spent much time caring for her mother; Jen is a single lesbian mother and has also been a foster parent; and Gayle is biologically childless but for the last 10 years has cared for John's sons.

Introduction to Issues and Approach

The focus of the increasing collection of work regarding the gendered aspects of academia has been not only on the differences in experience based on gender but also on the differences among and between women. In addition, there has also been attention paid to the issues of managing motherhood and work (e.g., Leonard & Malina, 1994; Munn-Giddings, 1998). As Leonard and Malina argue, there is a tension between roles at home and at work, one that is shaped by the ideological dichotomy between "altruistic mother" and "career woman." Leonard and Malina also highlight the ways in which both the family and academy are "greedy institutions"; that is, they are both places that require women to be constantly available and committed and where women are expected to cater to all the physical and emotional needs of others. In a parallel area, Munn-Giddings discusses the manner in which the notion of the "biological clock" conflicts and corresponds with the "career clock." Interestingly, Munn-Giddings argues that mothers within academia are more likely to receive support from other mothers, with nonmothers being less sympathetic, the evidence for which comes from her own experience.

Whereas we are happy to concur with many of the points made by Munn-Giddings (1998) and others regarding motherhood and work in higher education (e.g., David, Davies, Edwards, Reay, & Standing, 1996; Raddon, 2001), we remain concerned with the separation of women into "mothers" and "others," especially as it seems to be focused upon biological notions of both (Ramsay & Letherby, in press).

In this essay we seek to expand the discussion of motherhood, caring, and working within higher education to address the significant issues for women, men, parents, and nonparents. We believe that, from our personal experiences, it is possible to elucidate some broader lessons. As such, in the remainder of this essay we self-consciously draw on work we have done together, separately, and with others in the past. This work provides aspects not only of our knowledge creation but also of our own auto/duo/multiple/biographies and not only tells part of our chronological life history but also illustrates other elements of our intellectual autobiographies.

Personal Stories

In this explicitly autobiographical section, we each detail aspects of our life stories.

Jen

Since 1996 I have had a number of different experiences related to the competing requirements of work and care. First, I moved in with my (then) partner, who had only recently been diagnosed with two chronic, painful, and potentially life-threatening medical conditions. In this context, although she was and is self-supporting, I remained a day-to-day carer, and I had to balance work with such support, especially during frequent hospitalizations and periods of convalescence at home. Throughout, I would say that our relationship remained one of equals, yet there were definitely times when my share of domestic duties was vastly increased as well as times when psychological support was needed. Fortunately, this was more easily achievable in academia than in other professions.

My second experience of care was a period of a year when we fostered my partner's teenage niece. Very few people were aware I had care of a child, let alone one with educational difficulties and social needs. In fact, to this day, several years after this arrangement ended, very few people outside of friends and family are aware that this has been part of my life (and remains an important relationship—I've just become a foster granny!!!).

My current care responsibilities began in October 2000 when I gave birth to my son. This has had several implications for work, the most obvious being that my workday has become much more structured and constrained, because I am now a single parent. Interestingly, but not surprisingly, my status as a biological mother has masked my identity as a lesbian, and it has meant that other staff with child-care responsibilities (now or previously in their lives) include me as a member of their "club" in ways that I was never included as a nonmother.

As at least half of my work life to date has been without caring responsibilities, I feel that I am in the position to reflect on the subtle and not-so-subtle distinctions made at work. In some instances my "new" (biological) parenting responsibilities give me a "green light" to structure my work in ways that my first two experiences did not. Conversely, having spent so much time as one of the women deemed to have no responsibilities, I am very aware of the additional load this can create for nonmothers within academia (Ramsay & Letherby, in press). As such I am loath (as Munn-Giddings, 1998, reports) to use my responsibilities as an explanation for, say, requesting that meetings end prior to 5:30 P.M., for I am conscious that I will be perceived by some as not committed to my job and by others as "making excuses" not available to them and thus increasing their workload. It may be ironic that as a non(biological)mother, but as a foster mother and partner of a disabled person, I supported my colleagues who had caring roles, yet I am wary of assuming that others will be willing to provide that same support for me.

John

I became a single parent about 12 years ago, when my then wife and I split up. I had "custody" of our two sons. The emotional difficulties I needn't go into, although in different ways we all shared them and they have had a lasting effect. The practicalities of school, work, and food were the basic problems facing me. As a single parent, I had to organize my life and theirs in a much more thoughtful and preplanned way than I had done before. "Keeping up" with work in the areas I was teaching and researching had to compete with washing, ironing, cooking, housework, and so on.

In a sense, these immediate, practical problems made it more difficult to cement or maintain emotional ties, which, to me, were all-important and the reason why I wanted the kids in the first place. I can't say that I ever resented my situation, but I certainly regretted some aspects of it at times.

The ways in which other people responded to me were interesting, sociologically. First, there was an assumption that my ex-wife would have custody (predicated on the dominant mores of this culture and on the statistical realities of separation and caring). Also, and relatedly, there were doubts about whether a man could "mother" adolescent or preadolescent children adequately—the answer, of course, is no, but as hardly anyone ever meets the parenting ideal this makes me little different from all other mothers and fathers. Gendered expectations and assumptions stick in the strangest places. On reflection, of course, there is nothing strange about it, because gender—and the expectations and requirements associated with it—structures our lives as much as social class, ethnicity, sexuality, or age.

As far as the single male parent factor goes, that didn't last for long. Some months after the breakup of my marriage, I "met" Gayle, and we became partners. This, predictably, raised other problems—for all of us—not least because Gayle undertook some of the caring responsibilities in our new family.

The fact of being a single parent (or virtually a single parent, because their mother was always in touch and cared for them) is not at all unusual, but that, and the fact of having another partner who cares and provides for them, raises interesting issues about what *family* means.

Gayle

Twenty years ago when I was a married day-care worker working with small children, my main ambition in life was to become a mother, and I felt that I was only half a woman without a child. Any doubts I had concerning motherhood I denied. A miscarriage in 1985 added to my distress and sense of failure. I decided against pursuing pregnancy via medical assistance. By the time I started work on my doctorate (an exploration of the medical, social, and emotional experience—predominantly women's—of "infertility" and "involuntary childlessness"[2]) 14 years ago, my feelings were different. Although I still felt the desire for motherhood and felt a gap in my life, this issue did not dominate my every thought and action, as it had earlier. I no longer felt that I was a lesser woman or less than adult for not mothering children. I was also able to accept the equivocal nature of my desires. A part of me enjoyed the freedom I had because of my "childlessness," and I felt sure that if I did become a mother, I would feel opposing emotions in relation to that experience also. In the interim, I had also developed warm relationships with the children of several close friends through staying with and visiting them and their parents.

During my fieldwork, when asked about my hopes for the future, I sometimes said that I felt I still had plenty of time. Now several years on, at the age of 45 I find myself in the same position as Joanne Sundby (1999): "Sad not to have children, happy to be childless" (p. 13). I quite regularly feel distressed by the insensitivity of others who, if they don't know me very well, assume that I do have children or, if they do know me, assume that I know nothing about children and child care because I don't have children. A major (relevant) change in my life is my relationship with John's two sons (now aged 23 and 26). Although I would not describe myself as a mother, I do have parental relationships with them. Consequently, when asked if I have children, I sometimes feel that it is appropriate to say yes. Also, there are times now when I am an active participant in, or even initiate, a conversation about "troubled" and "troublesome" youth. These changes have made my daily experience both more comfortable and more challenging and have caused me to rethink my desire for a biological child. I no longer feel that I "need" children—I am confident that I would never go for "infertility" treatment, and I never use the word *cope* anymore. I appreciate that some people may interpret this as a rejection of motherhood, but in fact, it is far from that. As we think these accounts show, there are varieties of parenting and of relationships that are analogous or comparable.

Karen

My identity as a nonmother is a matter of choice: In my teens and 20s I actively prevented and terminated pregnancies, and for much of my 30s I identified as celibate. Now in my 40s, I am ambivalent about my identity as a nonmother, but I enjoy the freedoms that my choices have brought me. One aspect of this freedom is the time to reflect on the choices I have made.

My intellectual interests were shaped initially by a rejection in my teens and early 20s of my mother's choices to marry and bear children. At the same time, I identified with her and other women around me in terms of my lack of interest in formal education and the type of work I accepted: retail, service, and caring work. I returned to education as a mature student at 26, having 10 years' experience of "women's work" and a determination to do more with my life. My first degree, in organization studies, introduced me to women's studies, and I found my intellectual home in the interface of gender and organization. I furthered this interest in my MPhil thesis, which explored equal opportunity practice in academia. My main interests centered on women's experiences in paid employment, and I paid little attention to domesticity, the family, or motherhood.

Thus, the way that I "did" feminism in my 30s was very much in the public spaces of organizations, employment, pubs, and cafés. When Gayle and I met as postgraduates, we shared many of these interests and appreciated each other's different research topics. Although our research topics were very different to begin with, these individual topics have been intersubjectively shaped over the years by our friendship and our working relationship.

Up until my mid-30s I was able to act on my perception of myself as a career-oriented woman. The death of my father and later my mother's illness and death changed much of this. I lived in Bradford, but my parents had moved up to Scotland to be closer to other members of the family, and our distance necessitated long train and bus journeys for me to visit them. I began to reflect on my developing role as a carer. As a single woman with no children, I was viewed by some as available to care full time for my mother. I was not prepared to move to Scotland to do this, but I did want to be involved in the care of my mother. I eventually reached the hard compromise of regularly traveling to and from Scotland and negotiating care of my mother with other family members in Scotland and with social services and nursing staff.

The main issue that came out of this experience was that I acknowledged my own need to work and to have a clear and separate identity from a "family" (my parents or my own children). I experienced family life as all-consuming and desired a separate space for myself. At that time, my passion for my teaching and academic work gave me such an identity. Now, several years after my mother's death, I see myself disengaging from academia and less willing to make the sacrifices I see as necessary to have an organizational career. I want to be liberated from a full-time career, and although I recognize that I greatly benefit from the privilege of having such a career, to me, academia seems to be as "greedy" as the family is for many women.

Having recently trained to be a counselor, I intend to balance some teaching and research with some client work. Although this is another caring occupation, I am less concerned with striving to prove to myself and others that I am an adult, with a career as an alternative to the traditional female adult status as mother. I feel more rather than less ambivalent about not being a biological mother, and I am aware that I have consistently chosen occupations and practices that allow me to care without the long-term commitment or structure of the family.

Discussion

Here we discuss some of the political and personal choices, and responses to social and biographical events, that have influenced our experiences of caring and that have brought us to this shared interest in caring in academic life. Further, we reflect on the relationship between our identities as parent/nonparent, as carer/noncarer, and our status and roles within the academy. Finally, we consider the importance to us of managing home and work.

Political and Personal Choices and Influences

Each of us has been influenced by the relatively similar academic tradition of the social sciences, and we share a commitment to practicing our sociology and our politics in our everyday lives and in our work as academics. However, our four stories produce a richly textured picture of "care," and our experiences are shaped by different political and personal choices.

Personal politics permeate all four stories, and we each have explored (and sometimes rejected) different feminisms. For example, Karen describes a feminism that was very much about inhabiting public spaces but that later, and as a result of experience, became an exploration on private, internal space. Jen, writing with other lesbian academics (Marchbank, Corrin, & Brodie, 1993), describes how the traditions of patriarchal religion and party politics in West Scotland permeate academic culture. In this particular academic setting, women's studies was virtually excluded, and feminism was seen as biased. The struggle described by Jen and her colleagues to challenge both sexism and homophobia in the academy and other educational areas shaped their identities as feminist academics. Together with other women postgraduates, Karen and Gayle (Holliday, Letherby, Mann, Ramsay, & Reynolds, 1993) describe the process of forming an alternative to the traditional postgraduate culture, an alternative based on sharing physical and temporal spaces. We also describe the weaving of the personal and the academic, which clearly influenced how we practiced as academics. Both of these papers describe a concern with personal politics and with a shared understanding of our selves as formed through our relationship with others.

For each of us, "caring" is part of our political as well as our personal lives: For some of us, actively caring for others or supporting others in their caring responsibilities has been central to our identities as fathers, mothers, daughters, friends, and lovers. In some cases, this has involved reshaping what it means to be a father and a parent in a society that genders caring relationships. In other cases, caring has been an absence as much as a presence in our lives, and refusing to care for others has been an important part of our identity at particular points in our life stories.

Finally, we have come to academia from different directions, and our experiences of academic life have been shaped by class, sexuality, gender, and ethnicity. As such, at times we have experienced academic culture as hostile to "others." Nevertheless, we feel that it is relevant to our accounts that at least in some instances academic culture, which values personal autonomy, has allowed space for the complex balancing of private and public responsibilities.

In/visibility and In/validity

As Karen and Gayle have argued elsewhere in relation to the managing of choices, the issues of "work intensification" and "dedication to the job" are important (Ramsay & Letherby, in press). As we have previously noted, others have suggested that the academy as well as the family is a "greedy institution." Added to this, new managerial changes and increasing stress on quality mean that higher education as an institution has recently become much greedier, with academic and support staff being expected to provide more support to students than ever before (Cotterill & Waterhouse, 1998; Letherby & Shiels, 2001; Marchbank & Letherby, 2002). However, the tension between home and work roles and identities continues, and at different times mothers may feel marginalized at work because of their caring roles at home, and nonmothers with caring responsibilities may feel that these are denied in their working life. Yet, ironically, it is likely that maternal and feminine ideologies influence recruitment strategies: "[A]s women we feel we are at times expected to place the organisation at the centre of our emotional lives, and extend our mothering capacity to our students, colleagues and to the 'greedy institution.' . . . at times women 'without' children may be viewed as having no responsibilities outside of the organisation and therefore able to give all to work" (Ramsay & Letherby, in press). As our personal accounts demonstrate, we have all felt in/visible and/or in/validated at times.

Us as Educators

As two of us have argued elsewhere: "[G]enerally when men are responsive to students it is often seen as additional to their responsibilities and as more of a gift, whereas when women provide [care,] it is seen as a natural aspect of their femininity and part of their job" (Letherby & Shiels, 2001, p. 128).

In the current climate of expectations, "parenting" becomes obligatory rather than voluntary in that academics are squeezed or forced into a mode of "parenting" that they are not necessarily comfortable with—whether or not they have children (or dependent parents, or others) of "their own." Where issues of course development, management, and critique are concerned, there is no question that many students have a clear conception of "rights" but little consideration of the other accepted elements of "citizenship"—the acceptance of others' "rights," for example. In a way, this has been an inevitable result of the last 20 or so years of British politics, and it has affected not just the structure and organization of university courses but also the personal relationships involved within them. We are all involved in the complex balancing of private and public responsibilities. There are, of course, different, sometimes opposing or countervailing pressures within this balance.

As Thomas (1998) notes, the fact "that universities are patriarchal institutions where male hegemony is seen as natural and unproblematic" compounds the problems for women in the academy (p. 90). Walsh (2002), in a discussion of equal opportunities, adds the structural factors of "marketisation" and "new managerialism" to the mix (p. 40). Given this construction of problems and responsibilities at work, does the job/home experience of single-parenting men differ significantly from that of women?

Within the patriarchal, masculine, hegemonic culture (and often macho subcultures) of what seem, increasingly, to be becoming total institutions, John found that an initial response on "becoming" a single parent with the care of two children of preteen and early teen ages was one of support and sympathy from both management and colleagues (those who knew). This rapidly, and predictably, gave way to "business as usual." Similarly, although Jen's identity as mother "normalized" her with colleagues, she is still expected to be completely devoted and committed at work.

Our feeling is that single women and men parents (with important provisos in relation to social class, etc.) experience many of the same problems and pressures that, as other sections in this book indicate, are shared but that sometimes differ between different household structures.

Balancing Home and Work

Obviously, we are not the only ones to have considered multiple identity in this way, as our introduction demonstrates. Also, as academics we are aware that we are not the only ones who manage home and work. Students too have a heavy workload and increasingly manage a triple burden. Our *full*-time students often also have *full*-time jobs in the workplace and caring responsibilities of their own. As our previous section demonstrates, our students have caring expectations of us. Women lecturers in particular are expected to be accessible, caring, and "separate from the dominant patriarchal culture [but] on the other hand when students find the institution oppressive, they see us as contributing to, and responsible for, the system. It is in these circumstances that the students see their oppression as partly our fault" (Barnes-Powell & Letherby, 1998, p. 74).

Care (whether provided by women or men) has become a "maternal," feminized, and therefore marginalized activity in both the wider community and in the communities of higher education (Cotterill & Waterhouse, 1998). So although this activity is valued by students, there is little management value attached to it. Furthermore, the pastoral element of our workplace identity is just one among the multiple demands on us. We are also all affected by the demands of teaching, administration, and the publish-or-perish culture. It is also possible to argue that the recent changes in higher education have made the job more difficult, not least because within the current academic climate, where large numbers of students are intended to be processed through general-purpose courses as cheaply as possible (Epstein, 1995), academics may be viewed as providing a service or even selling a product (e.g., Epstein; Morley & Walsh, 1995; Skeggs, 1995). This is accentuated not only by the introduction of fees and student loans but also by the increased stress on support and evaluation systems that actively encourage students to see themselves as consumers (see Marchbank & Letherby, 2002, for further discussion).

All of this is relevant to the experience of the men who provide care in the academy as well as the women who do. However, although (as highlighted earlier) not all men adopt masculine models, they remain protected by the fact that they are men. Yet, men as well as women sometimes have to juggle the demands on them at work with the demands on them at home. As our personal stories demonstrate, we all have or have had caring responsibilities at home. None of us has been able to follow the traditional (male) linear higher education career model that starts with early undergraduate experience followed by a smooth upward progression through the ranks, not least because of our class backgrounds, our gender, and our caring responsibilities. In fact, this model is now increasingly outmoded, but the increased stress on accountability can inhibit opportunities for self-expression, leaving us little time to spend on things we think are personally and politically important.

Brief Reflections

In this essay we have presented aspects of our own work/home auto/biographies and reflected on these to demonstrate the complex interconnections between gender identity, non/parenthood, and care work within and outside of the institution. Obviously, if written by each of us individually or by different combinations of the group, this piece would be different. Presented as it is as a multiple auto/biographical reflection, this essay demonstrates not only our individual positions but our interconnections with each other and with ("absent") significant others. We hope that readers can make similar and different connections in their own home and work lives.

REFERENCES

Barnes-Powell, T., & Letherby, G. (1998). "All in a day's work": Gendered care work in higher education. In D. Malina & S. Maslin-Prothero (Eds.), *Surviving the academy: Feminist perspectives* (pp. 69–77). London: Falmer.

Cotterill, P., & Waterhouse, R. (1998). Women in higher education: The gap between corporate rhetoric and reality of experience. In D. Malina & S. Maslin-Prothero (Eds.), *Surviving the academy: Feminist perspectives* (pp. 8–17). London: Falmer.

David, M., Davies, J., Edwards, R., Reay, D., & Standing, K. (1996). Mothering and education: Reflexivity and feminist methodology. In L. Morley & V. Walsh (Eds.), *Breaking boundaries: Women in higher education* (pp. 208–223). London: Taylor and Francis.

Epstein, D. (1995). In our (new) right minds: The hidden curriculum and the academy. In L. Morley & V. Walsh (Eds.), *Feminist academics: Creative agents for change* (pp. 56–72). London: Taylor and Francis.

Holliday, R., Letherby, G., Mann, L., Ramsay, K., & Reynolds, G. (1993). Room of our own: An alternative to academic isolation. In M. Kennedy, C. Lubelska, & V. Walsh (Eds.), *Making connections: Women's studies, women's movements, women's lives* (pp. 180–194). London: Taylor and Francis.

Leonard, P., & Malina, D. (1994). Caught between two worlds: Mothers as academics. In S. Davies, C. Lubelska, & J. Quinn (Eds.), *Changing the subject: Women in higher education* (pp. 29–41). London: Taylor and Francis.

Letherby, G., & Shiels, J. (2001). "Isn't he good, but can we take her seriously?": Gendered expectations in higher education. In P. Anderson & J. Williams (Eds.), *Identity and difference in higher education: "Outsiders within"* (pp. 121–132). Aldershot, England: Ashgate.

Marchbank, J., Corrin, C., & Brodie, S. (1993). Inside and "out" or outside academia: Lesbians working in Scotland. In M. Kennedy, C. Lubelska, & V. Walsh (Eds.), *Making connections: Women's studies, women's movements, women's lives* (pp. 155–166). London: Taylor and Francis.

Marchbank, J., & Letherby, G. (2002). Offensive and defensive: Student support and higher education evaluation. In G. Howie & A. Tauchert (Eds.), *Gender, teaching, and research in higher education* (pp. 141–154). Aldershot, England: Ashgate.

Morley, L., & Walsh, V. (Eds.). (1995). *Feminist academics: Creative agents for change.* London: Taylor and Francis.

Munn-Giddings, C. (1998). Mixing motherhood and academia—a lethal cocktail. In D. Malina & S. Maslin-Prothero (Eds.), *Surviving the academy: Feminist perspectives* (pp. 56–68). London: Falmer.

Raddon, A. (2001, April). *(M)others in the academy: Positioned and positioning within discourses of the "successful academic" and the "good mother."* Paper presented at Gender and Education Conference, Institute of Education, London University, London.

Ramsay, K., & Letherby, G. (in press). The experience of non-mothers in the gendered university. *Gender, Work, and Organization.*

Skeggs, B. (1995). Women's studies in Britain in the 1990s: Entitlement cultures and institutional constraints. *Women's Studies International Forum, 18,* 475–485.

Sundby, J. (1999). Sad not to have children, happy to be childless: A personal and professional experience of infertility. *Reproductive Health Matters, 7*(13), 13–19.

Thomas, R. (1998). Incorporation or alienation?: Resisting the gendered discourses of academic appraisal. In D. Malina & S. Maslin-Prothero (Eds.), *Surviving the academy: Feminist perspectives* (pp. 90–100). London: Falmer.

Walsh, V. (2002). Equal opportunities without "equality": Redeeming the irredeemable. In G. Howie & A. Tauchert (Eds.), *Gender, teaching, and research in higher education* (pp. 33–45). Aldershot, England: Ashgate.

NOTES

1. *Nonmotherhood* in this context refers to the experience of women without biological children who may have other caring responsibilities—for children and adults—outside of the academy

2. We write *infertility* and *involuntary childlessness* in quotation marks to highlight the problems of definition.

22

The Life I Didn't Know I Wanted

Rachel Hile Bassett

From Feminist Intellectual to Selfless Mother and Back

As a freshman in college, I joined a feminist consciousness-raising group, excited to find one at the late date of 1989, well after the groups' heyday in the 1970s. I had been an outspoken feminist since my junior high school days, and I delighted in those evenings, sitting in a small circle with seven other women, talking about things women aren't supposed to talk about even with their closest friends. Throughout my college years, my proud self-identification as a feminist and an intellectual confirmed me in my idea that I was going to be Somebody. I was going to go to the top of my field, and people were going to know who I was. Sometimes I thought I wanted children, but other times it seemed that children wouldn't fit in with my fabulous career.

I chose academia, completing a master's degree and starting along the path to a PhD in English, but I grew increasingly dissatisfied with my quasi-religious understanding of intellectual and political life: the idea that my academic involvement and political commitment could give my life transcendent meaning (though I had little idea of what transcendence was). My disillusionment with academia and feminism made me ripe to see the merits of the opposite side. In 1998, two years into my doctoral work, I dropped out of graduate school because with my new goal in life—mothering a large family, homeschooling them through high school—there was no point in having a PhD. I enjoyed my academic work, but my image of what motherhood required made it inconceivable that I could do both at the same time.

What had happened to change the teenage feminist scholar into the woman who wanted to be a renunciatory full-time mother? Not as fundamental a shift as you might think. In 1996, two years before quitting my doctoral work, I joined the Catholic Church and switched from letting liberal feminist ideas and ideals shape my thinking and my choices to allowing the Catholic Church and, later, the ideology of attachment parenting to provide me with my perceptual framework. In both cases, I looked to others' ideas rather than my own experience in making decisions about my life. Certainly I had agency in these decisions, but I exercised my agency only to the extent of deciding which group to follow, not to the extent of synthesizing new ways of looking at the world based on my own experiences, relationships, and values.

But life doesn't fit neatly into boxes, however hard we may try to shape them to the contours of the life models our cultures give us. During my three years away from academia, I was sure I would never go back, never finish the PhD, and I was resolute in not reading anything about English Renaissance literature because I didn't want to awaken any desire. I had my son, Joey, in 2000, and when the fog of new motherhood lifted a year later, I found, despite my expectation of Total Fulfillment, that my intellectual self still yearned for expression. I reenrolled in grad school and finished my PhD in 2004, despite having intensified my commitment to motherhood with the birth of my daughter, Helen, in 2003. I maintained an ambivalent stance throughout my graduate career, fully believing that motherhood had to be my highest priority while nevertheless deriving great pleasure from my work.

What I want to write about here is how the academy itself has unwittingly given me the opportunity to experience something I didn't realize that I wanted or valued: an egalitarian marriage and a coparenting situation for my two children. Through this experience, I've come to realize that each life is different and that observing my own life and feelings is a surer guide to my own happiness than listening to the dictates of those who tell me what my goals as a woman should be. In the process I've arrived at a new understanding of my ways of being feminist, Catholic, mother, and scholar; a renewed appreciation of what work means to me; and a firm commitment to continue shared coparenting.

Shared Coparenting in the Academy

The flexibility of academic work makes coparenting seem more possible for academic couples than for couples whose jobs place more restrictions upon their time, but the academy's demand of total commitment means that when dual-academic-career couples have children, one member of the couple—usually the woman—often feels compelled to accept marginalized academic positions, thus granting priority to the other partner's career. Both Diane Ehrensaft (1987) and Francine M. Deutsch (1999) included academic couples with two full-time jobs in their studies of coparenting couples, but neither clarified whether one or both partners had achieved tenure before starting a family. Our story is slightly different in that we have become coparenting academics who both work part time, thus avoiding regular paid child care. Though the academy, by keeping my husband Troy persistently underemployed, did not intend to enable our egalitarianism, it could, by providing financial and policy support for job sharing, part-time tenure-track work, and the like, provide a model for the nonacademic world of a reconceptualization of work-family balance.

Now is not a good time to look for a tenure-track assistant professor position in English literature—it has not been a good time to do so at any point in the past three decades. Because of this, Troy has worked part time as an adjunct instructor ever since finishing his PhD two years ago; during that time, I've done freelance editing work part time while finishing my own PhD in English. Thus, the upside for us of the unspeakably bad job market in the humanities has been a family situation in which my husband and I share both breadwinning and child-care responsibilities. The downsides include the finances and the strain each of us feels from time to time at not perfectly fulfilling our culturally prescribed gender roles.

If the job market were better, we would already be firmly within traditional gender roles—Troy's finishing his degree two years before I finished would have meant that he would already be two years along the road to tenure. That fact, coupled with my limited prospects as the "trailing spouse," probably would have pushed me into shaping my life to fit the idea, reinforced repeatedly by Catholic and attachment parenting ideologies, that women should give priority to their maternal roles. It would be more than easy—indeed, it would feel downright "natural"—to live the dichotomized domestic ideology that requires one (male) "ideal worker" and one (female) family worker (Williams, 2000).

But it hasn't turned out that way, and what we've learned from the past four years of coparenting while both of us worked part time has changed our expectations of both family life and work life. Troy has experienced the pleasure of spending real *quantity* time with his children, and my positive experience of graduate work (supported by my husband's sharing the domestic work, including washing all the dishes, every day) has made me question my assumption that I would eventually give up my career to focus on child rearing. And the children? Both of them will grow up seeing both parents caring about intellectual work and achievement and also caring for them. I have faith that it will be easier for Helen to stick up for what she wants in her life, and that Joey will be more likely to respect women as workers and men as nurturers and participants in domestic life. I saw an example of this the other day when Joey wanted to play house. I was the mommy, Helen was the baby, and Joey was the daddy. "I'm the daddy, and now it's time for me to do some dishes," he announced proudly as he walked to the sink of his play kitchen.

Reawakening to My Self

We don't know how much longer our current arrangement will last. At least for the next year, neither my husband nor I will have a tenure-track job, and neither will be a trailing spouse; we will continue each working part time. Though the expected career trajectory for me involves working as an adjunct lecturer while I seek full-time tenure-track employment, one of the ironies of our position is that I can't afford to allow the academy to exploit me in that way: To support a family of four on two part-time salaries requires me to choose higher-paying editing work over teaching.[1] I don't know whether hiring committees will perceive this choice as a lack of commitment to academia. Perhaps it is. I'm so appalled by the shift to part-time and non-tenure-track staffing of university humanities courses that, even if I could depend on the luxury of a full-time income for my husband, I would be hesitant to participate in that system.

In the meantime, as we continue to search for full-time employment for one or both of us, we will continue to benefit from our unconventional work-family arrangement, which has led me to grow beyond the gender expectations I was so quick to adopt when I joined the community of the Catholic Church. Not having the choice to devote myself full time to motherhood over the past four years has made achievement in academia acceptable to me. As Lotte Bailyn (1964) pointed out decades ago, to the extent that women have a "choice" about whether to achieve outside the home, their achievement becomes less likely. I know that if my husband had been working full time, I would not have finished my PhD. If I had even tried—unlikely, because I would have been so committed to being the perfect full-time mother—intellectual work would have felt like a burden rather than a pleasure because I wouldn't have had enough hours in the day to enjoy the work. It was the pleasure of the work itself, my own life experience, that spurred me to question the validity of the cultural models of motherhood that I had previously accepted.

I have questioned as well the monastic model of the academic career. When I imagined that there was only one way to be an academic—involving late hours and total commitment—I said no thanks. People now sometimes imagine that I am that sort of academic because I managed to write my dissertation relatively quickly while taking care of two small children, but I am not that woman. Troy's part-time work means that I have dedicated work time during daytime hours, rather than minutes snatched during naptime or stolen late at night from my own sleeping time. If he hadn't been the other caregiver, I couldn't have done the work without guilt: For most of my graduate career, I was so tied up in ideas of the superiority of parental care that I couldn't have utilized paid care without unacceptable levels of guilt. So this arrangement has given me an experience of academic success that I didn't perceive as coming at the expense of family. With neither partner expected to perform as an "ideal worker," professional and family roles can be combined without any one role being shortchanged, and that has been true for Troy as well, who has continued to work on his research while teaching and searching for a full-time job.

My understanding of what I want from my work life and my family life has come a long way since my unquestioning acceptance that my role as mother should take priority over all my other roles, but it took the experience of living this life for several years to make me see the benefits of the arrangement. It was hard to feel the rightness of placing equal emphasis on several roles—mother, academic, wife, individual—because of opposing voices insisting with great confidence on the necessity of role hierarchies. Because I have been female in this culture my entire life, and because of my connection to the Catholic community and attachment parenting groups, my role as mother seemed more "true," even as I was delighting in my graduate work, and I did not question this. In this area, I simply could not see how culture had shaped my perceptions of children as requiring "intensive mothering" (Hays, 1996). Additionally, my acceptance of the tenets of attachment parenting, with its valorization of this parenting style as "natural," made it even harder for me to see the possibility of choice in mothering practices (Bobel, 2002). For me, the priority of my nurturing role was simply truth, and only the lived experiences of academic success and of the benefits of coparenting gave me the courage and the conviction to *believe* that choices were available to me.

I don't think I am alone in needing experience to teach me the truth of something. I know that many men perceive their roles as paid workers—as "breadwinners"—as their "natural" role in the family. Some such men are no doubt curious about their children or long to enjoy deeper bonds than they can build in an hour on weeknights and a few hours on weekends, but without living the actual experience of coparenting, how can they grow sure enough of their feelings to change things, to take the family leaves so many are afraid to take, to find a way to change the workforce to make family participation more accessible to men and success in paid work more available to women? Women's future in academia cannot depend only on women's efforts: To achieve gender parity, men are going to have to change, too.

Changing the Academic Work Culture

I am not describing the benefits I've received from coparenting in order to romanticize our situation, which has been sustainable only because of the lower cost of living in the Midwest, our freedom from student debt, and an almost ruthless frugality. We are not in this situation by choice, and, unless someone offers us a shared or split tenure-track appointment, both of us will probably eventually take full-time positions.

But rather than focusing on these drawbacks, I wish to suggest some of the potential of a situation that remains for most simply an idea: that parents really could share responsibility for both child rearing and bread-winning. Ann Crittenden (2001) reports on a survey of male and female college students' expectations for work-family balance. For a family with preschool children, the female respondents considered both parents working part time to be an ideal arrangement, whereas the men perceived a full-time working husband and a full-time homemaker wife as ideal. Noting that the men's model family describes reality in roughly one third of families with young children, while part-time work for both partners remains quite rare, Crittenden observes bluntly that "young men are more likely to get what they want out of life than young women" (p. 239). Young men are unlikely to spontaneously change their understanding of ideal work-family balance. More men living as coparents, experiencing the joys of nurturing, may be the only way for men to change such that they will share the goal of achieving systemic change (Chodorow, 1978).

But shared coparenting will remain rare as long as employers view full-time (and then some) work as normative for "serious" workers. Academia, with its flexible and independent workload, could lead the way in changing employer perceptions of how work could be structured. Policies for job sharing and part-time tenure-track work and provision of prorated benefits for part-time work (and efforts to encourage academics' use of such policies) would be inexpensive ways to change perceptions of what qualities are valued in a worker. A more radical, but more equitable, approach would be to make the academy more humane for *all* members, not just parents, by making job expectations and tenure requirements more in line with what mere mortals can accomplish in a reasonable workweek. Jerry Jacobs (2004) suggests as a first step to this more humane academy a shift to a focus on quality rather than quantity in academic work. Because of our acculturation within the academy, volume—number of hours worked, number of works published—can come to seem like a "natural" correlate of scholarly merit, but a revised academic culture might choose to emphasize intellectual quality instead of a capitalistic assessment of "productivity."

If academia or governments were to provide real support, our family and many others would find living on two part-time incomes not only possible, but desirable, especially during early-childhood years. Also, dual-academic-career couples with two full-time jobs would find coparenting a more realistic possibility if academic institutions scaled back their expectations of total commitment. My own experience gives me hope for how others could change their values through the experience of coparenting. My husband would never have known what he was missing if he hadn't had the chance to spend so much time with our children from their infancies. As for me, I didn't know what sort of life I wanted until I had lived it. Without my husband, the "daddy who does the dishes"—and changes diapers, plays with the children, and gets them lunch—my dissertation, this book, *my work* would not exist. And I might never have realized that I had lost something important.

REFERENCES

Bailyn, L. (1964). Notes on the role of choice in the psychology of professional women. *Daedalus, 93,* 701–707.

Bobel, C. (2002). *The paradox of natural mothering.* Philadelphia: Temple University Press.

Chodorow, N. (1978). *The reproduction of mothering: Psychoanalysis and the sociology of gender.* Berkeley: University of California Press.

Crittenden, A. (2001). *The price of motherhood: Why motherhood is the most important—and least valued—job in America.* New York: Henry Holt.

Deutsch, F. M. (1999). *Halving it all: How equally shared parenting works.* Cambridge: Harvard University Press.

Ehrensaft, D. (1987). *Parenting together.* New York: Free Press.

Hays, S. (1996). *The cultural contradictions of motherhood.* New Haven, CT: Yale University Press.

Jacobs, J. A. (2004). The faculty time divide. *Sociological Forum, 19,* 3–27.

Williams, J. (2000). *Unbending gender: Why family and work conflict and what to do about it.* New York: Oxford University Press.

NOTE

1. The institution where my husband works as an adjunct pays him a prorated portion of a full-time salary, which seems fair to us.

23

Living and Teaching Developmental Psychology in a Liberal Arts Setting: A Blending of Mothering Roles

Suzanne M. Cox

As a graduate student in human development in a program housed in a psychology department, I was intrigued with how becoming a mother might influence my own interpretation of my training, as well as the development of my career. I became pregnant with my first child during my sixth year of graduate school. At the time, I had finished my required course work and was in the throes of data collection for my dissertation, a study of attachment among preterm infants and their mothers. I was beginning to teach introductory and developmental psychology at local colleges and universities, but most of my energies were focused on interpreting attachment theory for understanding my dissertation study and my own development as a mother. I hadn't realized the degree to which such scholarly endeavors as teaching and researching attachment would be shaped by my experiences as a mother.

A basic tenet of attachment theory is that sensitive and responsive caregiving contributes to the development of secure infant attachment (Ainsworth, Blehar, Waters, & Wall, 1978; Bowlby, 1988; Cassidy & Shaver, 1999). My years of undergraduate observation while working as a day-care provider in a university infant and toddler day-care unit confirmed the research findings for me: The children who greeted their sensitive parents at the end-of-the-day reunions demonstrated secure attachment behaviors. I accepted most of the research findings on attachment theory and felt no need to acknowledge individual (or dyadic) differences for particular cases. The one area of parent-child relationship research that I questioned was that on sleeping patterns and sleep disorders among infants and children (e.g., Benoit, Zeanah, Boucher, & Minde, 1992).

As a soon-to-be coparent and as a teaching assistant for a course on attachment theory that brought into focus cultural differences in child rearing, I began to question the mainstream North American approach to sleeping patterns and sleep disorders among children and infants. Furthermore, I began to question the limited practice of breastfeeding children, particularly beyond the early weeks and months of infancy. I questioned the wisdom of encouraging parents to foster secure infant attachment via parental sensitivity during the day, but then to take a be-havior-modification approach to teach infants to cry it out so as to ensure a good night's sleep for all (Ferber, 1985). It made no sense to me to con-ceptualize sleep disorders in toddlers as a function of parents' attachment histories without also considering the functionality and implementation of breastfeeding and cultural differences (see Liedloff, 1975; McKenna, 2000; Small, 1998). I was committed to shared, egalitarian coparenting early on in my pregnancy, and I remember my graduate school advisers reminding me that biological functions such as lactation would, at least for a time, make my ideal of complete egalitarianism impossible. It took my becoming a breastfeeding mother of my own infant to learn how to interpret both research findings on maternal sensitivity and mainstream advice on ensuring sleep. Ten years later, the controversy around cosleep-ing still persists (see, e.g., O'Mara, 2002), while coparenting and attach-ment parenting are gaining popularity.

Currently I teach at a small, selective liberal arts college. I teach courses in general and developmental psychology (e.g., introduction to psychology, research methods, child growth and development, life-span developmental psychology, psychology of women, developmental psychopathology, and pediatric psychology), and I try to maintain an active student-faculty col-laborative research agenda. My experiences of motherhood influence my teaching in several of my courses in developmental psychology, whether I am teaching about pregnancy and childbirth, nutritional effects on growth and development, attachment from both the child's and parent's perspec-tives, or implications of attachment theory for humane intervention in foster care and hospitalization.

While an undergraduate student at a state university, I had focused most of my studies on psychology, but I was fascinated by the feminist perspective on the anthropology of women's health offered by a medical and cultural anthropology professor, Brigitte Jordan. My first exposure to cultural differences in the management and experience of childbirth was during my junior year in college when I enrolled in her course, the Anthropology of Women's Health. This course was perhaps the most influential course of my undergraduate career, as it has shaped both my teaching and my plans about how to birth (see Jordan, 1983).

Using feminist pedagogy when teaching my students about childbirth, I begin by eliciting their own perceptions and images of birth in mainstream North American culture. Themes of pain, fear, and medical risk inevitably arise. I then encourage my students to deconstruct their notions of birth by contrasting medical (or "technocratic" as in Davis-Floyd, 1994) and midwifery models of childbirth. Viewing videotapes of laboring women aids our analysis of birth management and experience. Emphasizing active student participation (e.g., shared identification of topics to be addressed, shared selection of readings and in-class exercises), we go on to continue to develop a provocative unit on childbirth that examines a myriad of theoretical themes. Although the unit is an effective vehicle for raising feminist ideas about women's health, it is also useful for addressing notions of women's sense and locus of control, discussing the empowerment of women, and drawing significant theoretical distinctions between attachment and bonding (Eyer, 1992).

Although I document the efficacy of woman-centered, family-focused midwifery approaches to childbirth (e.g., Katz Rothman, 1991; Kennell, Klaus, McGrath, Robertson, & Hinkley, 1991; Kitzinger, 1991; Sosa, Kennel, Robertson, & Urrutia, 1980) and try to remain unbiased and objective in my presentation, students inevitably want to know more about my doula-assisted, midwife-attended, three- to five-day–labored homebirths. Hard as I try to present "objective" data, my students are captivated by my anecdotal experiences of birth, extended breastfeeding, or combining the raising of a family with having a career. They are fascinated by the story of my first son's birth (I labored for five days), and I use my own case study to refute textbook examples of how a birth should proceed. My students also want to know about Adam's reaction to the homebirth of his brother, Ethan. I contrast the experiences of Adam's and Ethan's births with the high-risk situation I faced when my third-born son presented as breech during the final weeks of pregnancy. Noting the differences between high-risk pregnancies and what is the norm for 90 to 95% of women, I rejoice in telling the empowering story of Aidan, who found his way to be head first while I was in labor and who allowed me to safely birth him at home after all. Some students' fascination with my personal experience has translated to a deep commitment to learn more, as for an alumna who assisted as a doula in the recent homebirth of my daughter, Juliana. I have come to realize and adopt a feminist pedagogical stance that acknowledges that my experiences need not be kept private, as students in a liberal arts setting can benefit greatly from a real role model who can encourage them to explore these life issues not only in theory, but also in practice.

The part of my identity and experience that I keep from my students is the way in which my professional integrity has been questioned because of my choice to mother in ways that enhance healthy attachment experiences for all members of my family while pursuing a career that continues to be evaluated by colleagues adopting a traditional model of assessing scholarly productivity (see Rosen, 1999). Although the experience of blending my private and public roles of mothering has been intellectually and emotionally rewarding, a multitude of challenges for my professional integrity have arisen. In my role as a scholar, I have attempted to "mother" and "nurture" my students' intellectual curiosity by engaging in collaborative student-faculty research that focuses on mother-child interaction. Such a labor-intensive approach to research in a teaching-intensive institution does not always yield high volumes of publishable research reports or recognition for one's work productivity. For example, I have coauthored numerous conference presentations with students interested in specific areas of mother-child interaction, but the training involved in behavioral coding and the writing up of research findings with students who are about to graduate leaves me with limited time and energy to prepare manuscripts for publication. Conversely, focusing on publication would leave me with little time to serve as the midwife to my students' interests and ideas.

My goals as a teacher-scholar—and my needs as a mother combining motherhood and an academic career—are not always understood and valued by colleagues who prefer a dated model of performance. My need for on- and off-campus flex-time, which is rooted in my desire to remain active in my research as well as in my children's lives, presents obstacles during times of evaluation and consideration for promotion. Working at home preparing for classes, grading students' papers, or interpreting research findings allows me to also be available to my nursing toddler and older children. Some colleagues have viewed my pattern of on-campus time as a "liability" for our department and my need to close my office door so as to pump breast milk in private as "noncollegiality." Perhaps when my children are older I will not need to keep juggling multiple sets of needs. Now that I am tenured and have served as the chair of my department, I hope to offer colleagues another model of life-work balance.

Finally, I'd like to express the joy and challenges I face as a feminist mother of three sons. Having provided child care for several young girls while in college, my husband and I always envisioned raising daughters. I had anticipated difficulty with accepting the possible male sex of each of my sons when I was pregnant, but I have been relieved to learn that with each passing day, their sex and gender matter little to the mothering I provide them. This personal experience has permeated my teaching of developmental psychology in addressing gender identity and preferences. As my sons grow, I find myself growing defensive about "male-bashing" and the exclusion of sons from programs such as "Take Your Daughter to Work Day." I share with my students anecdotes about my own attempts to raise feminist sons, and I find myself helping my students focus more on emotional intelligence (Goleman, 1995) for all rather than accentuating gender or sex differences. I take some pride in knowing that my sons like it that their mom is a "doctor who teaches college students how kids grow." Now that I have a daughter, I am curious about the degree to which our family will acknowledge or challenge traditional constructions of gender. I look forward to serving as a role model for her as she is raised in a family in which both the males in the family and I are committed to being sensitive and caring for one another. Indeed, I could not actualize my goals as a developmental psychologist without my feminist, coparenting partner, whose family commitment and relatively flexible work schedule enable him to take equal responsibility for child care. From the beginning, he shared my belief in Chodorow's (1978) idea that coparenting is essential for eliminating sexism in child rearing and in society.

I live and breathe developmental psychology both at work and at home. I'm able to blend my mothering roles in a liberal arts college setting where students and faculty are encouraged to learn and grow together. Despite challenges in validating my professional contributions, I continue to find ways to combine my experiences of mothering with my identity as a developmental psychologist.

REFERENCES

Ainsworth, M. D. S., Blehar, M., Waters, E., & Wall, S. (1978). *Patterns of attachment: A psychological study of the strange situation.* Hillsdale, NJ: Lawrence Erlbaum.

Benoit, D., Zeanah, C. H., Boucher, C., & Minde, K. K. (1992). Sleep disorders in early childhood: Association with insecure maternal attachment. *Journal of the American Academy of Child & Adolescent Psychiatry, 31*(1), 86–93.

Bowlby, J. (1988). *A secure base: Parent-child attachment and healthy human development.* New York: Basic.

Cassidy, J., & Shaver, P. R. (Eds.). (1999). *Handbook of attachment: Theory, research, and clinical applications.* New York: Guilford Press.

Chodorow, N. (1978). *The reproduction of mothering: Psychoanalysis and the sociology of gender.* Berkeley: University of California Press.

Davis-Floyd, R. E. (1994). The technocratic body: American childbirth as cultural expression. *Social Science and Medicine, 38,* 1125–1140.

Eyer, D. E. (1992). *Mother–infant bonding: A scientific fiction.* New Haven, CT: Yale University Press.

Ferber, R. (1985). *Solve your child's sleep problems.* New York: Simon & Schuster.

Goleman, D. (1995). *Emotional intelligence: Why it can matter more than IQ.* New York: Bantam Books.

Jordan, B. (1983). *Birth in four cultures* (3rd ed.). Montreal: Eden Press.

Katz Rothman, B. (1991). *In labor: Women and power in the birthplace.* New York: W. W. Norton.

Kennel, J., Klaus, M., McGrath, S., Robertson, S., & Hinkley, C. (1991). Continuous emotional support during labor in a US hospital: A randomized controlled trial. *Journal of the American Medical Association, 265,* 2197–2201.

Kitzinger, S. (1991). *Homebirth: The essential guide to giving birth outside of the hospital.* New York: DK Publishing.

Liedloff, J. (1975). *The continuum concept: In search of a happiness lost.* Reading, MA: Addison-Wesley.

McKenna, J. J. (2000). Cultural influences on infant and childhood sleep biology and the science that studies it: Toward a more inclusive paradigm. In G. M. Loughlin, J. L. Carroll, & C. L. Marcus (Eds.), *Sleep in development and pediatrics* (pp. 99–124). New York: Marcel Dekker.

O'Mara, P. (Ed.). (2002, September/October). Sleeping with your baby: The world's top scientists speak out [Special issue]. *Mothering, 114.*

Rosen, R. (1999, July 30). Secrets of the second sex in scholarly life. *Chronicle of Higher Education,* p. A48.

Small, M. F. (1998). *Our babies, ourselves: How biology and culture shape the way we parent.* New York: Anchor Books.

Sosa, R., Kennel, J., Robertson, S., & Urrutia, J. (1980). The effect of a supportive companion on perinatal problems, length of labor, and mother-infant interaction. *The New England Journal of Medicine, 303,* 597–600.

24

Of Diesels and Diapers:
A Resident Alien in Motherland

Anna Wilson

My daughter knows about the construction of identity through representation. "Ruth!" she pronounces, pointing triumphantly at the camera or camcorder in my hand. Over breakfast, opening one or another of the photograph albums that pile up on the table, I struggle to narrate a plausible adoption story, pointing at the picture of her birth mother, gaunt and desolate at the ceremony in Vietnam, at another of me, grinning maniacally in the hotel dining room, a bewildered baby in my arms. Or we look at the pictures of the house where my partner lives on the East Coast: the car, the crib, the cats all carefully itemized against the peculiarity of our constant journeying back and forth between our home in England and her other mother's in America. "Mama!" Ruth says dependably, as we turn the pages.

Well, yes and no. I want to try to unpick the complex operations at work in that naming and in its reception outside an always already multiplied, nonoriginary, and fictionalized mother-daughter dyad. In doing so, I hope to put some pressure on the ways in which queer parenting and parenting in the academy have taken form in our contemporary cultural imaginary. The context in which I write both motivates and constrains: I think there are compelling connections to be drawn between the pressures on queer parents to perform in certain ways in order to survive in a larger social sphere, and the expectations under which parents labor in the academy, but it is also the case that this kind of writing is not the sort that is likely to enable my escape from the penumbral region where aging junior faculty lurk before slipping into retirement. Part of the material difficulty of my partner's and my project is, paradoxically, a direct consequence of that which academia apparently enables. On the one hand, parenting on both sides of the Atlantic is only as barely feasible as it is because we each have long periods when our presence in classroom or office is not absolutely required. On the other, it is the scarcity of tenured employment and its nonportable nature that keeps us apart in the first place. And it is not just cultural capital that locks us down: I do not have the right of residence in the United States (no green cards for queers, however partnered or domestic), and although my partner would be allowed to join us in England, to do so she would have to give up the salary that keeps all three of us afloat.

GREETERS ARE A RELATIVELY RECENT ADDITION to British superstores, so it was partly the shock of the new that hit a couple of years ago when the young men accosted me with "Can I help you, sir?" as I went about furnishing my new apartment in an unfamiliar postindustrial city. In the American small towns from which I'd just returned, the mall would be swarming with middle-aged women in button-down shirts and chinos, very few of whom would be lesbians; in that crowd, I could usually pass for female, or anyway pass unnoticed. My interlocutor's confusion, while a result of differing sartorial norms on either side of the Atlantic, also presumably signals anxiety, an urgent need to keep gender binaries in place. It is crucial that this hailing take place in public, be called across the crowded entrance to a store, and that the entity thus named is stilled, if only momentarily, halted midstride by a deeply encoded (mis?)identification. It's not, I suggest, that the store clerks really think I'm a man so much as that the body before them does not fit comfortably into the "woman" category in their taxonomy. This experience might lend itself to analysis through Diane Griffin Crowder's (1993) argument that the lesbian body undermines categories of sex and gender by "deconstructing femininity in physical appearance" (p. 66), or Cheshire Calhoun's (1994) contention that, falling out of the realm of "intelligible gender identity," I have slipped out of the category of either "woman" or "man" into the nebulous region inhabited by lesbians, "not-women" (p. 567).[2]

But Calhoun's (1995) suggestion that the capacity "to generate the question To which sex does s/he belong?" (p. 22) is coextensive with the capacity to represent lesbian difference is put under some pressure by the fact that, once I started carrying my daughter around with me, an appendage to the previously questionable body, the boys at the stores let me enter unmolested. The baby recasts me as "mother/mother substitute"—and apparently, mothers are reliably female. And yet, now that she's old enough to toddle away from me when set down, I get to watch another aspect of the process of gender and sexuality taxonomizing at work: How far away does she have to be before my identity as her mother, provided by proximity, is dislodged by the overwhelming unlikeliness that this gray-haired Anglo dyke should be found in official parental relation to that Vietnamese child? On our last trip back from the States, Ruth ran through the security gate while I was putting our carry-on baggage through the scanner. Then she turned around and ran back, past me, toward the wide-open airport spaces. Before either of us knew what was happening, a guard had raced after her, picked her up, and attempted to return her to a young Hispanic woman further up the line whom he had identified as suitable mother material. It took some time, and Ruth's attaching herself firmly to my leg, to get this emblematic scenario sorted out.

All of which is to say that the identity "mother" appears to overlay certain others, at least in public: As a mother, I am seen as female; this in turn has the effect of disidentifying me as a lesbian, for it is only as not-female that I am visible as the latter in the public sphere. At ten paces separation, however, the lesbian effect regains its power, and concerned onlookers pass effortlessly over me in their attempts to locate a suitable caregiver. We know, of course, that lesbian mothers exist, or at least that many claim, and live, this identity at the same time as its ontological possibility is subject to challenge both theoretically and legally.[3] I want to revisit the questions that arise from this particular conjunction of identities and the ways in which the silent third term *woman* is implied by the second term but, at the least, problematized by the first. Do I become more of a woman as a mother? Can I be a lesbian and a mother, if being the former means being not quite female? Can one be a mother and not be a woman? I do this here in part because these questions also resonate with the discomforts of academia in some potentially useful ways. The lexicon of parenting in the academy employs terms suggestive of creative division and multiplicity: "juggling," "balance," "wearing three hats," and the rest; a rhetoric of pluralism informs and justifies women's (in particular) efforts to be various things at once, while reinforcing the belief either that such activities or identities are not incompatible or, if they are, that they must be brought into harmony. This vocabulary might, viewed in an optimistic light, call up Teresa de Lauretis's (1986) formulation of a de-essentialized feminist subjectivity, "a multiple, shifting, and often self-contradictory identity . . . an identity that one decides to reclaim from a history of multiple assimilations, and that one insists on as a strategy" (p. 9). But what if each is toxic to the other? Is this necessarily a reactionary question? Is it, in other words, any more possible to be a (lesbian) academic parent than it is to be a lesbian mother, and how potentially subversive or normative are those positionings?

My department is tolerant, enlightened, and flexible. On a day-to-day level, the exigencies of transatlantic parenting are acknowledged and accommodated. But that does not mean that the criteria for excellence have shifted or that the promotion mechanism in place recognizes these factors. My colleagues are more productive and more successful: They do more of all kinds of academic work while I transport a small child backward and forward across time zones. Tolerance in a liberal institution translates into tolerance of failure, of the incapacity to attain standards that are structurally out of reach.

For the model of academic achievement remains resolutely unitary, a mountain that the fittest must scale in solitary vigor. The glory goes to the conqueror of the north face, he who chooses the fastest, most arduous route to the top. There may be other ways up, there may even be necessary work to be done in base camps at the tree line, but, like Sherpas carrying the white man's supplies, those on the lower slopes are intrinsically of lesser value.[4]

Mothering is in fact hard to accommodate within any of our existing models of participation in the public sphere. This incompatibility is both effaced and stabilized by the ideological construct within which motherhood is understood: that, fundamentally, motherhood *is* bliss. Linda Singer's (1989) claim that "the discourse of motherhood has been strategically deployed . . . [to] devalu[e] and effac[e] maternal labor, effort, and commitment which is therein reduced to the status of a natural aptitude" (p. 61) captures a crucial part of this mechanism, but de-emphasizes the (naturalized) connection between the natural and satisfaction of the self. Even feminist critiques of mothering (and mothers) continue to produce motherhood as a transcendent experience, completely satisfying (despite everything). Love conquers all. The bliss construct allows for any number of complaints and caveats but leaves an unshakeable hierarchy in place: The difficulties are social and contingent, the joys eternal.[5]

This is very useful. Belief in the primacy of bliss enables women to endure, by discounting, those myriad occasions when motherhood is miserable, inconvenient, and debased. Women will put up with almost anything, so long as the image of Madonna and child (insert your own culturally specific iconic model) as characterizing what they're really doing holds sway in some core segment of their mind.[6] Since the family is discursively produced as existing in the private sphere, specifically in the private sphere imagined as the other to the public sphere, as indeed a "haven in a heartless world" (Michaels, 1996, p. 54), there can be no structural acknowledgment of the extent to which the allegedly "private" is lived in and through the public. Women will be grateful for the "parent and child" parking slots near to the supermarket door, rather than wonder why such places do not offer child care. Why should social institutions or the architectural infrastructures of the public environment have to accommodate them, after all, when they are already getting the best that life has to offer a woman?

The academic "mommy track" that is now routinely proposed as a civilized solution to the difficulties of parenting in the academy is in essence another version of the parking space close to the supermarket entrance: We know you have to shop—everybody does—and as you are doing it burdened down with infants, we will shorten the distance you have to travel; we know it is going to take you longer to troll up and down the aisles picking up research off those shelves, longer to get to the checkout with sufficient scholarly work to feed the tenure committee, so we will give you an extra year or two.[7] The model is still unitary, founded on the assumption that we are not just aiming, but going to arrive, at the same place, the only place of value, in the end. The academic mother must operate in two allegedly separate spheres, public and private, the difficulties of the public being compensated for by private joy. And since her eyes are trained on that public, snowy north face, there shall be no seepage across the parent/academic boundary.

Reasons for rethinking this model—allowing, for example, for the possibility that the hand holding the diaper comes into direct contact with the hand holding the pen, that shit and ink mix, intellectually as well as psychologically—for thinking of how to accommodate this fluidity and difference in process and product rather than requiring that mothers pass as professors, might emerge from the further complication of the picture that the queer academic parent generates.

It goes almost without saying that when women become mothers they perceive themselves as getting not so much the transcendent experience as the transcendent female experience. A lesbian who becomes a mother simultaneously becomes inarguably a woman, however insecure that identification may previously have seemed to her or to others. What is at stake here is securely located in our explanatory system as a reimagining of the interior self: Motherhood is a state of the interior, and for lesbians a way to redefine and develop the internal self as female.[8]

As a child and as a young woman, I was quite clear about not wanting children; that avoidance went along with the rejection of a range of behaviors that attached to "woman" as it was then available to me. In the drenchingly conservative suburb where I grew up, maternity was synonymous with marriage, which was synonymous with female entrapment. My 1970s, early second-wave brand of lesbian feminism saw the decision to have children, especially on the part of lesbians, as a surrender to the most traditional expectations of femininity. This is not the place to rehearse the many plausible explanations for my personal shift, or for the demographic phenomenon in which my partner and I are participants: Suffice it to say that I am working on the assumption that lesbian motherhood can currently be plausibly inhabited as social engagement rather than as a retreat into domesticity.

Cultural rhetoric would have it otherwise, that the process of bringing up a child is driven by internally generated impulses: Biological clocks tick, desires to nurture rise from the psychological depths, and before these ultimate inner truths the differences of surface—the differences between heterosexual women and lesbians—fall away. But we experience much of the dailiness of motherhood on the surface, where appearances, and how those appearances appear to others, are crucial. Being a mother in any circumstances is a necessarily social act. And for the lesbian mother, I would argue, it is one that rubs up against the grain of the world at every moment.

Being a lesbian mother is a kind of public activism—especially if you can manage, despite the difficulty of invoking both categories at once, to look like one. Invisible lesbian motherhood is a kind of activism, too, I realize, because the relationship, and the child in that relationship, exists and impacts materially on the world, even if its presence is not manifest to the casual glance. But right now I want to make the case for the difference that being seen makes. One way of being a visible lesbian mother is to have two of you—arguably, indeed, this is the most effective political strategy, because it potentially hits assimilationist and subversive methods at once, providing an alternative model of adequacy for those inclined to fetishize two-parent families as well as allowing for the visibility of a few differences.[9] This approach also gets away from the historically contingent aspects of the kind of recognition I tend to privilege, my notion of what a lesbian looks like being both culturally and generationally specific, and extremely narrow. Still, for what it is worth, carrying on like a diesel dyke while carrying a baby will get you noticed. And if, as I contend, the core of motherhood is not the internalized, privatized dyad but that relationship as it plays out and is played back in the world, this is a matter of significance.

I am making no global claims here. Queer parents can, and do, seek simply to blend with the wallpaper, just as academic parents may aspire to dizzying alpine feats. I am suggesting that the potential and the necessity for some other way of being exists. Partly because queer parenthood is always embattled, the political discourses that we typically produce revolve around a claim to sameness. We only want the right to prove that we can do what heterosexual parents do: "We are two [lesbian] middle-class, working parents, two beautiful children, two cars, a new home, and more credit cards than we need. Our family fits together so simply, so perfectly, so naturally" (Drucker, 1998, pp. 46–47).[10] Others, in face of an awareness of the constraints of sameness, project the queer family as necessarily inculcating an unusual level of tolerance and open-mindedness: Their children may suffer from prejudice in others, but they will not inflict it in return. In other words, they are producing better people even if the children, just like their parents, have to suffer.[11] To admit this, however, is only to suggest that queer parenting is a happy segment of a pluralist, diverse social structure. What happens if we seek to locate the queer right to parent sufficiently elsewhere as to be outside that liberal consensus, abandoning our claim to the capacity perfectly to repeat what heterosexual parents perform?[12]

I want to be seen as occupying the social space that is labeled "mother." But (and this is the queer part) I need strategically and momentarily to claim that identity exactly in order to destabilize it, to put its provisional nature into play. A photograph in the lesbian journal *Conditions* that made a profound impression when I first saw it (such that when I was thinking about writing this essay a 20-year-old memory of it resurfaced) may help to exemplify this. Illustrating an interview with Doris Lunden titled "An Old Dyke's Tale" about her life as a butch lesbian in New Orleans and New York before Stonewall, the photo shows Lunden holding her young daughter and sporting what she describes in the accompanying text as "a slicked back Tony Curtis type hairstyle" (Bulkin, 1980, p. 36). Reading the journal in 1980, I kept coming back to that picture, poring over it as if there were some illicit pleasure to be gained from the collision of identities that it framed. It fascinated me partly because it repeatedly dislodged my assumption that mothers looked a certain way; I could look again and again and still be shocked and thrilled in a way I couldn't quite explain at the time by that juxtaposition: dyke/mother.

As a mother I intermittently perform that dislocation of expectation. Ultimately I see this as a key, socially productive aspect of queer parenting: The small shifts that are required to accommodate something unlooked for, out of place, are the shifts that can make a little more room for us to live. Kareen Malone and Rose Cleary (2002) articulate an aspect of this argument in "(De)Sexing the Family" when they suggest that queer theory's commitment to the antinormative properties of excess desire can be reintroduced into theorizing on the lesbian family, not as the desexualized family's other, but as part of what constitutes its difference. Jaqui Gabb (2001) similarly claims that sexuality, having been systematically erased from the lesbian family narrative in the interests of normalization, must be acknowledged as constitutive of the particular discontinuities of lesbian motherhood as a subject position: "Lesbians' trajectory into motherhood, irrespective of their sexual/conception narratives, takes them into an abyss of myth and incongruence" (p. 344). Whereas Gabb wishes to suture "lesbian" and "mother" into a "holistic self" ("I do not leave my maternal status at the bedroom door, or my lesbian identity at the school gates: I *am* a lesbian/mother" [Gabb, 2001, p. 344]), I would suggest that this stance reinvigorates the binaries that "lesbian" can destabilize.

Although "mother" reaches out the tentacles of femininity and of gender stability, its embrace can be resisted. The aspects of daily life that seem to me most clearly to encapsulate the state of motherhood are being the one who gets up to her in the night, the one who knows what her next two meals are going to be, and the one whose suitcase is full of her stuff when we go away somewhere. These functions could probably all be performed by a high-functioning lizard, of any gender—the lizard would just have to really want to do it. Impersonating a lizard to denaturalize gender, to disconnect mothering from femininity, might seem a bit extreme—at least until you come across me in the video store crushing copies of *The Little Mermaid* beneath my scaly feet.

My position in academia, too, might usefully be imagined as having something of the lizard in the video store about it. I have argued here that strategies for making academia more friendly to various disadvantaged forms of faculty—more flexible working hours, longer tenure tracks, and so on—are in essence aimed at enabling everyone to catch up to the same place. Were the university to be asked, however, to revise its social, architectural, or epistemological structures to suit large, cold-blooded, tail-endowed reptiles, the institution would likely, and not unreasonably, balk: There are limits beyond which accommodation to slithering difference is a step too far. It might be productive to think of the queer parent as sometimes as resistant to assimilation as your average saurian; it could be a way of freeing our thinking from the baggy monster of liberal pluralism that envelops us, of acknowledging that discomforting otherness, a distinctly reptilian view, shall we say, cannot always be addressed by the devices currently available. The lizard is intended to suggest not only the ineluctable difference of the queer parent but also the category-challenging qualities of the academic mother. Being a queer parent can threaten some apparently eternal verities, but so too, if we admit of the contingent nature of this institution likewise, can mothers threaten—or threaten to reimagine—the academy.

How might institutional structures be troubled? For example: A cultural formation (such as the queer academic family) that exists as much in its relations despite dislocation as in its sporadic occupation of temporarily domesticated spaces and ways of being, that steals time together in the interstices that noncongruent schedules allow, that becomes visible or invisible according to both its members' and its observers' shifting placement, creates what urban geographers call "pathways of desire." Pathways of desire are those routes marked out by bodies seeking another way from here to there than that officially designated: They do not feature on original plans, and can only be mapped by studying patterns of usage. What might an academy look like, were its structures to be denaturalized by unaccommodating mothers in lizard costumes? I have no idea.

REFERENCES

Allen, J. (1984). Motherhood: The annihilation of women. In J. Treblicot (Ed.), *Mothering: Essays in feminist theory* (pp. 315–330). Totowa, NJ: Rowman and Allanheld.

Allen, M., & Burrell, N. (1996). Comparing the impact of homosexual and heterosexual parents on children: Meta-analysis of existing research. *Journal of Homosexuality, 32,* 19–35.

Bohan, J. (1996). *Psychology and sexual orientation.* New York: Routledge.

Bulkin, E. (1980). An old dyke's tale: An interview with Doris Lunden. *Conditions, 6,* 26–44.

Calhoun, C. (1994). Separating lesbian theory from feminist theory. *Ethics, 104,* 558–581.

Calhoun, C. (1995). The gender closet: Lesbian disappearance under the sign "women." *Feminist Studies, 21*(1), 7–34.

Card, C. (1996). Against marriage and motherhood. *Hypatia, 11*(3), 1–23.

De Lauretis, T. (1986). Feminist studies/critical studies: Issues, terms, and contexts. In T. de Lauretis (Ed.), *Feminist studies/critical studies* (pp. 1–20). Bloomington: Indiana University Press.

Drucker, J. (1998). *Families of value.* New York: Plenum Press.

Firestone, S. (1970). *The dialectic of sex.* New York: William Morrow.

Flaks, D. K., Ficher, I., Masterpasqua, F., & Joseph, G. (1995). Lesbians choosing motherhood: A comparative study of lesbian and heterosexual parents and their children. *Developmental Psychology, 31,* 105–114.

Gabb, J. (2001). Desirous subjects and parental identities: Constructing a radical discourse on (lesbian) family sexuality. *Sexualities, 4,* 333–352.

Gilligan, C. (1982). *In a different voice.* Cambridge: Harvard University Press.

Glazer, D. F. (2001). Lesbian motherhood: Restorative choice or developmental imperative? *Journal of Gay and Lesbian Psychotherapy, 4,* 31–43.

Griffin Crowder, D. (1993). Lesbians and the (re/de)construction of the female body. In C. B. Burroughs & J. D. Ehrenreich (Eds.), *Reading the social body* (pp. 61–84). Iowa City: University of Iowa Press.

Hale, J. (1996). Are lesbians women? *Hypatia, 11*(2), 94–121.

Malone, K., & Cleary, R. (2002). (De)sexing the family: Theorizing the social science of lesbian families. *Feminist Theory, 3,* 271–293.

Mason, M. A., & Goulden, M. (2002). Do babies matter? The effect of family formation on the lifelong careers of academic men and women. *Academe, 88* (6), 21–27.

McNeill, K. F. (1998). The lack of differences between gay/lesbian and heterosexual parents: A review of the literature. *National Journal of Sexual Orientation Law, 4,* 10–28.

Michaels, M. W. (1996). Other mothers: Toward an ethic of postmaternal practice. *Hypatia, 11*(2), 49–70.

Pollack, S., & Vaughn, J. (Eds.). (1987). *Politics of the heart: A lesbian parenting anthology.* Ithaca, NY: Firebrand Books.

Robson, R. (1992). Mother: The legal domestication of lesbian existence. *Hypatia, 7*(4), 172–185.

Ruddick, S. (1989). *Maternal thinking: Toward a politics of peace.* Boston: Beacon Press.

Singer, L. (1989). Bodies—pleasures—powers. *Differences, 1*(1), 45–65.

Smith, A. -M. (1992). Resisting the erasure of lesbian sexuality: A challenge for queer activism. In K. Plummer (Ed.), *Modern homosexualities: Fragments of lesbian and gay experience* (pp. 200–213). London: Routledge.

Stacey, J., & Biblarz, T. (2001). (How) does the sexual orientation of parents matter? *American Sociological Review, 66,* 159–183.

Tasker, F., & Golombok, S. (1997). *Growing up in a lesbian family: Effects on child development.* New York: Guilford Press.

Wells, J. (Ed.). (1997). *Lesbians raising sons: An anthology.* Los Angeles: Alyson Books.

Wilson, R. (2001, November 9). A push to help parents prepare for tenure reviews. *Chronicle of Higher Education,* p. A10.

NOTES

1. The subaltern thus marked never found a good response to being addressed in this way: "No," is hopelessly defensive, whereas "I'm fine thank you, ma'am," is too patently as aggressive as the original, and its own play with binary-iden-tifications-as-insult only arguably parodic.

2. For the argument that gender uncertainty is not sufficient to shift the lesbian out of the category "woman," see Hale (1996).

3. For an attempt to quantify the number of lesbian mothers in the United States, see Bohan (1996). For a review of the current status of lesbian motherhood in law, see Robson (1992). For the argument that lesbian/mother is not an identity, see, for example, Smith (1992).

4. Data from the Study of Doctoral Recipients (SDR) show, for example, that women who have children within five years of completing their PhD are 24% less likely in the sciences and 20% less likely in the humanities to achieve tenure than men with children; interpretation of the SDR statistics points to "the unbending structure of the workplace, based on a male career model" to explain differences in achievement between single men, single women, men with children, and women with children (Mason & Goulden, 2002).

5. Feminist repudiations of motherhood as dangerous to female self-determi-nation and as necessarily complicit with oppressive patriarchal institutions do, of course, exist and continue to be produced: see, for example, Firestone (1970), Allen (1984), and Card (1996). But the argument that motherhood is a potential site of transformative engagement with patriarchy, as well as the quintessential female experience, has become normative, as is suggested by its iteration within both heterosexual and lesbian texts; see Ruddick (1989), Gil-ligan (1982), Pollack and Vaughn (1987), Calhoun (1994), and Wells (1997).

6. See Gabb (2001, p. 344) for the claim that the lack of this image in the lesbian imaginary is an index of the disconnection between cultural constructs of motherhood and of lesbian sexuality.

7. In 2001 the American Association of University Professors proposed as a solu-tion to inequities in the academic workplace that professors with newborn or newly adopted children be given up to two more years to prepare for tenure (Wilson, 2001).

8. For the argument that motherhood is a means to specifically lesbian psycho-logical health and development, see Glazer (2001).

9. For the argument that different reproductive strategies alone (the sperm in the

jar) disrupt heteronormative discourses of motherhood, see Michaels (1996, p. 56); for the claim that lesbian parenting disrupts social categories, see Gabb (2001).

10. Many narrative accounts and sociological studies seek to establish that there are no differences in outcomes between heterosexual and queer parents; see, for example, Flaks, Ficher, Masterpasqua, and Joseph (1995); Allen and Burrell (1996); Tasker and Golombok (1997); and McNeill (1998).

11. For a sociological study that makes claims for different, better outcomes for the children of queer parents, see Stacey and Biblarz (2001).

12. I am aware that parental sexuality is not always a crucially relevant factor in the struggle to moderate one's child's appetite for sugar or corporate-produced plastic ephemera. I am also not suggesting that lesbian mothers produce gay sons and lesbian daughters (much as we might secretly enjoy that prospect) or that indeed we have more than a fractional influence over children who are immersed in a heteronormative culture from the first breath they take.

Contributors

Christina E. Brantner received her PhD in German from Washington University, St. Louis, in 1987 and is currently an associate professor at the University of Nebraska–Lincoln. Her academic publications include *Robert Schumann und das Tonkünstler-Bild der Romantiker* (1991), but her true love is her creative writing, which includes *Der Hunger der Herbstzeitlosen, Gedichte und Impressionen 1983–1993* (1994), a collection of poetry. Her current projects include *German Women Writers of the Great Plains*, a German cultural history textbook, and a novel about a fictitious Jewish/Gentile family 1935–1995.

Lynn Z. Bloom, PhD, Board of Trustees Distinguished Professor and Aetna Chair of Writing at the University of Connecticut, is a specialist in autobiography, composition studies, creative nonfiction, and essays; her discovery of the contemporary essay canon is the subject of her 21st book, *The Essay Canon* (forthcoming). Her creative nonfiction includes "Teaching College English as a Woman," "Living to Tell the Tale: The Complicated Ethics of Creative Nonfiction," "Writing and Cooking," and "(Im)Patient." As her marriage approaches the half-century mark, she and her husband are happy to include grandchildren and daughters-in-law in frequent family parties and world travels.

Heather Bouwman has a PhD in English from the University of Illinois at Urbana-Champaign (1998). She is an assistant professor at the University of St. Thomas in St. Paul, Minnesota. A specialist in early American literature, Bouwman has published poetry, edited a recent instructor's manual for American literature (for the Harper Anthology single volume), and written essays on pedagogy and on early Native American preacher Samson Occom. She and her husband, Steffen Kellogg, have two sons.

Cindy Patey Brewer holds a doctoral degree in German Literature from the University of Utah. She is currently an assistant professor at Brigham Young University. Her research focuses on German women writers of the 18th and 19th centuries, and she is the associate director of *Sophie: A Digital Library* *of Works by German-Speaking Women* (http://sophie.byu.edu/). Her other research interests include raising children bilingually. Though a native English-speaker, she has raised her children speaking German in the home. All of her children are fluent in both languages. Recently, she has discovered a new passion. In a bid to reclaim her body after multiple pregnancies, Cindy successfully ran her first marathon in October 2004.

Marc Christensen is just shy of ABD status at Wayne State University in Detroit. His reviews of academic books and popular magazines appeared regularly in the *Detroit Metro Times* when he stayed at home with children. He now teaches English at Camosun College in Victoria, British Columbia, and might remember how to write something longer than a newspaper article sometime soon.

Suzanne M. Cox is an associate professor and recent chair of the Department of Psychology at Beloit College in Beloit, Wisconsin. She is the mother of four children (ages 12, 7, 4, and under 1). She earned her BS from the Honors College at Michigan State University and her MA and PhD degrees from the University of Chicago. She balances teaching courses in developmental psychology and women's studies with coparenting with her self-employed husband. Her research interests focus on the development of attachment in infants, children, and parents. She is currently engaged in a long-term follow-up study of children born preterm.

Rachel Fink received her doctoral degree from Duke University and is a professor of biological sciences at Mount Holyoke College in South Hadley, Massachusetts. Her research focuses on how cells migrate through the early fish embryo, and she has published articles in *Developmental Biology* as well as two video compilations, entitled *A Dozen Eggs: Time-Lapse Microscopy of Normal Development* and *CELLebration*. She has published about teaching bioethics in *Cell Biology Education*, and she won the Mount Holyoke College Faculty Award for Teaching in 2001.

Michelle M. Francl-Donnay is a full professor of chemistry at Bryn Mawr College, where she has been on the faculty since 1986. Her research area is computational chemistry, where she is best known for her work on methods for assigning atomic charges. In 1997 she ranked in the top 1,000 most-cited chemists. She is currently a member of the editorial board for the *Journal of Molecular Graphics and Modelling* and is active in the American Chemical Society. She is the proud mother of Michael and Christopher and shares the joys of parenting with her colleague in the math department, Victor Donnay.

Nancy Gerber holds a doctorate in Literatures in English from Rutgers University. She is the author of *Portrait of the Mother-Artist: Class and Creativity in Contemporary American Fiction*, a critical study of the mother as artist in fictions by Gwendolyn Brooks, Tillie Olsen, Cynthia Ozick, and Edwidge Danticat (Lexington, 2003). Currently she is completing a memoir entitled *Losing a Life: A Daughter's Memoir of Caregiving*, to be published by Hamilton Books. She teaches in the Women's Studies Department at Rutgers University–Newark and resides in Montclair, New Jersey, with her spouse and two sons.

Rachel Hile Bassett received her PhD in English literature from the University of Kansas in 2004; her dissertation research focused on issues of social status in Edmund Spenser's *Faerie Queene*. She and her husband Troy live in Lawrence, Kansas, with their two children, Joseph and Helen.

Lorretta M. Holloway holds a PhD in literature from the University of Kansas, an MA from the University of Michigan, and a BA from the University of Alaska–Fairbanks. She works as an assistant professor of Victorian Literature and Composition at Framingham State College in Massachusetts. She is coediting a book titled *Beyond Arthurian Romances and Gothic Thrillers: The Reach of Victorian Medievalism*. She is also revising a book about the Gothic tradition and women's survival.

Susan Jacobowitz is an assistant professor in the English Department at Queensborough Community College/The City University of New York. She received her PhD from Brandeis University, where she wrote a dissertation entitled *The Holocaust at Home: Representations and Implications of Second Generation Experience*, about depictions of survivor families. Publications include "'Hardly There Even When She Wasn't Lost': Orthodox Daughters and the 'Mind-Body' Problem," which appeared in the Spring 2004 issue of *Shofar: An Interdisciplinary Journal of Jewish Studies*, dedicated to Jewish American literature. She lives with her husband and two daughters in Forest Hills, New York.

Kathryn Jacobs, PhD, is a professor at Texas A & M–Commerce, where she teaches Medieval and Renaissance literature. Her first daughter was born while she was writing her dissertation at Harvard University; her twins were born four years later. Since then she has published a book, *Marriage Contracts from Chaucer to the Renaissance Stage,* and some two dozen articles and poems in journals such as the *Chaucer Review* and *Mediaevalia.* She is currently finishing her second book, *Chaucer through Shakespeare's Eyes.*

Shimberlee Jirón-King is a PhD candidate in the Department of English at Stanford University. She received an MA from Penn State and a BA from the Metropolitan State College of Denver. She plans to focus her dissertation on Latina/o and Chicana/o literary and cultural studies in the United States. She has brought her research interests to the classroom at Stanford teaching classes such as "The Rhetoric of Education and Minority Discourse." She lives in Modesto, California, with her husband and three sons.

Kathleen B. Jones is a writer, grandmother, political activist, and professor emerita of women's studies at San Diego State University. A graduate of Brooklyn College (1970) who received her PhD in political science from CUNY Graduate Center (1978), she also holds an honorary doctorate from Örebro University, Sweden. Author of scholarly books and essays on feminist theory and politics, and co-editor of *International Feminist Journal of Politics,* she has also published a memoir, *Living Between Danger and Love* (Rutgers University Press, 2000) and is writing a book about Hannah Arendt. She teaches creative nonfiction writing workshops in university and community settings.

Katharine Lane Antolini is a doctoral candidate in history at West Virginia University. Since the birth of her son, her academic interests have focused on the institution of motherhood and its historical variations. She is currently writing her dissertation on the relationship between the model of "scientific" motherhood and the rise of the consumer culture in the early 20th century.

Gayle Letherby is reader in the sociology of gender at Coventry University, United Kingdom, where she also holds the post of deputy director of the Centre for Social Justice. Gayle has published in the areas of motherhood and nonmotherhood, working and learning in higher education, crime and deviance, and research methodology. The latter interest is reflected in her book *Feminist Research in Theory and Practice* (Open University, 1993). Gayle's other books are *A Criminology Reader,* with Y. Jewkes (Sage, 2002), and the edited book *Gender, Identity, and Reproduction,* with S. Earle (Palgrave, 2003).

Jen Marchbank is head of undergraduate studies in the School of Health and Social Sciences at Coventry University, United Kingdom. Jen is a political scientist by background and has a publication record in the areas of childcare policies, women and conflict, working and learning in higher education, and research methodology. Jen's publications include the following books: *Women, Power, and Policy: Comparative Studies of Childcare* (Routledge, 2000) and *States of Conflict: Gender, Violence, and Resistance,* co-edited with S. Jacobs and R. Jacobson (Zed, 2000).

Donna J. Nelson obtained her PhD in chemistry from the University of Texas at Austin and did her postdoctorate at Purdue. In 1983 she joined the University of Oklahoma faculty; she received tenure and promotion to associate professor in 1989. She researches the comparison of correlations of reaction versus computational data applied to reaction mechanisms and synthetic design in organic and organometallic chemistry, as well as issues of diversity in science, which were the subject of two Capitol Hill briefings. Her awards include a Guggenheim Award (2003), a Sigma Xi Research Award (2001), and a NOW Woman of Courage Award (2004).

Andrea O'Reilly, PhD, is associate professor in the School of Women's Studies at York University. She is editor of six books on motherhood, including *From Motherhood to Mothering: The Legacy of Adrienne Rich's* Of Woman Born (SUNY Press, 2004) and *Mother Outlaws: Theories and Practices of Empowered Mothering* (Women's Press, 2004), and is author of *Toni Morrison and Motherhood: A Politics of the Heart* (SUNY Press, 2004). O'Reilly is founding president and director of the Association for Research on Mothering, the first feminist association on the topic of motherhood. Andrea and her common-law spouse are the parents of a 20-year-old son and two daughters, ages 15 and 18.

Karen Ramsay is a senior lecturer in organizational studies at Bradford College, United Kingdom. An organizational sociologist by background, Karen's research interests include gender and culture in higher education, motherhood and nonmotherhood, and research methodology. Key publications include "Emotional Labour and Organisational Research: How I Learned Not to Laugh or Cry in the Field," in S. E. Lyon and J. Busfield (Eds.), *Methodological*

Imaginations (Macmillan, 1996), and "So Why Are You Doing This Project? Issues of Friendship, Research, and Autobiography," with Gayle Letherby, in *Auto/Biography* (1999).

Janice Rieman lives in Charlotte, North Carolina, with her sweetie, their daughter, and their three dogs. She continues coming to terms with resigning from a tenure-track job in Ohio after relocating to North Carolina to devote her time primarily to her most challenging and rewarding project to date: family life. Dr. Rieman fulfills a large part of her scholarly self by teaching in the American Studies Department at the University of North Carolina at Charlotte.

John Shiels is a retired sociologist and criminologist who taught in higher education in the United Kingdom for over 25 years. John's research and writing interests include sociological theory, citizenship, and working and learning in higher education. Key publications include contributions to D. Jary and J. Jary (Eds.), *The Collins Dictionary of Sociology* (Collins, 1993) and "'Isn't He Good, But Can We Take Her Seriously?' Gendered Expectations in Higher Education," with Gayle Letherby, in P. Anderson and J. Williams (Eds.), *Identity and Difference in Higher Education: "Outsiders" Within* (Ashgate, 2000).

Tarshia L. Stanley is an assistant professor of English and film studies at Spelman College in Atlanta, Georgia. Her recent publications include "The Boys' Price in Martinique: Visions of the Bildungsroman in Sugar Cane Alley" in Murray Pomerance and Frances Gateward (Eds.), *Snips, Snails, and Puppydog Tails: Cinemas of Boyhood*. She is currently at work on the manuscript *The Trope of the Lock: Whoopi Goldberg or the Re-Presentation of the Black Woman's Body in Hollywood Film*.

Alison M. Thomas first experienced being an "honorary man" in academia as an undergraduate within the ivory towers of Cambridge, and obtained her PhD (on gender and identity) from the University of Reading. Becoming the mother of twins several years later opened her eyes to the challenges of maintaining a balance between parenting and academic life. In 1996 she and her family moved to Canada, and, after seven years with the University of Victoria, she now has a faculty position in Sociology and Anthropology at Douglas College in Vancouver. Her publications include work on masculinities, gender relations, and sexual harassment; she is currently researching fathers' involvement in "family work."

Norma Tilden is an assistant professor of English at Georgetown University, where she teaches courses in 20th-century literature, ecocriticism, and nonfiction writing. She is currently completing a study of the contemporary American nature essay and is also at work on *Animal Watch,* a collection of her creative nonfiction.

Gale Renee Walden teaches writing at the University of Illinois in Urbana. She is the author of *Same Blue Chevy,* a poetry collection.

Anna Wilson is a lecturer in American Studies at the University of Birmingham, England. Recent publications include *Persuasive Fictions: Feminist Narrative and Critical Myth* (Bucknell University Press, 2001) and "Sexing the Hyena: Intraspecies Readings of the Female Phallus," in *Signs* (2003). She is currently working on a study of the representation of queer bodies in American national narratives.

Index